A GUIDE TO LOCAL STUDIES IN EAST YORKSHIRE

edited by
BRIAN DYSON

HUTTON PRESS
1985

Hutton Press Ltd.
130 Canada Drive, Cherry Burton, Beverley
East Yorkshire HU17 7SB

Printed by Clifford Ward & Co.
(Bridlington) Ltd.
55 West Street, Bridlington, East Yorkshire
YO15 3DZ.

ISBN 0 907033 33 4

CONTENTS

To the memory of
Douglas H. Jones,
1906-1982

— B.D.

LIST OF CONTRIBUTORS

J. A. R. Bickford — formerly Physician Superintendent, De la Pole Hospital, Willerby

Arthur G. Credland — Keeper, Town Docks Museum, Hull

Jan Crowther — Local History Tutor, University of Hull

Jill Crowther — Local Studies Librarian, Central Library, Hull

Brian Dyson — Special Collections Librarian and Archivist Designate, University of Hull

Barbara English — Lecturer in Regional and Local History, University of Hull

David Foster — Head of the School of Humanities, Humberside College of Higher Education

Jane Lancaster — History Teacher, Kelvin Hall School, Hull

John Lawson — Reader Emeritus in Educational Studies, University of Hull

Faith Mann — formerly Local History Tutor, University of Hull

David Neave — Lecturer in Regional and Local History, University of Hull

Margaret Noble — Senior Lecturer in Geography, Humberside College of Higher Education

Geoffrey Oxley — Kingston upon Hull City Archivist

Leslie Powell — formerly Chairman, East Yorkshire Family History Society

6

LIST OF ILLUSTRATIONS

7

ACKNOWLEDGEMENTS

The editor wishes to thank the following for permission to use their photographs and illustrations:

Borthwick Institute of Historical Research: Figure 37
Broadgate Photograph Collection: Figure 53
Hull Central Library: Figures 38 and 39
Kingston upon Hull City Museums and Art Galleries: Figures 32-36
National Monuments Record of the Royal Commission on Historical Manuscripts: Figure 3 (Crown copyright reserved)
National Remote Sensing Centre, Royal Aircraft Establishment, Farnborough: Cover photograph
David Neave: Figures 16-20, 41-51
University of Hull Photographic Service: Figures 6-15, 30, 31
General Editor of the *Victoria County History*: Figure 29
Wellcome Institute Library: Figure 52
Yorkshire Archaeological Society: Figure 5

ABBREVIATIONS USED

BIHR   Borthwick Institute of Historical Research, York
BL   British Library, London
BPL   Beverley Public Library
DOE   Department of the Environment
ERAS   East Riding Antiquarian Society
EYFHS   East Yorkshire Family History Society
EYLHS   *East Yorkshire Local History Series*
FFHS   Federation of Family History Societies
HCRO   Humberside County Record Office
HLSL   Hull Local Studies Library
HMC   Hospital Management Committee
HUL   Hull University Library
IGI   International Genealogical Index
KHRO   Kingston upon Hull Record Office
LEAs   Local Education Authorities
LRO   Lincolnshire Record Office
MOH   Medical Officer of Health
NHS   National Health Service
NMM   National Maritime Museum
OS   Ordnance Survey
PRO   Public Record Office
TDM   Town Docks Museum, Hull
VCH   *Victoria History of the Counties of England*
VCH ER   *Victoria History of the Counties of England: Yorkshire, East Riding*
YAJ   *Yorkshire Archaeological Journal*
YAS   Yorkshire Archaeological Society
YML   York Minster Library

Figure 1: The East Riding of Yorkshire

PREFACE

Instantly recognisable on the map, from the air, or even, as the cover photograph shows, from space, there can be few regions in England which attract the devotion and loyalty of its inhabitants, be they native or otherwise, as does the East Riding of Yorkshire. A region bounded by the River Derwent in the north, the Ouse in the west, and to the east and south by the North Sea and the Humber respectively, cannot help but be a distinct locality both geographically and historically. I have no doubt that this *Guide* will not be the last book to be based on an administrative county which ceased to exist politically in 1974.

When I first invited potential contributors to take part in the preparation of the *Guide* I said that its chief aim was to provide a 'scholarly introduction to the study of local history in the East Riding of Yorkshire in order to meet the needs of practising and, above all, of potential local historians'. Its main concern is not the history itself but how to study it. I hope that the final product, this book, will be of use to all potential and actual students and scholars of the local history of this region, wherever they may live and whatever their age.

Of necessity, this *Guide* is a selective introduction to local studies in East Yorkshire. No one book could possibly cover every aspect of every topic even for a relatively small locality and then be available for sale at a reasonable price or without the aid of a wheelbarrow to take it home. Past guides written and published in this region and nationally have faced the same problem of selectivity. One such guide, issued in 1939, also helps to show how the study of local history has developed, particularly since World War II. The Local History Committee of the then University College of Hull produced a booklet for an exhibition held in the Mortimer Museum, Hull, between 20 March and 1 April 1939 which took the title *A guide to the history of the East Riding of Yorkshire*. The topics covered naturally concentrated on viewable exhibits, but did reflect the state of the art at that time: Holderness in the making; prehistory; Roman history; rural and urban East Yorkshire; and Hull between the seventeenth and nineteenth centuries.

Since 1945 the number of people interested and involved in local studies throughout Britain has grown enormously. Increased leisure time, nostalgia and the relative ease and comfort of relating to a distinct region, town or village in what is an increasingly complex and, to some, incomprehensible national and international society, are just a few of the reasons for this growth. Excellent introductory works designed to cater for historians

13

throughout the land began to appear, most notably the classic *Local history in England* by W. G. Hoskins in 1959, now in its third edition. The first important guide to local studies in this region came out in 1956 in response primarily to the needs of adult education and other students in the University of Hull. This little book, entitled *A guide to regional studies on the East Riding of Yorkshire and the city of Hull,* by A. G. Dickens and K. A. MacMahon, continues to be of use to the local scholar.

What follows in this new *Guide* is an up-to-date outline of the methodology and sources for local studies in East Yorkshire. The contributing authors are all acknowledged experts in their fields, and include university and college lecturers, librarians, a school teacher, a museum keeper, and an archivist.

At all times the intention is to explain how and where to obtain information, either generally or in relation to a particular topic. We begin with two chapters explaining the work and purpose of what for many scholars will be the most important repositories of raw material for their researches: the local studies library and the local record office. There then follows a number of topical chapters in which the individual authors give an introduction to the sources — both published and unpublished — for their subjects, with emphasis on those which are available locally. Each of these chapters is accompanied by an illustrative case study presented in such a way as to reinforce the earlier description of sources and methodology. These topical chapters offer a wide range of subjects representing a good selection of the interests of present-day local historians. They are: medieval history, church history and post-Reformation religion, family history, urban settlement, population, agriculture, maritime history, the history of education, the architecture and history of houses, and public health and private medicine. The case studies generally concentrate on a particular place within the region. These include: Eske, Lowthorpe, Holme-on-Spalding Moor, Great Driffield, Cherry Burton, Middleton on the Wolds, Hull and Burnby. Inevitably, the chapter on maritime history concentrates almost entirely on aspects of fishing, shipping and whaling in and from the port of Hull. The final chapter examines the provision of local studies teaching for the local historians of the future. This section on 'Local history in the classroom' offers a highly practical description of what teachers can do to stimulate and sustain what is potentially the most interesting subject in the curriculum and stresses the need for close liaison between teachers, local librarians and local archivists. The final sections of the book include a glossary of some of the more important terms used in the text, a select list of relevant libraries, record offices, museums, art galleries, societies and of educational establishments which currently run courses of interest to the local scholar. In addition, there is a select bibliography of the more useful publications which will help the reader wishing to study the subject further.

On behalf of a number of the contributors I have to thank K. D. Holt and his staff at the Humberside County Record Office in Beverley; Geoffrey Oxley, Kingston upon Hull City Archivist; Norman Higson, Archivist of the University of Hull; Jill Crowther, Local Studies Librarian, Hull Central

Library; and the Incumbent of St. Martin's Parish Church, Lowthorpe. Finally, a number of people have helped me — knowingly or otherwise — at various stages and to varying degrees in the preparation of this book. They include Keith Allison, Jan Crowther, Barbara English, Pat King, Alan Marshall, David Neave and David Pennie. The list of useful addresses and the index have been compiled by Karen Townsend. The maps were drawn by Wendy Munday. Above all, I should like to thank my wife, Philippa, for her patience, understanding, support and assistance. Needless to say, the responsibility for the content of the *Guide* is mine alone.

Brian Dyson,
Cottingham,
July, 1985.

15

1

A LOCAL HISTORY LIBRARY IN ACTION

Jill Crowther

The first public libraries in Britain were established following the Public Libraries Act of 1850, but for most local authorities, specialist libraries for local studies have been a comparatively recent development. In many cases, local material was at first collected haphazardly. Resources for acquiring, housing and exploiting it were limited, and it was little used except by a small number of historians. In the last twenty years or so, there has been an enormous increase in interest in local history at all levels, and local studies libraries are now developing very quickly to meet popular demand.

In East Yorkshire, the three main local studies collections are at Hull, Beverley and Bridlington, all now part of Humberside Libraries but before 1974, administered by separate local authorities. At Hull, the first public library was opened by Sir James Reckitt in 1888, and taken over by Hull Corporation in 1893. Hull's first permanent central library building was opened in 1901, but its local collection was not organised and made generally available until 1960. At Beverley, the two collections of local material belonging to the former Beverley Borough Library (opened in 1906) and East Riding County Services (established 1925) were amalgamated in 1974. The local collection of the former Bridlington Borough Library Service (established 1925) remains in the present Bridlington Library. There are also small collections of standard local works in most of the Humberside branch libraries.

As local history research becomes more sophisticated it is being increasingly realised that the history of a particular area has to be looked at, not in isolation, but in a regional and national context, and it is no longer sufficient for the local historian to study his own town or parish using only the resources of one library. One of the problems facing the users of local history libraries is the wide variation in arrangement and practice, and the reader who has become used to the layout and procedure of one library may well find that this is of little use elsewhere.

Security is now a problem for all local history libraries. A great deal of what seems to be ordinary material is valuable because it is irreplaceable. Books and pamphlets on local history are often locally published in limited editions on poor quality paper and do not survive in any quantity. Fragile materials are at risk through constant daily use, and photocopies and microfilms are now being offered to save the originals from further deterioration. The amount of access to originals varies, depending on the condition of the material and the resources available for making working copies. The dilemma for the archivist and librarian is how to serve the needs of today's readers, and at the same time ensure that the collections will survive for the future.

Libraries throughout the country have reacted differently to the security problem, sometimes providing very limited access only to single items under strict supervision, or allowing unrestricted use only to certain levels of reader. In East Yorkshire, the variations in ready access are related to the premises and staffing levels of the different libraries. The present coverage and arrangement of the three main collections is as follows:

Hull

Includes material on the City of Hull, the former East Riding of Yorkshire, and North Lincolnshire, with modern general printed works on the County of Humberside. This library has the main county collection for Hull itself.

Premises: Separate department seating twenty; full-time staff; selection of material on display.

Beverley

Includes material on Beverley and the former East Riding of Yorkshire. This library has the main county collection for Beverley itself, and has much material on the East Riding which is not available at Hull.

Premises: Administered as part of the Beverley Reference Library.

Bridlington

Concentrates on Bridlington and the surrounding area, with a small collection on the East Riding generally. This library has the main collection for Bridlington itself.

Premises: Separate Bridlington Room; administered from the Bridlington Reference Library.

Because these three collections were originally built up by separate local authorities, there is some overlap of historical printed material, and to make each library as self-sufficient as possible within its own area, there is also deliberate duplication of modern titles, such as local government publications and standard works.

Readers who are in doubt about which library to use are advised to check first with the Hull Local Studies Library (HLSL), which has the largest collection in the area. Its staff can contact Beverley and Bridlington if required, and it is well placed for visitors arriving by train or bus.

There is as yet no complete published bibliography of the holdings of the three libraries, but for a selective listing of the older material held at Hull, see R. F. Drewery's *Select list of books on Hull and district,* published in 1968, and for more general coverage the *Select bibliography of the County of Humberside,* published by Humberside Libraries in 1980, which includes some of the holdings of all three collections.

THE RESOURCES OF THE LOCAL STUDIES LIBRARY

The effective local studies library does not restrict its coverage to printed books. It will collect almost literally anything and everything on the history and present-day life of its area, regardless of format, so as to provide as much information as possible for the historian. It is this variety of material which makes local studies work so interesting, but which can be daunting for the beginner.

Because of the complexity of much of this material, the well-organised library has various finding aids such as separate indexes and catalogues. This makes the local studies collection more complicated to use than a general reference library, but means that, with their help, the reader will be able to find his way quickly into the contents of a wide range of sources.

The resources described here are mainly those of the HLSL. In the scope and depth of its material it is typical of the collections built up by the former county boroughs, which had long-established traditions of public library service, independent local government administrations, and large compact communities from which to draw revenue and readers. It is hoped that an account of the main features of the HLSL will introduce the reader to the kinds of resources and services which will be found, with variations, in the local studies libraries of the county. Notes on significant extra coverage elsewhere are included.

Printed books

The HLSL has about twenty thousand books as well as many pamphlets, which in some cases may be the only published accounts of a particular subject. To ensure complete coverage for the future, the library's policy is to acquire at least one copy of every title published, regardless of quality. This means that there will be items in the library which are not necessarily of a high scholastic standard, so it is advisable to cross-check printed facts whenever possible.

Finding aids: Classified card catalogue with subject and author/name sections; includes detailed bibliographical descriptions, and notes on copies available for loan.

Directories

Provincial town directories date from roughly the end of the eighteenth century. Hull directories were produced at intervals from 1791 to 1939, but the library also has the brief Hull sections from national directories from 1781. The constant shift of population during World War II made them impractical to continue, and there are no reliable directories after 1939. All Hull directories are selective, listing only a small proportion of the total population and concentrating on the business community. Early volumes are arranged by name only. By the 1840s there are listings by name, street and classified trades, which make them a useful source for tracing the geographical and economic development of the town as well as individual people. For East Riding villages, there are brief entries at intervals from 1823 to 1937, sometimes in a series covering the North and East Ridings, sometimes as an addition to the Hull volumes.

Finding aids: All directories are listed by date in the main card catalogue. For other locations of all known local directories see the East Yorkshire Local History Society *Bulletin*, no.3 (1971); see also *A guide to national and provincial directories . . .*, edited by J. E. Norton (London, 1950).

Newspapers

Local newspapers are one of the most valuable sources for the historian, because they provide the background and local reaction to national and regional events, as well as facts often not found elsewhere. The earliest English provincial newspapers date from the end of the seventeenth century and were well established by the mid-eighteenth century. As the largest town in East Yorkshire, Hull had the earliest newspapers. The main runs start with the *Hull packet* (1787-1886), and the *Hull advertiser* (1794-1867). Odd issues of the *Hull courant* survive from 1746.

Nineteenth century Hull, geographically isolated, but prosperous and fast growing, was able to support several daily and weekly newspapers at any one time, of which the longest running, in addition to the above, were the *Eastern morning news* (1864-1929) and the *Hull times* (1857-1984). The present *Hull daily mail* dates from 1885. The earliest newspapers are more useful for their advertisements and trade information than for news items, but by the mid-nineteenth century, the range of papers for any one year provides very detailed coverage, and offers different slants on the news, reflecting the interests and politics of the independent proprietors.

East Riding area newspapers, where they survive, will be found in the local collection for that area. At Beverley, the earliest files are those of the *Beverley guardian* (1856 to date). At Bridlington, the *Bridlington free press* (1859 to date) is filed only from 1925, but there are news cuttings from 1867. For other towns, surviving coverage is uneven, and there are sometimes no locally held files.

Coverage of Hull and East Riding events before 1784 can sometimes be found in the *York courant*, which dates from 1725. The Hull newspapers sometimes carry sections on village news, and the *Hull times* has different editions for different parts of the county.

Many newspaper files are now brittle and fragile, and to prevent further damage, users are generally asked to use microfilm copies wherever possible. The advantage of microfilm is that several editions of each paper can be stored, and items can be copied without damage to the originals. News cuttings files may provide a short cut to useful items.

Finding aids: For details of titles, runs and locations, including files at newspaper offices and the British Newspaper Library at Colindale in London, see *Yorkshire newspapers: a bibliography with locations*, by G. E. Laughton and L. R. Stephen (Harrogate, 1960); select published index to the *Hull advertiser*, 1794-1825; select card index to the *Hull daily mail*, 1964-72 and 1985 to date; index to *Bridlington free press* cuttings 1900-1942 (at Bridlington Library).

Census returns

Printed statistical returns have been published every ten years since 1801, except for 1941. The HLSL has separate East Riding volumes from 1921, and detailed small area statistics on microfiche for 1981. The full returns from which statistical tables are compiled are confidential for one hundred years, after which they are open for inspection and available to libraries on microfilm. The returns from 1851 onwards give full details of age, occupation and place of birth; those for 1841 are less exact. The full returns can be used for checking on individual people or families, or for analysing the development of an area through its growth, trades, occupations and population patterns.

Returns on microfilm for the East Riding are held in the HLSL for Hull and district, 1841-1881, and the East Riding parishes, 1851 only. The library at Beverley contains those for the East Riding for 1841-1881 as well as for Bridlington and other towns.

Finding aids: Indexes by street and reel for Hull and Beverley; by place and reel for East Riding villages.

Ephemera

The term 'ephemera' covers the varied range of material produced during the everyday life of an area, which is intended to provide immediate information and then be thrown away. Because of its transient nature, this material has rarely survived in any quantity, but it is now realised that it provides valuable background for the local historian, as well as conveying very well the 'feel' of the period in which it was produced.

Most local studies libraries are now collecting and indexing as much historical and modern ephemera as their resources will allow. Because of the difficulties of acquisition and storage, this is one class of material for which there is unlikely to be any overlap between libraries, so ephemera for, say, the Beverley area should be sought at Beverley, rather than at Hull.

The HLSL is currently collecting a range of ephemera which includes entertainment and sports programmes, handbills, posters, menus, election handouts, and the publicity material of local companies and tradespeople. The library's largest collection of historical ephemera is a series of about seven thousand local theatre bills dating from the mid-eighteenth century.

Finding aids: Some material listed in the main card catalogue; extra detail in the general Information Indexes; theatre bills separately indexed by theatre, date, and title of performance.

Illustrations

An illustration will often provide an answer where no published information exists, and the collections of photographs, drawings, paintings and prints of the typical local studies collection are of increasing value for providing a permanent record of a rapidly changing environment.

The illustrations collection at Hull has over seven thousand items dating from the eighteenth century, with the emphasis on nineteenth and twentieth century Hull, although there is some material on the East Riding. There is also a separate collection of over one thousand photographs of eighteenth and nineteenth century Hull housing, scheduled for improvement or demolition at the turn of the century, which are a record of a Hull now vanished. The illustrations held by the Hull Museums are a useful source for early views of Hull, and complement the holdings of the HLSL. There is also a large illustrations collection on Beverley and the East Riding at Beverley, and the Bridlington Library has views of the resort and surrounding villages.

Finding aids: Separate classified card catalogue, with full details of date and copyright; photocopies in folders for browsing; checklist of housing photographs (in progress).

Maps

Like illustrations, maps can often provide an answer where narrative sources fail, so the collections of Ordnance Survey (OS) and other maps held in local history libraries are valuable sources of information, particularly when used with the evidence found in other material. The main classes of maps in the HLSL are as follows:

Town maps

When these exist for old-established settlements, they predate the official OS maps by several centuries. Contemporary single sheet historical maps of Hull date from the sixteenth century, with conjectural plans back to 1293. Town maps for other areas will be found with the local collections for that area.

Finding aids: Separate card catalogue, arranged by place and date. For a description of all known historical Hull maps see *The evolution of Kingston upon Hull as shewn by its plans,* by T. Sheppard (Hull, 1911).

OS maps

For this area, these date from the early 1850s, and since then have been produced at various scales and dates. The collection in the HLSL covers Hull and the whole of the East Riding; the holdings elsewhere are not as wide.

Finding aids: Various grid indexes supplied by the OS; street index to modern fifty inches to the mile series. For a general guide to all series and their interpretation see *Ordnance Survey maps: a descriptive manual,* by J. B. Harley (Southampton, 1975).

Subject maps

There are also various special subject series, including enclosure, geological and agricultural maps. For a more detailed description of holdings, see the HLSL's *Notes for a village study* handout.

Special collections

In many local studies libraries there are special collections built up because of some particular activity or interest associated with the area. Where these exist, they become standard collections of world-wide interest. The most important collections at Hull are summarised below.

Wilberforce and slavery

Originally built up because William Wilberforce (1759-1833), who led the fight for the abolition of the British colonial slave trade, was born in Hull. The collection includes material on all aspects of slavery, ancient and modern, but especially on the slave trade, and biographies of slaves and abolitionists. The stock of about thirteen hundred items contains all

21

printed material, with no manuscripts. Included is the ninety-four volume set of reprints of British parliamentary papers on the slave trade. There are some loan copies, especially of Wilberforce biographies. The collection should be used in conjunction with the materials in the Wilberforce House Museum and the Kingston upon Hull Record Office (KHRO).

Finding aids: Separate card catalogue with author and subject entries; select bibliography, *William Wilberforce* . . . published by Hull Public Libraries in 1959.

Andrew Marvell

Born in 1621, this poet and politician was educated at Hull Grammar School, and was Member of Parliament for Hull from 1659 until his death in 1678. The collection of about two hundred titles includes first editions, biographies and criticisms. There are some loan copies, especially of modern publications. A quantity of original Marvell material can be found in the KHRO.

Finding aids: Separate card catalogue, with author and subject entries.

Whaling

The town of Hull played an important part in the British whaling trade up to 1869. The collection of about five hundred titles includes material on all aspects of whaling and the whaling trade, particularly items associated with Hull and Whitby, and including modern whaling and the zoology of the whale. There are also twenty original whaling log books, and microfilm copies of logs held at Hull Town Docks Museum (TDM) and Hull Trinity House. There are some loan copies, especially of modern publications. The collection should be used in association with material at the TDM.

Finding aids: Separate card catalogue with author and subject entries.

Winifred Holtby

Born at Rudston, near Bridlington, and best remembered as a novelist, Winifred Holtby (1898-1935) was also a journalist, and active in the feminist, pacifist and trade union movements. The printed book collection of some fifty titles includes various editions of her works, including foreign language editions, and biographies. There are some loan copies. The archive collection is the largest on Winifred Holtby in public ownership in the world and totals approximately twenty-five thousand manuscript and documentary items.

Finding aids: Printed books listed in main card catalogue; duplicated checklist of main classes of manuscripts.

Information indexes

Because of the complexity of many local history enquiries and the frequent lack of information in book form, all local studies libraries have some form of indexing system to exploit the contents of their material and supplement traditional catalogues. The HLSL has a series of information files which include answers to earlier enquiries, and references to the contents of books, journals, and other sources. All correspondence is also indexed. As well as a general subject sequence, there are separate biographical, shipping and companies indexes.

Background collection

The HLSL is building up a collection of titles which it is hoped will be of help to readers who are beginning local history and may need general advice on techniques and sources. It includes books on genealogy, on the use and interpretation of records, introductions to the study of local history, and guides to national archives. To make the department as self-sufficient as possible, there is also a selection of frequently used general reference books.

Finding aids: Separate classified card catalogue, with author and subject sections.

FACILITIES AND SERVICES

Searches

Limited searches can be made for enquiries received by letter or telephone. Where an answer cannot be found in the time available, the staff will try to suggest search lines which can be followed up, and advise on the location of other records.

Loan collections

Humberside Libraries are acquiring extra copies of published works for home reading. There are still small collections of local history titles at branch libraries but the main loan collections are now in the County's local history libraries. The HLSL has a large loan collection covering Hull and the East Riding, with copies of most standard histories and modern publications, and can borrow from other libraries in Humberside as needed.

Microfilm/fiche readers

There are facilities in all libraries for using microfilm and microfiche. The HLSL currently has two microfilm readers in the department. Advance bookings are not taken because if these are in use, local material can be used on the machines in other parts of the building.

Photocopying

Local material can be copied on self-service photocopiers depending on the regulations of the different libraries and the requirements of the Copyright Act. The HLSL has its own copier, with others in the different reference departments for larger items. Fragile or easily-damaged material may not be copied. The staff can print microfilm extracts from newspapers as required. These usually need to be ordered well in advance, as demand is heavy.

Visits

The HLSL staff will visit local organisations free of charge to talk about the work of their department, or lecture on set local history topics. Tours of the libraries can be arranged. It is necessary to write well in advance to book this service.

Publications

The HLSL sells the complete set of booklets produced by the East Yorkshire Local History Society, and other selected local publications. It also stocks and sells a number of local interest publications produced by Humberside Leisure Services. There are duplicated lists of all titles currently in print, all of which can be ordered through library service points.

SERVICES TO EDUCATION

The growing trend of introducing local history work into educational studies means that local history libraries are now dealing with very large numbers of students at all levels. Humberside Libraries have as yet no Education Officer to work full-time on educational projects, but the library staff will give whatever help they can. The HLSL offers the following assistance to teachers and students:

Advice on projects

Teachers planning class projects and adult students working on theses or dissertations are advised to visit the library to check the stock and talk to the staff before deciding on subjects for study. The uneven coverage of all local history collections means that for some topics there will not be enough source material, so whilst library staff cannot provide titles or plan projects, they may be able to advise on whether particular topics are feasible, and/or suggest other places where material can be found. Teachers are asked not to refer individual children to the library until their projects have been planned and the background work on sources completed.

Visits

Class visits can be arranged to suit the needs of particular groups. The library staff will give introductory talks on the resources and organisation of the HLSL, or on course materials for particular topics. Small groups of up to ten students can work in the department; for larger groups or for lessons, there is separate classroom space where teachers can work with students on materials provided from the local collections. Because of the pressure on space and resources, teachers are asked to indicate their needs in advance, so that suitable arrangements can be made.

Booklists and study sheets

In Hull schools alone, up to ten thousand children a year are now undertaking local studies projects, either informally, or as part of examination work. The library staff will help teachers to compile book lists, and will provide duplicated copies for use in school or library. The Library's own series of free study sheets covers the following subjects so far:

No.1   *General guide to the Hull Local Studies Library*
No.2   *Notes for a village study*
No.3   *Amy Johnson, aviator*
No.4   *Entertainments in Hull*
No.5   *Zeppelin raids on Hull in World War I*
No.6   *Sources for a project on Hull streets*

Loans and photocopies
Students holding a ticket for any Humberside library can borrow spare copies of published books. Collections for classroom use can be made up for teachers. Photocopies of standard source materials can be provided where the originals cannot be lent.

HELP FOR GENEALOGISTS

Family history is one of the growth areas of local studies. Not all the necessary materials can be found in local history libraries, but they are normally one of the first places visited by the genealogist, because the sources which they have are fairly straightforward for the beginner. Also, since they are part of the public library service, they usually have longer opening hours and less administrative restrictions than archive or record offices.

The family historian is likely to use different libraries during his research, and will meet the variations in stock and organisation described earlier. The HLSL offers the following:

Source materials
1. Census returns 1841-1881
2. Directories 1781-1939
3. Electoral rolls 1834 to date
4. Newspapers 1787 to date
5. Parish registers: Complete series of volumes published in the Yorkshire Parish Register series, plus several privately published volumes and a few manuscripts and microfilm transcripts.

Background guides
The HLSL's collection of background material for local history includes general introductions to family history searching, guides to archive collections, and text books on the use of particular classes of material, which it is hoped will help the genealogist with queries as they arise.

Biographical indexes
The Library's Information Indexes have a name section which lists

newspaper and periodical references and the results of searches already made. An alphabetical card index to the obituary columns of the *Hull advertiser* from 1800-1850 is now in progress.

Searches

Because of the very large numbers of family history enquiries received, the Library cannot undertake detailed or continuing research. Where possible, however, the staff will do limited searches such as checks of directories or specific census addresses to provide the genealogist with basic facts. Lists of local contacts willing to undertake paid searches can be supplied.

2

A LOCAL RECORD OFFICE IN ACTION

Geoffrey Oxley

Local record offices exist to preserve material created in and relating to their areas. As such they fit into a network of archive services throughout the country. Addresses and telephone numbers of the more important of these may be found in *Record repositories in Great Britain* (London, 1982). A more useful guide is *British archives*, edited by J. Foster and J. Sheppard (London, 1982). This covers a much wider range of repositories and gives fuller details of holdings and published finding aids. The most significant gap in these publications relates to archives held by businesses, for which the best available guide is the *Directory of corporate archives* compiled by John Armstrong and published by the Business Archives Council (London, 1985).

National archives

Most repositories may be thought of as operating at one of three levels: national, regional or local. At the national level are the archives organisations serving the whole country or operating in many areas. The largest of these is central government whose records are preserved in the Public Record Office. They include not only the records of ministries past and present but courts of justice, quangos and some nationalised industries. The importance of these records is often overlooked by local historians but one only has to consider the role played in Hull by, for example, Customs and Excise, the armed forces (Hull Garrison, naval shipbuilding), the Board of Trade (merchant shipping matters) and the nationalised transport undertakings to realise how significant they are.

Other national organisations whose archives contain a significant element of local material include businesses, churches, and learned, professional and trade associations. Some of these have deposited their records in public repositories; others provide their own archive service. A rather different form of national resource is provided by collecting institutions of which the foremost is the British Library in London. Some of these have general or regional collecting policies while others concentrate on a particular theme and have become major centres of research in their chosen subject. Such is the breadth and range of nationally held archives that it is impossible to give any guidance here beyond saying that there will be some national material relevant for almost all aspects of local history. Most local record offices see it as part of their function to gather information about local material held elsewhere. Such information will inevitably be incomplete but it provides a starting point. Another is to follow up clues in information already obtained; references to individuals whose interests lay largely elsewhere or to national organisations may sometimes give hints as to where additional information may be found.

Regional archives

At regional level there are two repositories of especial interest to East Yorkshire. The Yorkshire Archaeological Society was collecting archive material long before most of the public repositories were established and has extensive collections relating to all parts of the ancient county. The Borthwick Institute of Historical Research at York is chiefly concerned with the records of the higher administrative levels of the Church of England but it also holds parish records for the York area and deposited records.

Local archives

Locally the main archive repositories are the Kingston upon Hull Record Office (KHRO) which holds records relating to the City itself and is the main subject of this chapter, and the Humberside County Record Office which holds records relating to the remainder of the area. Needless to say, both repositories hold material relating to the area of the other since former administrative areas and the ways in which depositors organise their business are no respecters of modern administrative borders. Similar overlapping occurs between Humberside and its neighbours. Local archive material is also held in Hull University Library and some of the public libraries which have local history collections. Nor should local archive repositories in other parts of the country be overlooked. References in the local records to individuals or organisations whose primary sphere of activity was elsewhere will often suggest where relevant records might be found.

History of archive services in Hull

Although Kingston upon Hull City Council may be said to have established an archive service in the formal sense with the appointment of its first full-time archivist in 1968, this was the culmination of many years' work during which the arrangement, listing and accessibility of the records had been progressively improved. This process began just over a hundred years ago. Before that time records were dealt with on an *ad hoc* basis as the needs of current business demanded, but by about 1880 they were forcing themselves upon the attention of the Council both as a problem and as an opportunity. The problem was the familiar one of bulk. It is clear that papers had been allowed to accumulate without any consideration of their relative merits and with no policy for the disposal of trivial or routine material at regular intervals. But as soon as any attempt was made to identify material for destruction, it became apparent that among the duplicated and routine papers was an archive of considerable importance which should be preserved, arranged and made available to historians.

It was in response to this twofold problem that the Council appointed the local journalist and artist of antiquarian leanings, T. Tyndall Wildridge to the post of records clerk in 1884. He held this post until early 1895 when it was considered that he had completed his original task. There is no doubt that a great deal had been achieved. As far as reducing the bulk was concerned he disposed of 144 hundredweight of paper in the first eighteen months with more to follow in later years. His list of what was destroyed makes depressing reading. It includes petty sessions papers, Poor Law records, militia lists, poll books, insolvency records and accounts, to name only the more significant items. On the positive side he was responsible for creating the format/subject (i.e. deeds, leases, parliamentary, docks, railways, etc.) arrangement of the records which remained in operation until their reorganisation on archival principles in recent years. He also carried out much detailed work such as listing of deeds and transcribing charters which formed the foundations for the work of his successors.

About a year after Wildridge's dismissal J. R. Boyle offered his services to the Council. This offer was accepted and the chief product of his work on the historical records was his translation of the charters which were published in 1905. Boyle spent a good deal of his time indexing minutes and processing current documents into the numerical system which he initiated and which remains the basis of record keeping in the Town Clerk's Department. Indeed, the burden of this work became so great that it was necessary to provide him with an assistant and it was one of these, L. M. Stanewell, who succeeded Boyle on his departure in 1905. The appointment of an insider rather than someone with a background in historical scholarship as had been done in the past only served to emphasise the fact that work on the historical records would in future have to be fitted into whatever time could be spared from current adminis-tration. Thus Stanewell's achievement in compiling his *Calendar of the ancient deeds . . .* , which was published in 1951, is all the greater for having been completed under such unfavourable circumstances. However, this progressive reduction in the time available for work on the historical records meant that by the 1960s it was clear that the only way to make the substantial and important achives held by the Council available to the growing number of scholars and others wishing to use them was to appoint an archivist who could devote his whole time to creating a modern archives service.

This was achieved in 1968 but only then did it become apparent how much needed to be done. In Hull, record keeping had stood still since the turn of the century while archive methods elsewhere had been transformed. By modern standards the storage accommodation was totally unaccept-able, there was no proper provision for readers and Wildridge's format/subject arrangement of the records took no account of provenance or organic structure and was quite unable to cope with the many records which did not fit into its rigid structure. The accommodation problem was solved by the acquisition of 79 Lowgate. As a former bonded warehouse it was well adapted to the needs of an archive repository and its central position close to the Guildhall made it accessible to both Council staff and the general public. The first phase of conversion for Record Office use was completed in 1979 and provided offices, a search room, reference area and library and two floors of storage space which, when fully shelved, will contain about eight thousand feet of records. The new building has provided all that was expected of it, ample and attractive working space for staff and readers, proper conditions for the storage of documents and substantial gains in efficiency through having everything under one roof.

The rearrangement of the holdings and the compilation of lists which reflect the provenance and organic growth of the records has been a longer job. Much has been achieved but the task is by no means complete. However, progress has been sufficient for it to be possible to describe the current holdings in terms of their archive groups, covering not only the records which were inherited in 1968 but the far greater quantities of records which have been received by transfer from other departments or by outside deposit since that date.

THE HOLDINGS OF THE KHRO

Borough Corporation and City Council records

The core of the archives holdings are the records of the Borough (later City) Corporation, its post-reorganisation successor the City Council and the various bodies from which they have inherited powers and functions. The story of these bodies has been described in G. W. Oxley, *An introduction to the history of local government in Kingston upon Hull* (Hull, 1975) and may be briefly outlined here.

When the reformed Corporation was established in 1835 it inherited most of its functions from the chartered borough which it replaced. The most significant of these were the provision of the water supply and the management of the corporate estate, including the markets. The new Corporation also took over the task of providing a police force from the improvement commissioners. These had been established in 1801 (for Sculcoates) and 1810 (for Hull and Myton) to provide the paving, lighting and watching of streets and other environmental services. Under the 1847 Public Health Act their remaining powers, with those of parish highway authorities, were absorbed into the local Board of Health which had more extensive powers to control the physical environment in the interests of public health. This body was merged with the Borough Council in 1876. By means of similar mergers the work of the School Board, established in 1871, was absorbed by the Corporation in 1903 and that of the Poor Law Unions, established in 1837, in 1929.[1] Throughout this period additional powers were being conferred directly upon the Corporation. There were also periodic removals of powers such as those lost as a result of nationalisation in the late 1940s and to the County Council and Water Authority in 1974.

The records of the Corporation and each of the bodies it replaced follow a similar pattern. The main record was the minutes of the governing body and any committees which it may have established. They have survived well and since they contain all the major decisions they can be used to reconstruct the history of each authority or of a particular aspect of its work. Subsidiary to the minutes were the correspondence, reports and working papers. These have survived less fully than the minutes, but where they have, their bulk can be substantial and their value as a means of filling out and providing background to the decisions which are briefly reported

30

in the minutes is considerable. Financial records have also survived well and are complementary to the minutes in that while the latter are predominantly concerned with new policies, practices and services, the former have more to say about the continuing work of established activities. Indeed, they are one of the few sources which do deal extensively, if in a rather specialised way, with the routine activities of the public services.

Over and above these common and central classes of records each authority developed other classes which were peculiar to its particular activities. These fall into three main areas: the provision of public services, the supervision and regulation of private activities and the management of resources. Although the outline history given above indicates some of the broad areas of services provided by the local authorities it does no more than hint at a few salient features of a range of activities, the scope of which is so broad that special finding aids have been devised to assist the enquirer to gain access to the relevant records. At the centre are lists of the duties assigned to each of the Council committees from 1876 onwards which, taken together, give a full account of Council responsibilities at any given date. Subsidiary to this is an index of Council properties which have been many and varied and have ranged from prisons and hospitals to bridges and refuse destructors. This index is especially valuable because it focuses on an area which is well documented. A sheet is provided for each property. It identifies the responsible committee and relevant documents such as the legal records of site ownership, building contracts and the purchase of capital equipment, the design records of architects and engineers and the financial records. Together these provide a full and detailed picture of how each property was acquired, constructed, altered and improved.

The supervisory and regulatory functions were as wide and varied as the public services. They range from major tasks such as planning and building control to the licensing or registration of such specialised groups as dealers in scrap metal and the export of horses. The full range of these activities is best derived from the lists of committee duties but for many of the smaller functions records other than references in the minutes have failed to survive.

Local authority assets may be considered under three headings: money, staff and property. The first of these has already been considered in the context of accounting records. The second represents a very large area which includes, besides professional and clerical workers in central departments, specialists like teachers and police and many kinds of manual workers, especially in the trading departments. The employment of staff on such a scale generates a great deal of routine paperwork which it has never been practicable to retain and information is, therefore, scattered between references to appointments and retirements in the minutes and specialised records like national insurance contribution books and the records which were kept for some of the early superannuation schemes.

It is, however, in the area of property management that the records are the fullest. Starting in the middle ages the local authorities have built up a

31

substantial portfolio of commercial property including farm land, shops, offices and factories. The main documentation consists of a series of rentals from 1527 and of leases and tenancy agreements from 1399. Letters from tenants, actual and prospective, and from agents are to be found throughout the correspondence of the unreformed Borough and of the Property Committee after 1837. Documentation relating to individual properties may be traced through the Council property index described above. Together these records constitute a remarkably comprehensive source for all aspects of property management over a long period of time and, indirectly, for the tenants of the properties and the economic activities in which they were engaged.

Semi-official records

A much wider range of subject matter is to be found in the records of those activities and organisations over which the Council exercised varying degrees of control but were not part of the Council itself. One such was the Hull Charterhouse, an almshouse endowed by the De la Poles in 1384. The family retained the advowson, or right to appoint the master of the Charterhouse and, after their fall, it was granted to the Hull Corporation in 1552. When the Charterhouse was reorganised under a Charity Commissioners scheme in 1902 the Town Clerk became clerk to the trustees and the archive passed into his custody. The greater part of it is concerned with the estate which is of particular interest in that it included agricultural land in Cottingham and elsewhere, chalk quarries at Hessle, a high class residential development in West Hill, Hessle and buildings in the commercial centre of Hull. The ownership and administration of these properties is fully recorded in deeds, leases from 1410 onwards, glebe terriers, plans, correspondence and accounts. By contrast the master and brethren (as the inmates were called) are very poorly documented. For the former there is very little more than formal appointments and for the latter, occasional lists or registers.

Another section of the former De la Pole estate which the Corporation acquired in 1552 was the lordship of the manor of Myton. The manorial records relate to the transfer of property in the small portion of the manor which was held by copyhold tenure. These areas were developed early in the nineteenth century as the town spread westwards and the court rolls therefore provide a full and detailed record of the process of urban development and of urban land ownership. Quite different are the records of public meetings which were called by the mayor at the request of groups of citizens. They were generally concerned with matters of topical interest and relate to such varied subjects as opposition to the proposals of the proprietors of the Aire and Calder Navigation in 1774, the East India Monopoly in 1829, destitution in the highlands and islands of Scotland in 1837 and assassinations in Dublin in 1882. The interest in these records is derived not only from their subject matter but also from their indication of who felt strongly on particular issues and, occasionally, from the diverse points of view expressed. Other groups of records in this category relate to charities managed by the Corporation, taxes levied on shipping, the service for weighing lead passing through the port, rates levied for the payment of the vicar's salary and, more recently, the records of the Humber Bridge Board.

The history of the County of Kingston upon Hull has been complex. The Borough itself was given county status in 1440 and the neighbouring townships of Hessle, North Ferriby, Swanland, West Ella, Kirk Ella, Tranby, Willerby, Wolfreton, Anlaby and Haltemprice were added in 1447. Under the Municipal Reform Act of 1835 the county was abolished and the jurisdiction over the whole area transferred to the East Riding Quarter Sessions. In 1837 Quarter Sessions for Hull was reestablished with jurisdiction over the area within the town boundary. This continued until abolition in 1971. Since these powers and functions have been fully described elsewhere we may concentrate on certain groups of records which are unusual and of particular interest.[2] Among these are the assessments for national taxation which are most numerous for the seventeenth century and include ship money, to finance the army during the Civil War, and for various later taxes, including the tax on marriages etc., of 1695-97, the assessment of which involved listing every inhabitant. Two groups of records which have survived in exceptional detail from 1837 to 1900 are papers relating to prosecutions at Quarter Sessions and to coroners' inquests. In addition to the formal papers there are statements by the eyewitnesses which detail the circumstances in which the crime or death took place and, in so doing, give a vivid picture of the ordinary life of the period.

Although the records of Quarter Sessions have generally been housed alongside the Council records they are not legally records of local government but of central government. As such they are one of several groups of records which have been deposited in or donated to the record office by central government under the Public Records Act of 1958. Among other important groups of records which have been received in the same way are the records of the registration of shipping and motor vehicles, valuations for the 1910 tax on land values, hospital records and trawler crew lists, 1884-1914.

Deposited records

In addition to official and semi-official records the record office seeks to preserve and make available records relating to all aspects of life in Hull by receiving records by gift or deposit from individuals and organisations of all kinds. While the staff are regularly approaching organisations known to have records, especially if they appear to be in danger, as in the case of businesses in liquidation or receivership, this is an area where a substantial contribution to the preservation of the local heritage can be made by the general public informing the record office of records which might be available for deposit or are threatened with destruction. Books and papers which may appear dull or even unintelligible to one person can provide vital historical information to another and archivists are always ready to inspect material in order to ascertain its suitability for preservation.

As befits a large commercial centre the chief source of deposited records has been local businesses. Among records held are those of engineers, trawler owners, corn millers, land agents, printers, retailers, paint manufacturers and fruit merchants. The balance of the contents of the archives varies greatly. The legal requirement to keep formal records relating to shareholders and directors means that they figure prominently in the archives of companies which have ceased to exist but by the same token are absent from the deposited records of extant businesses. If the product was of a durable capital nature detailed records of design and sales were compiled to assist in the manufacture of replacement parts and the promotion of future sales. In Hull it was more often a case of producing a standard product such as flour, oil, or fish in large quantities. Such industries rarely retained repetitive sales records and production figures are, at best, periodic, global figures. Some businesses, notably professional firms, preserved records relating to the firms they served so that deeds of business property, contracts and partnerships often come from solicitors' offices and financial records from accountants.

Another type of record which throws light on organisations other than the one which created the record are the data which some firms collected as a basis for management decisions. Thus the records of property sales, including auction catalogues and advertisements, which Hebblethwaite and Company maintained from 1850-1930 as a basis for their valuation work provide a mass of information about the condition, occupancy and management of all kinds of property. Similarly trawler owners recorded the catch of every vessel discharging in the port in order to assess the relative merits of different skippers, fishing grounds and types of ship. The information thus gathered provides a basis for studying the history of the whole industry and not just those firms whose records happen to have survived. Another way in which business records may be used to illuminate a wider area than the history of the individual firm is through the comparison of material relating to a particular theme such as design, production, marketing or accounting procedures from a number of businesses. Nor should it be forgotten that business and its records are as important as any other element in the study of a particular locality.

The scope of other deposits is very wide. Some are from voluntary associations, which have come into being during the last two centuries for the pursuit of common interests, the propagation of particular views, the search for mutual protection, or through the desire to benefit humanity. Among them are the records of churches, trade unions and associations, charities and ethnic organisations. Other records have been received from individuals. Whether they be correspondence, photographs or papers relating to employment, investment or the membership of organisations their survival is often a matter of chance but their value as a counterweight to the institutional nature of most surviving records is considerable.

The role of the record office

The primary duty of the record office is to secure the preservation of its holdings which are now in the region of eight thousand shelf feet of records. Keeping them in secure strong rooms with fire protection and the correct atmospheric conditions provides the basic requirements but many documents have already deteriorated owing to heavy use or unsatisfactory storage. In such cases restoration and repair work is necessary. This work is the chief responsibility of the office's conservator who also undertakes related duties such as the binding of lists and mounting documents for exhibitions.

Using the record office

When the necessary conservation work is complete the records can be made available to readers. This is generally done by means of a personal visit because, although staff can answer specific enquiries by telephone or letter, their primary function is to make the records available to all and to advise on how they might be used for particular lines of research, but not to undertake detailed enquiries on behalf of individuals. A list of professional searchers can be made available to anyone who is unable to visit the office in person.

The first step for most prospective readers is to obtain copies of relevant introductory leaflets. They can be supplied on receipt of a stamped addressed envelope and at present cover *General information, Finding aids, Genealogy and family history* and *Photocopying.* Other titles are in preparation. In some cases a preliminary discussion with a member of staff may also be advisable. Having established in broad terms that relevant material is available the next step is to move on to the finding aids. These are arranged at three levels. The top level is the working guide which is designed to give a general overview of the holdings. It is still in preparation and will consist of summaries of the classification system arranged alphabetically and on a structured basis and a summary description of each group of records. At the second level are the lists which describe each item in each of these groups. They are arranged in alphabetical order of class letters. When the document required has been identified it may be obtained by completing a requisition slip and handing it to a member of staff. The third level of finding aids are the indexes of names, places and ships. They are derived in part from the lists and in part from original documents such as the shipping registers, letter books, prosecution papers and coroners' inquests which are virtually unusable until indexes have been provided.

The number of people visiting the office has been increasing at the rate of 25% a year for several years. The largest group of readers are those engaged in education either as students or teachers. As far as the students are concerned their use of the office falls into three main areas. First are those for whom the visit is an end in itself. Here the intention is to make the students aware of the office and its resources, often as part of a programme involving visits to other similar establishments. The second area concerns groups or classes pursuing a common project. This approach is especially popular at primary school level and can be very successful when there is sufficient material and adequate preliminary planning. The third and commonest area is individual project work. Here careful preparation is even more vital because it is necessary to match a topic for which there is adequate material with the time available and the ability of the student.

Most archive sources are specific and detailed and lend themselves to similarly specific and detailed studies. They can also be used for work of a more general nature but experience shows that at school level students have neither the time nor the experience to work through and bring together the range and quantity of source material that this requires. The processes which brought archives into being and secured their preservation mean that their coverage is highly selective. It is therefore also essential to choose project topics for which sources actually exist. These considerations may at first appear very restrictive but they do have one positive advantage in that they force students to abandon vague generalised projects in favour of asking specific questions of their sources and, in seeking the answers, to learn something of the historian's craft.

Of the remaining groups of readers the largest contains those using records for practical reasons. It includes Council staff consulting official records which have been transferred to the record office, the staff of cognate institutions such as museums and the Hull Heritage Centre, outside professionals such as architects, engineers and solicitors and private individuals who need information from the records. The smallest groups are those pursuing some personal interest and family historians. This may seem surprising in view of the way in which the latter activity has expanded in recent years but it must be remembered that there are no parish registers or wills in Hull and that the materials available are therefore fairly limited in scope and, often, of a specialised nature.

Although the use of the record office has grown steadily in recent years there is a continuing need to make the public aware of the services it provides. This is partly because these services are growing and changing as new records become available, partly because people do not take in the message until it relates to a perceived need, and partly because of the difficulty of making individuals aware, not of the service in general, but of that particular area which relates to their interests. Various strategies have been adopted to overcome these problems. One of these is an active publications programme through which guides to various sections of the holdings,[3] the results of work on the archives[4] and the texts of individual documents (now published in conjunction with Malet Lambert High School) are made available to a wider public. More specialised audiences are reached through notes and articles in their publications and the KHRO staff regularly give talks about their work to local societies and adult education classes or arrange for them to visit the offices at their normal time of meeting. Occasionally the record office mounts exhibitions in which its own holdings are the dominant element but in view of the limited visual appeal of most archive material the preferred approach is to contribute documentary items to shows drawing on a wider range of exhibits. A small display is also one of the attractions provided when the KHRO opens its doors to the general public as part of the open house programme of the annual Hull Festival. This event is valuable because it is the one occasion on which people who have no specific reason to visit a record office can come inside and learn something of the service in an informal way.

Although *action* is perhaps not what one would immediately associate with the atmosphere of studious serenity which we cultivate in our search rooms, a great deal of action is needed in order to create the service which is provided there. Finding, collecting, storing, listing, indexing, publicising and producing records all require action both physical and mental. But, however demanding these activities may be, it is important to realise that they are not an end in themselves. Ultimately archives will be judged not by the quantity of records held or by the number of readers signing the book but by the contribution which taken as a whole they make to the cultural and intellectual life of the community which brought them into being.

Notes for chapter 2

1.   For details of the records of these bodies see G. W. Oxley, *Guide to the Kingston upon Hull Record Office, part 1: Records of local authorities whose areas or functions were taken over by the former county borough of Kingston upon Hull* (Hull, 1978)

2.   F. G. Emmison and I. Gray, *County records* (London, 1977)

3.   L. M. Stanewell, *Calendar of the ancient records, letters, miscellaneous old documents in the archives of the Corporation of Kingston upon Hull . . . 1300-1800* (Hull, 1951); G. W. Oxley, ed., *World War II* (Hull, 1979); G. W. Oxley, ed., *Transport by sea, rail and inland navigation* (Hull, 1984)

4.   C. W. Chilton, *Early Hull printers and booksellers, an account of the printing, bookselling and allied trades from their beginnings to 1840* (Hull, 1982); J. A. R. and M. E. Bickford, *The medical profession in Hull: a biographical dictionary, 1400-1900* (Hull, 1983); R. Horrox, *The changing plan of Hull, 1290-1650: a guide to documentary sources for the early topography of Hull* (Hull, 1978)

3

MEDIEVAL HISTORY

Barbara English[1]

'Medieval' (sometimes 'mediaeval') is an adjective constructed from two Latin words meaning the middle age — the middle of what? The middle of three phases of history, the interval between the age of Greece and Rome, and modern times. The term seems to have been invented in Italy, in the fifteenth century: men of the great Italian city states, living in a time of intellectual change, believed themselves to be living in a new age, a rebirth of a culture lost for centuries, a rebirth which became known as the Renaissance. They felt they were reviving the great traditions of the classical civilisations of Greece and Rome. The time in between the classical age and their own was to men of the Renaissance a time of little importance, of intellectual and cultural stagnation, which they labelled 'the Middle Ages' and everything belonging to the Middle Ages was 'medieval'. It was to be several centuries before the Middle Ages began to be recognised as an era of great interest to historians, a time which saw the foundations of modern society, and in addition left a great artistic heritage.

Like most historical labels, the terms Middle Ages and its derivative medieval are imprecise, and the span of centuries described in these terms varies from subject to subject, and from place to place. In East Yorkshire, the medieval period probably begins when Roman Britain was finally overwhelmed by the barbarian invaders: around the year A.D. 410. It probably ends around 1536, when the centuries of Roman Catholicism, associated with a complex structure of church and monastic organisation, and a unified cultural tradition, were largely demolished by Henry VIII. Historians might choose to omit the first centuries after A.D. 410 (sometimes called 'the Dark Ages'), and also might decide that 'early modern England' began in the late fifteenth century, perhaps with the death of Richard III in 1485 and the replacement of the Yorkist dynasty by the Tudor kings, rather than taking the date of the Reformation of the church as decisive: it depends on the historian's individual view of history.

For historians of East Yorkshire, 1066 is a convenient date to begin the study of the medieval history of their locality, as evidence before that date is almost entirely archaeological. From the date of the Norman Conquest, and more particularly from the compilation of Domesday Book in 1086, there are some historical records, both written and unwritten, for most places in the region; and from about 1300 there are enough sources to allow the historian to make judgements with some confidence. The case study that follows at the end of this chapter begins around 1066: but the terminal date is much less precise; it is difficult to know in what century to end, for history has a unity that is difficult to divide.

As in many areas of research in different subjects, it is best to start with the known and easily accessible, and work back into the unknown. In the study of a medieval community, the 'known' may well be a surviving building (a church, or much more rarely, a castle), or a landscape (earthworks, parish boundaries, traces of medieval farming). This may set the historian on the long trail through books, documents, maps, photographs, ditches, hedgerows, thistles and brambles to a final goal, a day when he believes that all possible sources have been investigated.

Medieval source material is not so overwhelming in bulk as for, say, a nineteenth century topic. Most topics in history have a medieval dimension, but in many areas the evidence is fragmentary. A historian could choose a subject such as 'the position of women in East Yorkshire during the Middle Ages', or 'the wine trade of the Humber in the fourteenth century', and then find that months of research would produce very little evidence, perhaps ten short and unrelated extracts. In local studies of the Middle Ages, it is best to select subjects which it is possible to research *because* the evidence exists, rather than the alternative way of deciding on a topic and *then* looking for evidence, which may no longer exist, or may never have existed.

Most people working in local history are likely to be interested in a community, or group of communities, and this is an area in which some sources can always be found. But even here, survival of records is partial, and the history of other communities may have to be used, to round out the picture. For instance, if there is no record of how many people in your community died in the Black Death of 1349, you might have to study other communities in the neighbourhood which did have some records of mortality, to see what was likely to have happened in the community you were studying. Working in some areas and periods of medieval history is like deciphering a code, or trying to complete a crossword of which only some clues exist, and no more may ever be found. It may sound difficult; but many people come to enjoy this challenge, which may represent a more purely intellectual challenge than sifting vast quantities of material to reach a conclusion. If you were writing an account of the Battle of Stamford Bridge in 1066, you would have access to the site itself, and a small number of medieval narrative accounts of the battle, all incomplete and all flawed, some of which had not been written down until centuries after the event. There would be no new sources to discover. However, if you studied the site, the available sources, other eleventh century battles and the essentials of military strategy and tactics, you might create a more accurate recon-struction of the battle than had been achieved before.

Most medieval topics in local history are not so restricted in sources as the Battle of Stamford Bridge, and often you will find documents that no one else has used. There is a finite number of sources, however, and in medieval local history you have the chance of reading every source that still exists for a topic, and making your deductions on that basis. In an industrious life, you could read every medieval source that survived from the borough of Hedon in the Middle Ages: whereas if you were studying Hull in the Second World War, you could only study a minute fraction of the surviving material, and hope that your conclusions would remain valid if you had read the other half million documents. . . .

The written documents of medieval history show obvious differences from modern historical sources. They are usually in Latin, and sometimes (much harder and fortunately rarer) in Old French. The handwriting and some forms of letters, such as the long 's', the backwards 'r', are unfamiliar. The Latin words are usually heavily abbreviated: some of these abbreviations have survived, for instance A.D. in connection with a date (Anno Domini) and etc. (et cetera), but many would be unfamiliar to the reader new to the Middle Ages. On the positive side, however, medieval documents are usually very short — one of William the Conqueror's few surviving letters would be one piece of parchment about five inches by three inches: one of Queen Victoria's letters might be ten or more larger pages, and there are thousands of them. Medieval writing, once you have learned to read it, is (unlike later handwriting) very clearly written, with each letter formed separately, and the abbreviations have a logical, and consistent, meaning. The writing is often very elegant, written as a form of artistic expression. The analogy of William the Conqueror's letters (called 'writs') and Queen Victoria's letters illustrates another great advantage of working on medieval sources: all known letters of King William I are in print (and if another were found it would immediately be published), whereas Queen Victoria's letters are not all published and are unlikely to be so. A comparatively large proportion of medieval sources has been published, and virtually all the earliest documents, as publishing policy for the last 150 years has been to begin at the chronological beginning, at A.D. 1150, rather than, say, 1400. So paradoxically it is easier to work from printed sources in the twelfth century or early thirteenth century than in later centuries. A number of books has been written to help students translate and date medieval documents: some of these are listed in the bibliography of this book. Most record offices and some universities organise courses to help students decipher medieval writing and the format of medieval documents ('palaeography and diplomatic' courses).

Research into written history for any topic or period should begin in the local history library nearest to you, where the librarians will show you what has already been published about your community. The published bibliographies relating to East Yorkshire are listed at the end of this book. If the *Victoria County History* (VCH) has published a volume on your area, that is an excellent reference point. Failing that, most communities have some kind of written history, often concentrating on the manor and the church. The local history library may also be able to find for you articles in journals, maps going back to the first edition of the Ordnance Survey (OS) in the mid-nineteenth century, aerial and other photographs, and medieval documents in print. Do not, however, expect the local history librarians to do your research for you. You will find, as you read through the printed histories that footnotes or other references will lead you further and further into your subject. It is worth while, too, reading histories of other medieval topics or communities, to see if the author has made ingenious use of some source that might not otherwise have occurred to you.

Published histories are classified as secondary sources, several steps removed from the raw material of history. After working through all the

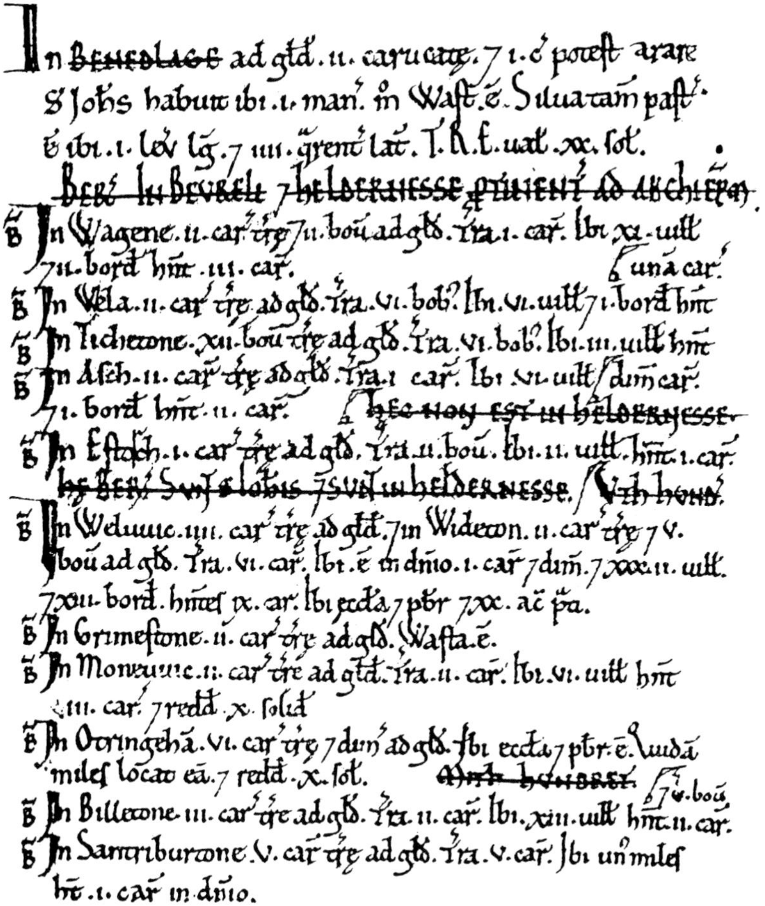

Figure 2: Extract from Domesday Book, describing part of the land of the Archbishop of York in Bentley, Wawne, Weel, Tickton, Eske and Stork (facsimile)

secondary sources, the next stage is to look at primary sources, that is, those created at the time of the events or past conditions being investigated. Again, it is easier to start with those most accessible, the documents in print, produced by the operation of central government or in the shire.

As has been written above, most central government records before c.1250 have now been published. For the whole set of government records in print you may have to use the University Library at Hull (HUL) or York, the Minster Library at York (YML) or the Lincolnshire Archives Office.

41

Domesday Book, the first central government record, has been published in its various editions, from facsimiles of the original text (see figure 2 for an example) to English translations. Many medieval records for East Yorkshire from both central and local sources have been printed by societies such as the Yorkshire Archaeological Society (YAS), or the East Riding Antiquarian Society (ERAS). The historian should search these publications before moving into the realm of unpublished documents, for it is very irritating to spend days transcribing a difficult document and finding later that it has already been published.

Unprinted records of the Middle Ages are for the most part either still in the county, or in the Public Record Office (PRO) or the British Library (BL) in London, with some in neighbouring counties and (because several important collections were bequeathed there) in the Bodleian Library, Oxford. Boroughs have preserved a certain amount of source material for the Middle Ages, and in East Yorkshire the towns of Beverley, Hedon and Hull have good medieval records which are now in the Humberside County Record Office (HCRO), or Kingston upon Hull Record Office (KHRO). It is not usual to find any surviving archives of local government of the Middle Ages in the county, except in some places in the form of manor court rolls; there are virtually no medieval parish records (registers, for instance, were not kept until 1538), but references to parishes can be found among the records, now in the Borthwick Institute of Historical Research at York (BIHR), kept by the Archbishop and other officials of the diocese of York, and also in the records of monasteries such as Bridlington, Meaux, Swine and Kirkham.[2] Monks were much better at keeping records than laymen, and monasteries had property all over the county, so that some information about almost every place can be found in one or other monastic chronicle or cartulary. Monastic chronicles are listed by A. Gransden in *Historical writing in England c.550 to c.1307* (London, 1974) and *Historical writing in England c.1307 to the early 16th century* (London, 1982); and cartularies by G. R. C. Davis in *Medieval cartularies of Great Britain: a short catalogue* (London, 1958). Excellent local sources for the Middle Ages are contained among the archives of the great landowning families, such as Hotham, Chichester Constable of Burton Constable, Bethell of Rise. These archives are almost invariably deposited within the county in the HCRO, KHRO, HUL, or at York in the BIHR or YML. All these record offices have detailed catalogues of documents, and the medieval documents are described very carefully, and sometimes completely translated.

Central government records of the Middle Ages are kept at the PRO, Chancery Lane, London. The *Guide to the contents of the Public Record Office* is essential; a large number of other lists and indexes can be found in the university libraries and some record offices. Both the BL and the Bodleian have published detailed catalogues of charters, manuscripts and other documents, and these catalogues can be found in the largest libraries.

Searching for material in London and Oxford can be expensive. The best solution seems to be a well-planned 'raid' in which the historian visits

London for the shortest possible time, perhaps on a day trip, looks at as much material as he can (which must be ordered in advance of the visit) and, without trying to transcribe it at the time of the visit, orders a photocopy or a microfilm of anything which looks useful. Seven hours work at Chancery Lane or the BL, using this system, can produce enough microfilm for months of work, much more economically, at home or in the local library. The London institutions and the Bodleian require the historian to obtain a reader's ticket, and this should be applied for in advance.

Not all medieval history comes from books and from pieces of parchment in record offices. The work of W. G. Hoskins and M. W. Beresford persuaded historians to leave their studies and get their feet muddy by going out to see what traces of the medieval past they could find. Local history at the end of the twentieth century encompasses a large proportion of field work, studying surviving earthworks, parish boundaries, standing buildings, the whole shape of the community — for the houses in a street may date from the nineteenth century, but they may be built in a street that has remained unchanged since the early Middle Ages. The siting of settlements, the placing of the church in the community, the road or river systems, all these elements of what Beresford called 'History on the ground' may tell the researcher something of the Middle Ages. It is in this area that maps and plans become essential tools, and aerial photographs, which often show landscape features hard to discern on the ground, can be a key to the re-creation of a medieval landscape (see figures 3 and 4).

CASE STUDY: THE DESERTED VILLAGE OF ESKE

For many years I had known that there was the site of a lost village at Eske, some miles north east of Beverley, near Tickton and Hull Bridge.[3] All the inhabitants of the area marked on the modern map as 'Eske' now live in one of two farmhouses, High Eske and Eske Manor (sometimes called Low Eske) or in the associated farm cottages. Yet there were signs that the parish of Eske had once been much more densely populated. Walking on the bank of the River Hull, it was possible to see, between the river and the seventeenth century manor house (see figure 6), the earthworks of the deserted village: that is, the old village streets, the boundary bank that once enclosed the cottages, and the corrugations in the fields which represent the old ridge and furrow of medieval and early modern farming. Curiosity about the earthworks of an old settlement first led me to investigate Eske. What had happened to the village? When was it first mentioned, and when and why did it disappear? How large had it been at its peak: how had the villagers lived, and why had they abandoned their houses, leaving the roofs to fall in, the grass to grow over the cottage walls, and the village street to become a green lane leading nowhere?

The first clue, therefore, was the site and the earthworks, which I found by chance on a picnic. Deserted villages nearly always have footpaths or bridle paths leading to them, survivals of the past, although even if there is

Figure 3: Aerial photograph of Eske taken in July 1970 and showing the
earthworks of the deserted village, roadways and ridge and furrow

a right of way it is diplomatic to ask the farmer for permission to visit the
site: you may also learn a considerable amount about the history of the site
from the farmer or his family. Once the earthworks had been found, I
looked at the modęrn OS map, but there was no 'site of the village of Eske'
marked, as is sometimes the case; however, any parish name on the map
without a centre of settlement may, in the East Riding, indicate a deserted
village (there are over a hundred such sites in the former county). I turned to
the literature on deserted medieval villages, dominated, in Yorkshire
particularly, by the work of Maurice Beresford. His description of the site
of Eske, in the *Yorkshire Archaeological Journal* (YAJ) for 1952, began with
the information that it was recorded in Domesday Book, gave some
medieval tax figures, reported that in 1801 thirty-two people lived at Eske,
cited evidence of ten house-plots in 1280 and seven in 1458 and continued:
'The air photograph is very clear and a number of two- and three-roomed
cottages can be seen. The village appears to have centred around a road

44

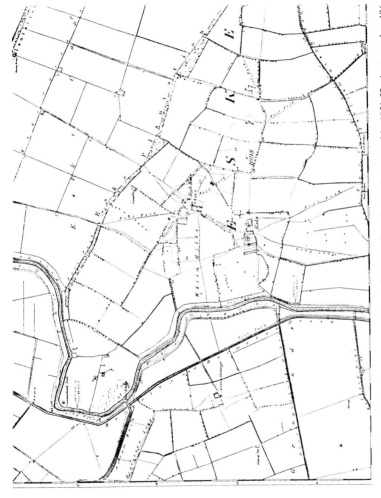

Figure 4: First edition of the Ordnance Survey map of Eske (extract), surveyed in 1851-52, sheet number 196

45

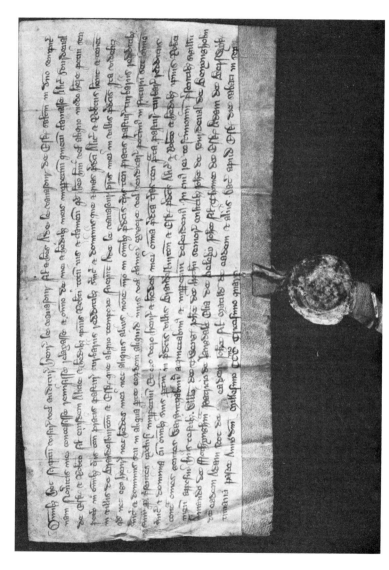

Figure 5: Charter of 1334 relating to property at Brandesburton and Eske (Yorkshire Archaeological Society MD 120 V6a)

46

Figure 6: The seventeenth century manor house at Eske

down to the ford'; the brief account was accompanied by an aerial photograph taken by the Royal Air Force in the 1940s.[4]

The VCH volume which will include Eske has not yet been published, but the editor of the East Riding volumes, Dr Keith Allison, has nearly completed his work on the parish, and I learned much from discussions with him, and he also provided me with valuable references. Next I turned to one of the massive nineteenth century histories of our area, George Poulson's *History of Holderness*, knowing that he would have published all he could find about Eske either in his *Holderness* volume or in his *Beverlac*: one of the problems of the place I was investigating was that sometimes it was deemed to be in Holderness, sometimes in Beverley. Poulson devoted seven pages to Eske; he was not a totally reliable historian, and made many errors in transcribing medieval documents; but he did normally give his sources.[5] Here I was lucky: one of those days when the researcher feels extraordinarily privileged. Poulson had copied a number of extremely interesting early medieval documents from the collection of another historian called J. R. Walbran: Walbran's own copy of the Eske documents was in the YML and I was able to obtain a copy of them.[6] They included thirteenth century charters relating to Eske and in particular a survey of the pasture there in 1278, which contained a considerable amount of information about land tenure and farming in early medieval Eske. Beyond Walbran's copy I reached a dead end; he had transcribed his Eske charters from a medieval original or originals in the possession of a great, perhaps the greatest, English collector of manuscripts, Sir John Phillipps. The Phillipps manuscripts were sold after the collector's death, and in spite of more searching of catalogues and letter writing, I have not yet been able to find where the original Eske charters are now; however, I do have Walbran's transcripts.

Poulson used in addition central government records: almost all those he used are now in print, and I would have found them in any event, but it is useful to have a cross-check. In any medieval research, the same references turn up several times in different secondary sources. The historian should try to get as close as possible to the original primary source, to eliminate mistakes in transcriptions by others.

Having exhausted the secondary sources for Eske, I searched through central government records in print — financial, legal and administrative rolls.[7] Apart from the Curia Regis Rolls for the later thirteenth century and beyond, most of these have been published in good modern editions and a week's part-time working through the indexes of the volumes completed the search of these printed central government records. It is infinitely easier, of course, to look for a place or a family name than for an abstract subject such as 'military service' or 'harbour works'. After searching central government records, I looked through all the indexes of the *Transactions* of the East Riding Antiquarian Society (ERAS), the YAS's *Record* series, the Surtees Society's volumes relating to East Yorkshire, and the Selden Society's publications of Yorkshire civil and criminal court rolls: all of these series print medieval records. During the course of a previous piece of research, I had read at the PRO all Holderness sources before c.1300, so that the main gaps in my knowledge of Eske in central government records were now those of the later Middle Ages and early modern England. I have not yet managed to look at all the documents that might be relevant for these later centuries: I have only looked at the most obvious sources, and these are described below.

A good source for the history of a community is the collection of central government tax records; there is a series of lay subsidies, clerical subsidies, and, perhaps the most useful but existing for a short time only, poll taxes, which taxed the people of a community at so much per head (per 'poll'). The poll tax was levied on 'adult' heads, a classification which may have been interpreted in different ways, but probably included every person aged fourteen years and over. In Eske in 1377 sixty-three people paid poll tax;[8] obviously the community at that time, with well over a hundred inhabitants if children were included, was well populated. By 1539, however, a surviving muster roll of men suitable for military service,[9] found only seven such men in Eske, the smallest number in any Holderness community, and the only number in single figures. This is not intended to be a history of Eske, but a case study in methodology; it seemed important, however to demonstrate that at some time between 1377 and 1539 the number of villagers had drastically declined. In which decade, and for what reasons, is still not clear.

Central government was interested in drainage problems in the flat marshy land of Holderness, Eske being partly on carr land beside the River Hull. Government interest led to a long series of surveys in the Middle Ages and later, which occasionally described parts of Eske. The surveys, from the fourteenth century on, can be found in the Patent Rolls,[10] in Sir William Dugdale's *Imbanking and drayning*,[11] in Poulson's *Holderness*[12] and in the later archives of the Holderness drainage boards, and they help to reconstruct the medieval landscape.

Because Eske belonged in the early Middle Ages to the Provost of Beverley Minster, there are references to the parish in the Minster Chapter Act Book.[13] The Chapter Act Book includes a tantalising reference to a 'church' at Eske, which Dr. Allison thinks is probably a chapel, attached to the manor house, as no other reference to a church at Eske has been found. The tithes of Eske belonged to Beverley Minster all through the Middle Ages, and then were sold or granted to successive landowners until about 1650, when the land was described as 'tithe free'.[14] Church records are little help in decoding the history of Eske.

Had Eske belonged to a great family, such as Constable of Burton Constable, or Percy of Leconfield, a family that survived into the twentieth century; or had it belonged to a monastery such as Meaux or Nunkeeling, there might have been more sources. The canons of Beverley Minster were not particularly good at keeping records, and the gentry families who held the manor in the Middle Ages, families such as York, Hebden, Vavasour, Surdeval, Grimston, have vanished and left trace save four or five charters in the BL, the Bodleian or in the YAS at Leeds. Estate archives, therefore, were not very useful in the case of Eske.

Late in my searches I wrote to the Deserted Medieval Village Research

Group in London, which keeps files on all deserted village sites.[15] The secretary of the group generously sent me a photocopy of all the references to Eske that the group had found, mainly in central government records; by this time most of the references were familiar to me, but one or two were additional, and the cross-check was very useful.

Archives only record part of the history of Eske, however, and all through the years of (intermittently) searching for Eske material, I had visited the site, at all seasons and with different ideas of what to look for. The basis for the fieldwork on the ground was maps and aerial photographs, and there was constant reference from the site to maps and photographs and back to the site again.

The earliest map depicting Eske in any detail (it occurs earlier on county maps) is one made in 1668 by John Osborne, showing the course of the River Hull from the Humber to North Frodingham. This map was described by T. Sheppard in 1939; the original map was deposited in Hull Museum in 1939 and was almost certainly destroyed in the bombing of the Museum in the Second World War. It now exists only in a photocopy in the BL and in the Map Room of HUL, and will not reproduce satisfactorily. It is difficult to know how accurate Osborne was — or even if he intended to show Eske as it was, or if he was just drawing some houses to represent a settlement. The number of houses shown by Osborne, however, agrees with the number of houses at Eske in the Hearth Tax of 1671.[17] Eske is shown on some of the drainage maps of the eighteenth and nineteenth centuries; the landowners of Eske commissioned a map of the township in 1833, and then in the 1850s the great series of OS maps begins (see figure 4).[18] These maps may eventually be useful in discovering the early history of the village: at present they are potentially rather than actually helpful.

There are some useful aerial photographs of Eske (one is printed as figure 3) which show the former village earthworks quite clearly. Aerial photographs can be obtained from various sources: the local planning office (district or county), the Royal Commission on Historical Monuments (in 1985 renamed English Heritage), and the Aerofilms Library. Local history libraries often have reference copies. A friendly civil pilot or crop sprayer may take a photograph for you, or take you up to make your own: but the effects of light at different times of the day, the season and the state of the crops mean that photographs taken by a professional air photographer used to working for archaeologists and historians are almost invariably much the most successful. It is said that a kite or radio-controlled model aeroplane can be adapted to take aerial photographs, but I have not yet risked my camera in such an experiment.

Finally, a complex site such as Eske deserves a measured plan of the surviving earthworks. With students I have undertaken ground surveys at Eske. Even if our mapping skills are rudimentary, which seems unfortunately to be the case, the exercise of measuring, drawing, trying to interpret, speculating and arguing, helped greatly in the understanding of the earthworks. It is unlikely that Eske will ever be excavated: but if I can, in time, look at all the documentary sources, and visit the site (which is a scheduled site and cannot be ploughed) again and again, and compare the deserted village with others in the area, I hope by the end of the century to have arrived at some tentative conclusions about what the village was like, what happened to the villagers, when they left, and why. Research of this type in medieval history is a slow process; but great satisfaction comes from successfully solving part of the jigsaw that the history of the Middle Ages represents.

Notes for chapter 3
1.   I should like to thank the following individuals and institutions for their help: Dr. Keith Allison, C. B. L. Barr, Mr. and Mrs. Ellerington (who farm the site of Eske), Dr. John Hurst, Alan Marshall; British Museum Map Room, Brynmor Jones Library of the University of Hull, Humberside County Record Office, National Monuments Record, and the Yorkshire Archaeological Society
2.   Ecclesiastical records are discussed more fully in chapter 4
3.   The National Grid reference for the site of Eske is 99 TA 056433
4.   M. W. Beresford, 'Lost villages of Yorkshire, part 2', YAJ, 38 (1952), p.61 and plate I
5.   G. Poulson, *The history and antiquities of the Seigniory of Holderness*, 3 vols (Hull, 1840-41); G. Poulson, *Beverlac; or, The antiquities and history of the town of Beverley . . .*, 2 vols (London, 1829)
6.   YML MS Add. 271
7.   For central government records, see G. R. Elton, *England 1200-1640* (Cambridge, 1969) and W. B. Stephens, *Sources for English local history*, rev. ed. (Cambridge, 1981)
8.   Beresford, p.61; confirmed by Dr. K. J. Allison, from PRO E 179/202/60, m.68
9.   The muster roll is printed in *Letters and papers of Henry VIII*, vol. 14 pt 1 (1539), pp.306-319, State papers (London, 1864-1929)
10.   For the Patent Rolls, see Elton, pp.36-7
11.   W. Dugdale, *The history of imbanking and drayning*, 2nd edition (London, 1772)
12.   Poulson, *Holderness*, pp.116-140
13.   A. F. Leach, ed., *Memorials of Beverley Minster: the Chapter Act Book . . .*, Surtees Society publications 98 and 108, 2 vols (Durham, 1898-1903)
14.   'Parliamentary survey of benefices,' ERAS *Transactions*, 2 (1894), p.51
15.   Deserted Medieval Village Research Group, 67, Gloucester Crescent, London, NW1
16.   ERAS *Transactions*, 28 (1939), p.153
17.   Microfilm of the Hearth Taxes in HCRO
18.   The 1833 map is in the HUL at DDCV 165/6

4

MEDIEVAL CHURCH HISTORY

Faith Mann

The purpose of this chapter is to examine the sources which one needs to consult in researching the history of a church in the Middle Ages. I have concentrated on the period 1066-c.1540, because it can be argued that these two dates serve as natural boundaries for the study of the medieval church, since the mid-sixteenth century saw a very dramatic change in English church life, with the Reformation and the dissolution of the monasteries. The great value of the study of churches is that these buildings can enable us to gain insight into medieval society. The church was a focal point of its community; it was enriched by the nobility of the area; it was enlarged to accommodate a growing population, or parts of it were allowed to fall into decay if the population declined in number. Evidence as to the relative popularity of medieval saints comes from the dedications of churches, and from the records of special altars and chantries at which specific saints were venerated. Sometimes, the church can even give a clue as to the occupation or interests of members of its congregation.

An example of a church which illustrates the pattern of growth and decline of the medieval population is St. Augustine's, Hedon. Much of the building here belongs to the thirteenth century, when Hedon was an important East Riding port, before the development of Hull and the silting of Hedon Haven. There is only a little fourteenth century work, indicating the economic problems which beset the town in this period, but by the fifteenth century it was possible for the parishioners to add some features to the building, notably the crossing tower. Examination of the outside walls of the church reveals that the south transept is earlier than the north, indicating a gradual process of building — whether because the population grew only slowly, or because funds were not immediately available to construct both transepts simultaneously, is not clear. There is also evidence of the existence of east aisles to the transepts, and a chapel on the south side of the chancel, all of which were destroyed, presumably because the community was no longer in need of the space afforded by them, or was not able to continue their maintenance.[1]

One very important aspect of the medieval church is monasticism. By the end of the Middle Ages, the monasteries owned a large proportion of the land in England. Many parish churches were appropriated to monasteries, and as centres of learning, of hospitality and care for the sick etc., the monasteries played a vital part in medieval life. In East Yorkshire we had a variety of religious orders, as follows:

House	Order	Date of foundation
Meaux	Cistercian	1150
Watton	Gilbertine	1150
Bridlington	Augustinian	In the reign of Henry I

Cottingham	Augustinian	c.1324
Haltemprice	Augustinian	c.1324
North Ferriby	Augustinian	c.1138
Warter	Augustinian	1132
Kirkham	Augustinian	1122
Burstall	Benedictine	c.1115
Swine	Cistercian nuns[2]	c.1150
Nunkeeling	Benedictine nuns	1152
Nunburnholme	Benedictine nuns	In the reign of Henry II
Thicket	Benedictine nuns	c.1200
Wilberfoss	Benedictine nuns	c.1150
Hull	Carthusian	1378

As well as the monasteries, there were the religious communities set up by friars — Franciscans and Dominicans at Beverley, and Carmelites and Augustinians at Hull — and the collegiate establishments, at Beverley, Howden, Hemingbrough, Sutton and Lowthorpe.

The collegiate establishments fall basically into two categories. The first of these, to which the earlier colleges usually belong, is that which encompasses churches built to be administered by a quasi-monastic establishment of canons, without any specific initial duty to pray for the souls of certain individuals. In many of these cases, a school was attached to the college, and the schoolmaster was treated as one of the brethren, and was subject to the same restrictions of behaviour.[3] Such establishments were usually based at a large church and the impetus for their attainment of college status often came from another ecclesiastical establishment, e.g. Howden and Hemingbrough were both the property of Durham — the former belonging to the Bishop, and the latter to the Prior and monks. Howden was made collegiate in 1267 and Hemingbrough in 1426.

The second category of college is the smaller, and usually later, establishments, which quite often are virtually indistinguishable in function from glorified chantry chapels, in that they seem to be preoccupied with the provision of masses for the soul of the founder and his family, rather than the maintenance of a school, or the fulfilment of a more general religious function. The staff of such colleges could be small in number, e.g. eight at Sutton, and the impetus for founding them often came from laymen.

After 1279, the foundation of any religious establishment was made a more difficult and costly procedure than heretofore by the introduction of the Statute of Mortmain. This sought to limit the amount of land which should fall into the 'mort main' or dead hand of the church (dead in that it was exempt from payment of feudal dues and lay taxes) by decreeing that all who wished to give land to the church should first obtain a licence to do so from the Crown. This procedure could cost the would-be benefactor a fair sum of money, and there is little doubt that the passage of the Statute did limit the number of grants to the church in the fourteenth and fifteenth centuries.

SOURCES

The parish church

The most obvious source for the study of a church and its relationship with the community around it is the building itself. One needs to be able to read the architecture, in order to ascertain at what periods building work was in progress, and thus be able to draw conclusions as to the relative wealth of the community, or its phases of growth and decline. There are many books on the general subject of English ecclesiastical architecture, but for more specific information relating to a particular building in our area, the best sources are the relevant volume of Pevsner's *Buildings of England* series, and of the *Victoria County History* (VCH). A further source for information and interpretation of the architecture is the church history, or guide, if one exists. Again, these often include references to documentary sources as well as the purely architectural.

The church guide and, usually, Pevsner, will also make reference to any interesting tombs, stained glass, examples of heraldry, etc. which may occur within the church. Further details about such items can be gleaned from the *Yorkshire Archaeological Journal* (YAJ) and the East Riding Antiquarian Society *Transactions*, both of which have published articles about subjects as varied as pre-Conquest sculpture, fonts, glass, and effigies of the Middle Ages. Other journals, notably *Archaeologia*, have published very detailed analyses of specific features within certain churches.

In some cases, important features have been removed from the church, so the casual visitor might be unaware of, and unable to discover any obvious information relating to, a significant aspect of the church's history. Museums have become the repositories of some of these missing features, while others are in private collections. The Stone Room in the Yorkshire Museum, York, contains some fragments of pre-Conquest and medieval sculpture from various parts of Yorkshire, including the Norman font from Hutton Cranswick.

Occasionally, a piece from one church turns up in another. This usually happens when the original home of the piece concerned becomes derelict. Perhaps the most striking local instance of this, because of the quality of the pieces involved, is the example of the three fragments of late twelfth/early thirteenth century sculpture which have been moved from the derelict church at Holme on the Wolds to Etton. Information as to the original location of such pieces can usually be found in the church guide, or in Pevsner, and more detailed information might be discovered by studying the churchwardens' accounts for the buildings concerned.

Churchwardens' accounts are indeed a very important primary documentary source which one ought to consult when trying to piece together the post-Reformation changes which took place in the church. Here are itemised details relating to collections of money for various purposes, references to contractual agreements with builders, etc., and information regarding the maintenance of the church fabric. However, such documents are quite rare for the medieval period. The most common early documents relating to churches are the grants and charters concerning them which were made usually by the upper classes in society. Some such charters are to be found in the Borthwick Institute of Historical Research (BIHR), and the British Library (BL). Many of the charters which are of especial interest to an historian of East Yorkshire were published in Farrer's *Early Yorkshire Charters*, which appeared in twelve volumes between 1914 and 1965.

Documents such as these often make it clear that a particular church was given to a religious house, in which case one can search the cartulary of the relevant monastery for further details relating to the parish church. It is because Meaux abbey had the right to appoint to the living of Keyingham, for instance, that we know of the terrible fire which broke out in that church in 1396 and which created so much havoc that it was feared the whole building would have been lost, if it had not been for the posthumous influence of Philip Yngleberd, a previous incumbent, who was buried within the church and who was venerated locally almost as a saint.[4]

Wills are another very useful documentary source relating to the church, for it was a matter of common piety in the Middle Ages to leave money to the church — often in the form of chantry bequests, but also as grants to the fabric fund. Some such grants were very detailed, and can be used as evidence for the period at which a particular feature was constructed. An example of this is the will of Robert Holme, who in 1449 left money to the building fund for the tower at St. Mary's church, Lowgate, Hull.[5]

Further information which can be obtained from wills includes the dedication of altars within the church, an indication of the number of chantries and religious guilds within the church, charities to be administered, etc. The relevant volume of the VCH contains a detailed list of chantries and other endowments in the parishes which it covers. Some of the Yorkshire wills have been published by the Surtees Society, in the *Testamenta Eboracensia* volumes, while registers of Yorkshire wills are published by the Yorkshire Archaeological Society (YAS). The original documents are for the most part in the BIHR, although some are in local record offices.

The BIHR is the repository for another important series of source documents — the ecclesiastical visitations, which were carried out at regular intervals by the archbishops. Yorkshire has one of the most complete series of such documents for the Middle Ages, and they can give a lot of circumstantial detail, not only about the fabric of the church, but about the behaviour of priest and parishioners. The Surtees Society has published several of the registers of medieval archbishops of York, which include references to visitations, as well as other administrative matters relating to the medieval church. The YAS has published the post-medieval visitation records of Archbishop Herring, and the BIHR has published a Catalogue of the Register of Archbishop Scrope.[6]

As well as the BIHR, York Minster Library is a useful centre to which one might direct one's researches into parish churches. This building houses an assortment of documents relating to churches and church building in Yorkshire. There is also one other very important source which has not yet been mentioned and that is Domesday Book.

The value of Domesday Book is that it sometimes refers to the presence of a church in a particular manor and so it can be the earliest documentary reference to a church in that area. In many cases, any architectural evidence for the existence of a pre-Conquest church has disappeared, so without the Domesday reference it would be uncertain how long there had been an ecclesiastical building on the site. However, we must bear in mind that the survey enshrined in Domesday Book did not give an exhaustive account of churches in this region. Some churches which incorporate pre-Conquest features survive today, yet are not mentioned in Domesday Book. Perhaps at the time of the survey, these churches had fallen into disuse owing to the harrying of the north; perhaps the survey was only dealing with churches of a certain value and over; or perhaps the Domesday commissioners did not feel able to carry out a very intensive survey of property in this region. It is impossible to say, but what is certain is that, even though Domesday does not mention a church, the village which one is researching may have had a pre-Conquest building, and only architectural evidence if there is any can be conclusive here.

There are several editions of the Yorkshire folios of Domesday Book. The best, and probably the most accessible, is the version done in volume two of *VCH Yorkshire*.

As stated in the introductory paragraph, the scope of this chapter ends with the mid-sixteenth century. In this period, a new type of documentary source was created — the paperwork which resulted from the Reformation. It is not until the reign of Edward VI that the religious changes of this period begin to make much impact on the contents of parish churches. In c.1535, a survey of the goods of chantries had been ordered, and an inventory of church contents was carried out in 1547, but no further action was taken. In the reign of Edward VI, however, the Protestant movement gained more influence and there were positive moves to eradicate traces of what was considered to be superstition from the churches. This involved the destruction of images and rood lofts, the whitewashing of wall-paintings, the seizure of vestments and plate and the closure of chantries and colleges.

The documentary returns made by these Chantry Commissions, both for the examination of the chantries and of church goods, are housed in the Public Record Office (PRO), although not all the documents have survived. The Surtees Society has published the lists of Yorkshire church goods,[7] and reference is made to the returns of the Chantry Commissioners in the relevant volumes of the VCH. There is also an article by C. J. Kitching which deals with the East Riding chantries.[8]

Monastic sources

As with the parish church, the most obvious source to consider for the pattern of growth and decline of a monastic building would be the architecture itself. However, in this case, the events of the dissolution of the 1530s and subsequent plundering of monastic sites for building stone has meant that in most instances the monastic buildings survive only in a ruinous state. In the East Riding we are most unfortunate in that no remains survive of the only Cistercian house in the Riding, Meaux having been used as a quarry for stone to be used on the defences at Hull. When the monastic establishment lay in or near a town, however, there was a chance that the church building at least might survive by being adapted to become a parish church. This happened at Bridlington, and the south wall of the church still bears traces of the range of cloisters and other buildings which adjoined the church when the house was an Augustinian community.

One feature of monastic churches is that they are usually quite large. They were considered to be the most important buildings on the site, and the money and care of the community were lavished on them. Quite often, therefore, when such churches were handed over to the parish in the sixteenth century, they were found to be too large for the needs of the lay community. This was the case at Bridlington, where the Priory church was 333 feet long. For this reason, the present east wall was built to block off the chancel of the church at the crossing, leaving the original east end of the church to decay.

Collegiate churches were usually stripped of their status at the Reformation and handed over to the lay community to serve as parish churches. Like the monasteries' churches, they were often quite large and placed too great a strain on the resources of the parish. Today, the east end of the church at Howden stands in ruins as testimony to this, and the maintenance of Beverley Minster was a great problem to the townspeople of Beverley.

The case of the friaries is rather different from monasteries and colleges, in that the friars did not usually build large or elaborate buildings. The comparative poverty of the friaries is well illustrated in the accounts of the dissolutions. Since the friars often occupied land in a central position within the town, their property was usually eagerly sought after and redeveloped after the closure of the religious houses, which is why so very few friary buildings remain today. The Beverley Friary is one of those which has survived, but in Hull and most other towns the story was very different.

Turning to documentary sources for the history of monastic establishments, the cartulary or chronicle of the house in question is a very important source. Such books usually went through a process of frequent revision and up-dating in the course of the Middle Ages, and they preserve details of the foundation and later grants to the house. Such documents often survive in more than one copy, and can be scattered through several collections. The BL and the Bodleian Library, Oxford, have good collections, and many monastic chronicles have been published, notably, for our area, the Meaux Chronicle, published in the Rolls Series, and the Bridlington Cartulary, abstracts of which were published in 1912 by J. Whitehead & Son.

Charters and other documents relating to grants to religious houses have been published in Farrer's *Early Yorkshire Charters*, and in occasional volumes of the YAJ and the ERAS *Transactions*.

Like the parish churches, religious houses were subject to the Archbishop's visitation, and reference to visitation documents can be found in volume three of *VCH Yorkshire*. There are also the published registers of archbishops to which reference was made earlier in connection with parish churches. Monastic visitation evidence gives a vivid picture of some of the problems related to this type of organisation. Although much of the surviving evidence has to do with discontented monks and nuns, and records cases of laxity regarding the observance of the monastic rule, it is important to remember that the visitations, by their very nature, were bound to take a greater interest in houses where there was need for improvement rather than in establishments which were being well run. Good news meant no news, so where a house was run along satisfactory lines, there was no need to report this.

The dissolution of the religious houses began on a large scale in the 1530s. In the winter of 1535/6 the Crown sent commissioners to visit religious houses and report on the conditions they found. The commissioners were not members of the religious orders, but were Tudor civil servants, apparently with an interest in finding the type of information that their masters required, so it is not surprising that their report presents a very bleak, not to say immoral, picture of life in an English monastery. After this report, the Act for the Dissolution of the smaller religious houses, with a value of £200 per annum or less, was passed, and this was followed by the act for the closure of the larger religious houses in 1539. The friaries were not directly affected by these acts, but were closed down independently in the course of the 1530s.

In order to handle the large amount of property which was taken away from the dispossessed religious houses, the government set up a Court of Augmentations. This dealt with acquisitions of property and with claims to part of erstwhile monastic possessions, or requests to lease such property.

The documentary material produced by the surveys and closures of religious houses is lodged in the PRO. Some of it is accessible to the local researcher, in the following published forms: Letters and State Papers of Henry VIII; Calendar of Patent Rolls for the relevant period, and some more local publications, e.g. the YAS has published some of the papers relative to the dissolution in its Record series.[9] Reference to the appropriate sections of the dissolution papers is made in volume three of *VCH Yorkshire.*

CASE STUDY: ST. MARTIN'S CHURCH, LOWTHORPE

I have chosen to deal with Lowthorpe since it was at one time a collegiate church, being therefore more than a parish church, but less than a monastery in terms of medieval church life. To trace its development, one needs to refer to more varied sources than would usually be necessary for the study of a parish church. The case study divides into two sections, the first dealing with the church building and the second concentrating on documentary sources.

The church building

The earliest feature in the church is an Anglo-Saxon carved stone cross-head (figure 7), presumably part of a standing cross. It is roughly carved

Figure 7: St. Martin's Church, Lowthorpe: Anglo-Saxon stone cross-head
(background) and fourteenth century double effigy possibly connected with the
Heslertons (foreground)

Figure 8: St. Martin's Church, Lowthorpe: south wall of nave and Chancel

60

Figure 9: St. Martin's Church, Lowthorpe: blocked window in chancel, showing reticulated tracery

Figure 10: St. Martin's Church, Lowthorpe: niche in buttress on south side of east wall, showing what may be the remains of sedilia

Figure 11: St. Martin's Church, Lowthorpe: the Salvin brass — knight in armour and inscribed plate

63

Figure 12: St. Martin's Church, Lowthorpe: west window of tower

Figure 13: St. Martin's Church, Lowthorpe: infilled arched window in east wall

Figure 14: St. Martin's Church, Lowthorpe: piscina in east wall of old chancel

Figure 15: St. Martin's Church, Lowthorpe: vaulted decoration inside piscina

with an interlace pattern and both style and design suggest a late Saxon date for the piece — tenth or eleventh century.[10] Reference to the Domesday Book proves that there was a church at Lowthorpe in 1086, so if the cross belongs to this site and has not been transported here from some other village — something which is possible, considering how small the piece in question is — it may be all that remains of the church mentioned in Domesday. The cross head was found in the churchyard, about 1934,[11] but there is no way of knowing whether it had lain buried there for almost a thousand years or whether it had been brought from another settlement, put aside and forgotten.

The architectural story of the building begins in the thirteenth century, to which the main part of the nave belongs. The windows in this part of the church are of the lancet type, although they have been restored in the post-medieval period. The south window between tower and porch is of a simple lancet form, whilst those further to the east are lancets with Y-tracery, although there is evidence of modern alteration (figure 8). In the fourteenth century improvements were carried out, and the chancel was built. It is likely that this part of the church was built to replace a smaller, earlier chancel. On the south side of the church, the plinth of the wall continues under both lancet and fourteenth century traceried windows, but stops after one bay (figure 8). Probably the point at which the plinth ends marks the limit of the earlier chancel.

The evidence for fourteenth century construction of the chancel extension comes from the style of window tracery used here — a type called reticulated tracery (figure 9) which is associated with the early part of the fourteenth century. The chancel itself was originally longer by at least one bay, because the buttresses at the sides of the east window include traces of window jambs (figure 8) and on the north side of the south east buttress is a large rectangular niche which, it has been suggested, may be the remains of sedilia (figure 10).[12]

Documentary evidence tells us that the church was made collegiate by Sir John de Heslerton in 1333, a date which coincides nicely with the chancel building. Inside the church is a monument which may be associated with the Heslerton family (figure 7). It is a double effigy, representing a couple dressed in the loose, flowing robes of the fourteenth century and covered by a sheet over which is a network of branches which terminate at the sides in children's heads — seven by the side of the male figure, and six by the side of the female. Could they represent sons and daughters? At the foot of the monument are shields, which presumably may once have been painted with heraldry. Although there is no certainty as to whom this monument commemorates (one tradition says that it came from Ruston Parva) it has been suggested that it may represent Sir Thomas de Heslerton who died in the later fourteenth century, and who founded a chantry at Lowthorpe in 1364.[13]

There is one other funerary monument inside the church which is worthy of note, and that is a small brass of a knight in armour of the late four-teenth/early fifteenth century (figure 11). Beneath the knight is a brass inscription which commemorates George Salvin, knight, who died in 1417, and his wife Elizabeth, who died in 1416. The stone from which both the knight and the inscription have come is still in the chancel, just behind the brick wall which now marks the easternmost extension of the present church. The stone also has an indent for the figure of a lady, now lost, and towards the foot of the stone are two shield-shaped indents which would probably have enclosed the heraldry of the two families concerned.

The fifteenth century saw further additions to the fabric of the church, notably the west tower, which dates from the late fourteenth/early fifteenth century, although its brick top was added later (figure 12). In the sixteenth century the tower was furnished with a new, square-headed west window, and it has been suggested that the chancel arch may belong to this period also.[14] In both cases, these sixteenth century additions would have replaced material already *in situ*, so they can be seen as modernisations rather than extensions to the building. Obviously there must have been a chancel arch constructed in the fourteenth century, if not before, and it is clear that the present west window replaces an earlier aperture, for figure 12 shows that the window is not placed centrally to the square hood moulding that runs over its top.

The sixteenth century saw Lowthorpe's decline in status from college to parish church, and it would seem to be about this time that the east end of the church was shortened by a bay or so: the old east wall contains an arched window which has been infilled partly by dressed stone, and partly by a mullioned, seventeenth century window (figure 13). The shape of the infilled window makes it unlikely that the church was shortened to this length during the seventeenth century, as has been suggested,[15] since it does not seem likely that rebuilders of this period would bother to use old window frames. They could more easily insert their mullioned window into a blank wall. Another point which makes it unlikely that the shortening of the chancel dates from the seventeenth century is the piscina in the east wall inside the church. Such things were cast out of churches in the reign of Edward VI and were not reinstated. It is surely too great a coincidence that the piscina should have been used as building stone, and should have been reset in a position that would be next to the altar, and in this process, should have managed to remain intact — even down to its vaulted roof, with roof-boss (figures 14 and 15). It seems more likely that the shortening of the chancel took place at a time when the piscina was still in use, i.e. before the Reformation, and this may be evidence to suggest that even prior to the Reformation the college at Lowthorpe was struggling to survive in the face of decreasing local enthusiasm for its maintenance, and of inflation which was eating away at the value of its original endowments.

After the seventeenth century insertion of a window in the east wall of the church, the next stage in the architectural history of Lowthorpe is the building of a brick wall behind the chancel arch, to shorten the length of the church to the size of its medieval nave, with a small extension into the old chancel, to provide some space behind the altar. This was done in the eighteenth century, in the same period as the brick upper stage of the tower.

Inside the church is a drawing of the building which dates from before the 1859 restoration. This shows the nave south wall to have had a reticulated window like those in the chancel, and the nave to have been the same height as the chancel, with an embattled parapet.

Restoration of the building took place in 1859, when the new nave windows were put in place, and a porch was built. Lowthorpe today presents a picturesque aspect of neglect over several centuries, though this is mitigated to a large extent by the care given to the present church and churchyard, and recent work done to tidy up the overgrown chancel.

Thus, quite graphically, the decay of Lowthorpe epitomises the problems encountered by collegiate establishments on the eve of, during and after the Reformation, when their medieval buildings were too large to be fully utilised by the small local community.

Documentary evidence

The first documentary reference to Lowthorpe is in Domesday Book, which makes it clear that the village consisted of three manors in 1086. One of these was held by the King, one by St. John's College, Beverley, and the third by a thegn called Game. This last manor, four carucates in extent, included a church. It is perhaps significant that this manor also has the largest recorded population — six villeins, whereas no inhabitants are mentioned in the King's manor, and only one farmer on St. John's manor.[16]

The next reference which mentions a church at Lowthorpe is the entry in Archbishop Gray's Register in 1226 concerning the presentation of Thomas de Thurkleby as rector of Lowthorpe.[17] This entry makes it clear that the right of presentment was made to Stephen de Meynil, overlord of the Lowthorpes, because the heir to the Lowthorpe estates was not yet of age. By 1281, the family of de Heslerton has come onto the scene. In that year, Thomas de Heslerton presented Walter de Thurkleby to the living of Lowthorpe, and did so by right of his status as guardian of the heir of Thomas de Lowthorpe.[18]

By 1312 Lowthorpe had been enriched by the acquisition of the chapel at Ruston, though the exact date at which the two came together is not known. However, in 1312, Archbishop Greenfield sent an order to the official of the archdeaconry of the East Riding, to excommunicate anyone violating the sequestration of the chapel of Ruston, described as being the parish of Lowthorpe.[19]

The acquisition of Ruston presented something of a problem, since the rector at Lowthorpe was bound to celebrate services at Ruston also, but the situation was alleviated somewhat after Lowthorpe became collegiate, served by several chaplains, one of whom could also take responsibility for Ruston, so that services could be maintained at both places. It was in 1358 that Archbishop Thoresby granted permission for this solution to the problem to be carried out.[20] Even so, this course of action was not without its setbacks, for a Papal Letter of 1414/15 records that the priests at Lowthorpe had sent a petition to the Pope complaining that they were finding it difficult to afford the maintenance of services at Ruston, and that a further problem was that they were all sworn to perpetual residence at Lowthorpe, so that none of them could actually reside at Ruston. The

Pope's response was to grant an indult to allow them and their successors to say the offices at Ruston and to govern it, despite the rules of residence at Lowthorpe.[21]

Lowthorpe's rise to college status came in 1333 when licence was granted to Sir John de Heslerton to found the establishment. The licence was confirmed by Letters Patent on 3 May 1334.[22] The founder's grant set up a college with a master and six priests. Each of the latter was to serve in a chantry chapel and these were dedicated to the following:

1. The Holy Trinity.
2. St. Mary.
3. Chantry of the Archbishop, where prayers were said for all archbishops, past, present and future, and also for Edward II.
4. Chantry of the Chapter of York, with prayers for Deans and Canons of York (past, present and future) and also for William de Ros, sometime lord of Hamlak.
5. Chantry of the Founder: prayers for Sir John, his wife, their children, parents, descendants, etc., and for John de Hotham, Bishop of Ely.
6. Chantry of the Patron.

The regulations of the chantry made detailed arrangements for the division of duties between the priests, and also stated what kind of clothing they should wear, and how they should be accommodated in a house within the manse of the rectory. Within the manse they were to have a hall, chambers, kitchen, bakehouse, brewhouse and a loft, and also a garden and turbary, and also each had an annual stipend of six and a half marks.

As well as the priests, the grant stipulated that there should be three clerks, at least one of whom should be a deacon, and another, if not a deacon, was to be a sub-deacon, and they were to be present at all church services.

In 1364 the original grant was augmented by Thomas de Heslerton, who obtained a licence to give his property at Lowthorpe to the college, and who, in the same year, founded a seventh chantry.[23] In 1372 Simon de Heslerton obtained licence to give his lands at Lowthorpe to the college.[24] At about this time, the rights of the priests were extended to allow them to nominate one of their number to become rector, and he was to receive a stipend of ten marks a year.

By the end of the fourteenth century, therefore, Lowthorpe college was an important local landholder. We can see the activities of the college in land transactions quite clearly in a number of published documents.[25]

The lay patronage of Lowthorpe, it is obvious, moved from the Lowthorpe family to the Heslertons some time in the fourteenth century. By 1329 the Heslertons were exercising the right to present the rector and in that year, master Robert de Heslerton, son of Sir John, took the living. However, in 1392, John de Westhend was presented as one of the chaplains of the church by Sir John de Hotham, and the Hothams, and sometimes their assigns, or representatives, continued to present to the college and church until well after the dissolution. The right of presentment seems to have passed from one family to another by marriage. It passed from the Lowthorpes to the Heslertons when the daughters of Thomas de Lowthorpe married Robert and John de Heslerton, and later in the fourteenth century, Agnes, the daughter of Sir John de Heslerton married Sir John de Hotham, who died in 1370.[26] The connection between the two families is perhaps one reason why John de Hotham, Bishop of Ely, should be included in the prayers said at the Founder's chantry.

In 1548 the dissolution of the chantries began. There was some doubt as to the exact nature of the establishment at Lowthorpe, whether it was a college or a parish church with chantry priests. Ultimately, it was treated as a college. The visitors working for the Crown found that the community at Lowthorpe had already declined from the numbers stipulated at the college's foundation. In 1548 there was only the master, John Brandsby, and four chaplains — Thomas Fugaille, William Revell, Robert Sharpe and Richard Bellard. Of these four, only Thomas Fugaille, aged twenty-seven, was under forty. Might this again be evidence for the idea that the establishment at Lowthorpe was no longer so attractive to priests as it had once been? There were also two sub-deacons in 1548 — Robert Busby and Thomas Jeffrayson, aged twenty-four and twenty-eight respectively. The commissioners allowed John Brandsby to remain as rector of Lowthorpe and to each of the chaplains they agreed to pay a pension of £5 per year.

The value of the property at Lowthorpe was also assayed at the dissolution. The minister's account shows land valued at £1 3s 3½, in the hands of free tenants, plus glebe land worth £25, land held at will worth £31 1s 10d and tithes worth £4 9s 5d, giving a total value of over £60.[27] A further valuation of the goods of the late college is as follows: Corn to the value of £5 12s 4d, cattle £12 5s 8d, and household goods, items of husbandry, etc., worth £5 8s 6d, making a total of over £83.[28] There was also plate, as follows: twelve silver spoons, two parcel gilt salts, a maser with a band, a great horn decorated with silver, and three bells.

The fate of the portable church goods of high value, like the silver plate, was to be transferred to London and usually to be melted down. Excess bells were to be melted down for ordnance, while lands were sold or leased out. This latter is what happened at Lowthorpe, whose sixteenth century landlords included the Earl of Huntingdon in the 1580s, when he was President of the Council of the North. By 1630 Lowthorpe manor belonged to the Pearson family. Tombs of the Pearsons can still be seen at Lowthorpe, to mark their connection with the church. In 1720 the manor was sold to the St. Quintin family, whose main seat was at Harpham, and this is the period when the physical decline of the church building, and the final reduction in its size took place.

After the dissolution, Lowthorpe continued to operate as a parish church. In 1552, therefore, it received another visit from royal commissioners, when the inventories of church goods were made. The purpose of this survey was to discover which churches still had articles which belonged with the old Catholic faith, e.g. vestments, extra chalices, etc. Such goods were to be itemised and confiscated. The precious things thus obtained by the Crown were to go to London and the less valuable were to be auctioned locally. At Lowthorpe, the commissioners found many rich vestments which were presumably used by the collegiate priests in the pre-Reformation period. These included 'one suyt of blak velvet ryped with gold' and 'one cope of silk flowered with gold'. The other properties included some items which may be the same as those mentioned in 1548 — i.e., two crewetts (the salts of 1548?) and three bells in the steeple,[29] although it would seem that some of the goods listed in 1548 had already been confiscated.

Thus, in 1552, the last remaining portable articles belonging to the collegiate church at Lowthorpe were itemised and seized. The remaining links with the past were the church itself and the curate of 1552, Thomas Fugaille, who had been a chantry priest at Lowthorpe and who became rector in 1557.[30] After his time, the links with the medieval past were severed. Like many other collegiate churches, Lowthorpe declined in wealth as in status. Perhaps this case study has shown how we need to use a variety of disciplines to elucidate the full progress of so many of our churches, which served at the heart of the medieval community.

Notes for chapter 4

1. For a discussion of the progress of Hedon, see VCH ER 5 (1984)

2. There is some doubt as to whether Swine was founded as a house of Cistercian nuns, since it was established at a time when the Cistercian order did not admit women. However, the nuns themselves seem to have regarded themselves as Cistercians, see J. E. Burton, *The Yorkshire nunneries in the twelfth and thirteenth centuries*, Borthwick papers, 56 (York, 1979), for more details of nunneries

3. A. F. Leach, *Early Yorkshire schools*, YAS record series, 27, 33, 2 vols (Leeds, 1899-1903)

4. E. A. Bond, ed., *Meaux Chronica*, Rolls series, 43, vol. iii (London, 1866-8), pp. 193-4

5. J. Raine, ed., *Testamenta Eboracensia: wills registered at York*, Surtees Society publications, 45, vol. iii (London, 1864), p.182 note

6. R. N. Swanson, *A calendar of the register of Richard Scrope, Archbishop of York, 1398-1405*, Borthwick texts and calendars: records of the Northern Province, 8 and 11, 2 vols (York, 1981-85)

7. W. Page, ed., *The inventories of church goods for the counties of York, Durham and Northumberland*, Surtees Society publications, 97 (Durham, 1897)

8. C. J. Kitching, 'The chantries of the East Riding of Yorkshire at the Dissolution in 1548', YAJ, 44 (1972), pp.178-94

9. [*Yorkshire monasteries: suppression papers*], YAS record series, 48 (Leeds, 1912)

10. The chronology of Anglo-Saxon carving in Yorkshire is discussed by W. G. Collingwood in articles in the YAJ, vols 19, 20, 21, 23, 28 (1907, 1909, 1911, 1915, 1926)

11. See note in YAJ, vol. 31 (1934), p.4

12. N. Pevsner, *Yorkshire: York and the East Riding*, Buildings of England series (Harmondsworth, 1972), p.308

13. Pevsner, p.308

14. VCH ER 2 (1974), p.277

15. VCH ER 2, pp.276-7

16. VCH York 2, pp.204, 215, 287

17. *The Register of Archbishop Gray*, Surtees Society publications, 56 (Durham, 1870), p.14

18. *The Register of Archbishop Wickwane*, Surtees Society publications, 114 (Durham, 1907), p.114

19. *The Register of Archbishop Greenfield*, Surtees Society publications, 145 etc., 5 vols (Durham, 1931-40), p.203

20. *The Register of Archbishop Thoresby*, folio 198d

21. *Calendar of Papal Letters*, vol. vi, p.511

22. *Calendar of Patent Rolls, 1330-1334*, pp.426-8

23. *Calendar of Patent Rolls, 1361-1364*, p.435

24. *Calendar of Patent Rolls, 1370-1374*, p.161

25. ERAS *Transactions*, 21 (1915)

26. N. A. H. Lawrance, ed., *Fasti parochiales*, YAS record series, 129, vol. 3 (Leeds, 1966), p.53

27. Kitching, p.190

28. W. Page, ed., *The inventories of church goods for the counties of York, Durham and Northumberland*, Surtees Society publications, 97 (Durham, 1897), p.85

29. *Inventories of church goods*, p.23

30. *Calendar of Patent Rolls, 1555-7*, p.504

5

POST-REFORMATION RELIGION

David Neave

The documentary and printed sources for the study of post-reformation religion in the East Riding are vast yet little exists in print for the period after 1660 that is not solely sectarian or institutional history. Little attempt has been made to portray the overall religious life of the county or individual communities and, as is vital, to set such studies within their social and economic background. Margaret Spufford, *Contrasting communities* (Cambridge, 1974), a study of religion and landholding in three Cambridgeshire villages in the sixteenth and seventeenth centuries and J. Obelkevich, *Religion and rural society: South Lindsey 1825-75* (Oxford, 1976), are excellent recent accounts examining religion within a wider local context. Anyone writing the history of a Methodist chapel who does not take into account its relationship to the overall religious, social and political life of the community, its geographical position in relation to the Anglican church and urban centres, the pattern of landholding in the parish and the principal changes in its economy, will not produce an effective study. In the same way anyone writing the history of the village who, other than referring to the existence and architecture of its churches and chapels, makes no attempt to examine its religious life will be guilty of overlooking an essential feature. It is, however, only the framework and social content of religious life rather than the quality of the spiritual life for which one can find adequate evidence.

What were the religious divisions of the county and individual communities? When did the various nonconformist sects emerge? From what social and occupational groups did their members come? How can one account for the immediate impact of Quakerism, and Wesleyan and Primitive Methodism? What role did the Anglican church play in the life of village and town? To what extent did popular beliefs survive? These are some of the questions a local historian should ask and some of the sources are outlined below. The main sources are located in the Borthwick Institute of Historical Research (BIHR) for which the guides by D. M. Smith and W. J. Sheils should be consulted.[1]

It is not until the later seventeenth century that an overall view of the religious persuasion of county and community can be obtained. The so-called Compton Census of 1676 provides the first countywide information on the religious divisions of individual parishes. The returns give the numbers of people in each Anglican parish of sufficient age to receive the communion and then the numbers of Roman Catholics and dissenters among them. The original survey for York diocese is in the Bodleian Library, Oxford, of which there is a microfilm in the BIHR.[2] Unfortunately the particular denomination of the dissenters is not identified although by then various sects had become clearly established.

The development of Protestantism, Puritanism and Catholic recusancy in the century after the Reformation has been the subject of a number of studies drawing on the wealth of material at the BIHR in the archbishops' registers, act books of the Chancery Court 1558-1642 and visitation court books from 1567. A. G. Dickens has written on *Lollards and Protestants in the diocese of York 1509-1558* (Oxford, 1959) and two booklets on *The Marian reaction in the diocese of York*, (York, 1957). The growth of Puritanism is examined in R. A. Marchant, *The Puritans and the Church Courts in the diocese of York 1560-1642* (London, 1960), and in two unpublished theses by J. A. Newton, 'Puritanism in the diocese of York 1603-1640' (London Ph.D. 1955), and H. I. Dunton, 'Religion and society in East Yorkshire 1600-1640' (Hull M.A. 1956). Many examples from visitation books and court records relating to East Riding parishes are to be found in J. S. Purvis, *Tudor parish documents of the diocese of York* (Cambridge, 1948).

Religious life in Hull 1558-1642 is covered in volume one of the *Victoria County History, East Riding* (VCH ER) and Claire Cross has written two useful articles about the development of Protestantism in the town.[3]

Recusancy is dealt with in detail by H. Aveling in *Post-Reformation Catholicism in East Yorkshire 1558-1790* (York, 1960). In appendix 1 Aveling lists by township all references to recusants from a wide range of sources. From the late sixteenth to the early nineteenth century the survival of Roman Catholicism in the area depended largely on the support of a handful of landed families who provided protection, priests and meeting places, the principal families being the Constables of Burton Constable, the Constables of Everingham, and the Langdales of Houghton and Holme. Details of the estates of Roman Catholics 1716-24 are to be found amongst the Quarter Sessions records in Humberside County Record Office (HCRO) and there is interesting recusant material in the Constable of Everingham collection in Hull University Library (HUL).

The majority of dissenters recorded in the East Riding in 1676 were probably Quakers for this was by far the most successful and widespread of the early dissenting sects in the county. Independents, Presbyterians and Baptists had established meetings, some with large congregations at Hull, Beverley, Bridlington, Howden, Cottingham and in a number of other villages to the west of Hull by the eighteenth century but their early records are few. See J. G. Miall, *Congregationalism in Yorkshire* (London, 1868); B. Dale, *Yorkshire Puritanism and early nonconformity* (Bradford, 1910); and Yorkshire Baptist Association, *Baptists of Yorkshire: centenary memorial volume* (1912). For a recent intelligible general account of the various dissenting sects see M. R. Watts, *The dissenters: from the Reformation to the French Revolution* (Oxford, 1978).

The establishment of the Society of Friends (Quakers) in the East Riding may be said to date from the winter of 1651-52 when George Fox paid an extended visit to Yorkshire. His journal records visits to Selby, Beverley, Malton, Pickering, Cranswick, Ulrome and through Holderness to Hull. Clearly he met many there already of the same views and there were enough followers for a regular weekly meeting to be established in the East Riding as early as December 1652 by William Dewsbury of Allerthorpe, a leading Quaker 'minister'. By the early 1660s meetings were being held in villages throughout Holderness, the Vale of York and on the Wolds. In Holderness the sect was supported by three leading families: the Acklams of Hornsea, the Hartas of Ulrome and the Storrs of Hilston, who provided protection for their growing numbers. The rapid organisation of Yorkshire into weekly, monthly and quarterly meetings and the careful preservation of their records by the Quakers allow a much fuller picture to emerge of the development of this important sect. After 1669 the East Riding area was covered by five monthly meetings, Kelk, Owstwick, Elloughton, York and Malton, the first three being completely within the county. The minute, account, sufferings and register books for these three meetings are in the HCRO and Hull Local Studies Library (HLSL) and they show the strength of the sect and the severity of persecution of its members. Numbers declined by the early eighteenth century and by the mid-nineteenth century Hull was the only sizeable meeting left. Kelk Monthly Meeting was renamed Bridlington in 1712 and Elloughton was renamed Cave in 1743. In 1773 Bridlington Monthly Meeting was dissolved and split between Owstwick and Cave Monthly Meetings, and in 1784 the last two were joined together and in 1803 were renamed Hull Monthly Meeting. For the introduction and development of Quakerism in the East Riding see N. Penney, ed., *The first publishers of truth* (London, 1907), and W. P. Thistlethwaite, *Yorkshire Quarterly Meeting of the Society of Friends 1665-1966* (Harrogate, 1979).

Quakers were still to be found in a number of villages, particularly in Holderness, in 1743 when Archbishop Herring sent out a detailed questionnaire to each of the clergy of the diocese which provides a full survey of the state of the Anglican church and the presence of dissent. Amongst a range of questions on residency, services, communicants, schools and charities the clergy were asked to state the number of dissenting and recusant families in their parish. These returns are available in print.[4] Twenty-one years later in 1764 Archbishop Drummond sent out an identical questionnaire and the returns, which are in the BIHR, record the beginnings of Methodism, a movement that was to revolutionise the religious life of the East Riding.[5]

The 1764 returns mention the existence of Methodists in twenty-three parishes chiefly in the west and north of the county for the movement seems to have spread initially from York although the first 'converts' were made in Hull in 1746. For the early days of Methodism in these two centres see J. Lyth, *Glimpses of early Methodism in York and the surrounding district* (York, 1885) and W. H. Thompson, *Early chapters in Hull Methodism* (Hull, 1895). John Wesley made some twenty visits to the East Riding between 1752 and 1790 and his early journal entries recording attacks made by mobs give way later to glowing accounts of new chapels and massive congregations.[6] In 1786 he preached in the new chapel at Market Weighton. This building still stands and is the earliest Methodist chapel in the area. For the early development of Methodism in the area see the unpublished Liverpool University doctoral thesis by B. Greaves 'Methodism in Yorkshire 1740-1851' (1968).

In the 1820s Wesleyan Methodism, as it was then known, lost ground to the new evangelistic sect, Primitive Methodism, which had arrived in the county in 1819 and was overwhelmingly successful. The religious enthusiasm engendered by the tours of William Clowes and 'Praying Johnny' Oxtoby is recounted in the various biographies written about them, e.g. J. Davison, *Life of the venerable William Clowes* (London, 1854); G. Shaw, *Life of Johnny Oxtoby: 'Praying Johnny'* (Hull, 1894). By mid-century the East Riding had become proportionately the strongest area of Primitive Methodism in the country. An entertaining account of the development of the sect in the rural East Riding with a great deal of information on individual villages is to be found in H. Woodcock, *Piety among the peasantry: being sketches of Primitive Methodism on the Yorkshire Wolds* (London, 1899). See also H. B. Kendall, *The origin and history of the Primitive Methodist church,* 2 vols (London, c.1906) which has photographs of early members and chapels.

The most important sources for the history of Methodism are the original circuit and chapel records which have been largely unexplored. In the HCRO there is an extensive collection of material covering the Wesleyan and Primitive circuits of Beverley, Bridlington, Driffield, Hornsea, Market Weighton, Pocklington and Withernsea.

Much on the history of local Methodism can be gleaned from the lives of preachers, e.g. T. Jackson, *Recollections of my own life and times* (London, 1878); and G. Shaw, *Life of the Rev. Parkinson Milson* (London, 1893). The *Arminian magazine* (which became *Methodist magazine* in 1798 and *Wesleyan Methodist magazine* in 1822) and the *Primitive Methodist magazine* collections of which, with substantial gaps, are in HUL and Hull Central Library Reference Department, contain hundreds of biographies of local Methodists and accounts of chapel openings. F. Baker, *The story of Methodism in Newland* (Hull, 1958) is an excellent example of a local history.

The Congregationalists and to a lesser extent the Baptists experienced new growth in the wake of the religious revival of the later eighteenth century. Baptist chapels had been opened at Bishop Burton, Driffield, Kilham, Cranswick, Beverley and Newbald by the mid-nineteenth century. The Congregational expansion centred on the Fish Street Church in Hull built in 1782, which in addition to supporting chapels in Howden, Pocklington, Market Weighton and Thorngumbald, directly established eleven chapels in Holderness between 1798 and 1820. For more details, see C. E. Darwent, *The story of Fish Street Church, Hull* (London, 1899). Some records of both these sects are in the HCRO.

An invaluable guide to the strengths of the various religious groups in the early Victorian period is the official census of religious worship taken in 1851. The original returns are in the Public Record Office but there are microfilm copies of the returns for East Yorkshire at HCRO, HLSL and the BIHR. The returns show that in the registration districts within the East Riding there were 235 Anglican places of worship, 362 Methodist, sixty-two other dissenters, and ten Roman Catholic. Out of the total attendances of 130,052 at a place of worship on Sunday 30 March 1851, Anglicans accounted for 37%, Methodists 47%, other dissenters 13% and Roman Catholics 3%. A hundred years before, the visitation returns had shown dissent as a minimal and possibly declining feature in the county.

The remarkable development of Protestant nonconformity can be charted for individual communities through the registration of dissenters' meeting houses which after the Toleration Act of 1689 had to be licensed by diocesan officials or magistrates at Quarter Sessions. The early eighteenth century East Riding Quarter Sessions files in HCRO contain a number of petitions for registration, and the record office has a few registrations for the period 1822-52 in class QDR. At the BIHR petitions for registration survive for the periods 1712-1799 and 1836-52, and certificates are registered from 1737 in faculty books, and from 1816 to 1852 there is a separate series of registers of dissenting meeting houses. Before 1800 the entries rarely state the specific denomination but the petitions are usually signed by the leading members of the congregation. The dates of the building of chapels and meeting houses can also be obtained from the religious census returns of 1851 and from local directories although the dates from these sources need to be treated with caution. The East Yorkshire Local History Society has recently undertaken a survey of all surviving nonconformist meeting places in the East Riding and it hopes to publish the material in the near future. Detailed information on Hull chapels can be found in B. W. Blanchard 'Nonconformist churches in the Hull district,' unpublished dissertation, Hull School of Architecture, 1955.[7] Indeed all towns and villages already covered by the VCH ER will be provided with excellent information on the development of nonconformity.

The neglect and alienation of the populace by the Anglican church are often quoted as major reasons for the growth of nonconformity and irreligion in the eighteenth century. Correspondence, cause papers, and visitation records in the BIHR recording the extent to which the church pursued the payment of tithes and the prosecution of parishioners for moral lapses alongside widespread non-residency and pluralism on the part of the clergy provides ample evidence for such a view. In 1764 less than a third of the parishes in the East Riding had a resident incumbent. Much of the work was carried out by poorly paid and overworked curates with the best livings securely in the hands of clerical dynasties, former fellows of Cambridge colleges or the near relatives of wealthy patrons. A number of clergy became major landowners as a result of allotments in lieu of tithes at the enclosure of the open fields. If a list of clergy for a parish does not already exist one can be compiled from institution act books at the BIHR. An entertaining attack on the state of the church in Holderness is contained in G. de Sawtry, *The churches of Holderness* (Hull, 1837).

The new breed of active clergy who came into the parishes in the 1840s imbued with the ideals of the Oxford Movement and the Cambridge Ecclesiologists were unable to retrieve much of the lost ground. The Reverend F. O. Morris made over 130 'improvements' at Nafferton within a year and a half of his arrival in 1844 but this did not endear him to his new parishioners. Later nineteenth century parish records in the BIHR and

HCRO, registers, vestry books, service registers and communicants lists along with parish magazines in Hull and Beverley Libraries all bear witness to this increased concern by Anglican clergy for the spiritual and social welfare of the community. Visitation returns at the BIHR for 1865, 1868, 1871, 1877, 1884, 1900, 1912-22 are, however, full of complaints by clergy of the indifference of their flock. In 1865 in reply to a question concerning the number of dissenting chapels in the parish the vicar of Hutton Cranswick wrote: 'Alas! There are three. The Independents, the Methodist and the Ranters places — The Masses being steeped in Poverty and Ignorance frequenting these Schismatic Displays as they would theatres'; and in 1894 the vicar of Lund complained of the 'Utter indifference of the people. Not a real churchman among the whole population. This is the result of past years'.

CASE STUDY: RELIGIOUS LIFE IN HOLME-ON-SPALDING MOOR, 1650-1900

Holme-on-Spalding Moor covering over 11,500 acres was the largest parish in the former East Riding and its pattern of landownership, size, topography and the dispersed nature of the settlement help explain the vigorous and divergent religious life it exhibited from the mid-seventeenth to mid-twentieth centuries.[8] Throughout this time the three main strands of post-Reformation English religion, Anglicanism, Roman Catholicism, and Protestant nonconformity were strongly represented in the parish and the divisions so created permeated the life of the community. A wealth of documentary material has survived from which something of the story is recounted in the following short case study.

The medieval parish church of All Saints high on its hill top (see figure 16) is half a mile from the centre of the village and over four miles from the more distant parts of the parish such as Hasholme and Bursea. The village itself is a widely spread settlement with its distinctive parts being given names such as Water End, Runner End and Moor End. Before drainage and enclosure by 1780 the greater part of the parish consisted of the vast unenclosed and unimproved 7000 acre Spalding Moor which was impassable at times. The land was in many hands but in the late eighteenth century there were three major resident landowners, the Langdales who were Catholics, the Anglican incumbent and the Clarksons who were Methodists. The religious affiliations of the landowners only partially explains the range of churchmanship in the parish, for although clearly Catholic or Anglican tenant farmers were preferred the small freeholders, tradesmen, craftsmen and those who sought a meagre living from the common showed an independency in religion as well as other matters.

The Ellithorpes, a prominent farming family, exhibit well the variety of religious persuasion already existing in the parish in the century after the Reformation. Richard Ellithorpe left money for the 'repayringe and amendment of the Church of Holme' in 1585, while in 1581 Jane Ellithorpe had travelled eighteen miles from Holme to York to hear a Catholic Mass

Figure 16: All Saints' Church, Holme-on-Spalding Moor

81

where she was arrested and imprisoned. Also during this decade two other members of the family are recorded as Catholic recusants. The following century however the family's dissent changed its complexion. In 1638 Thomas Ellithorpe was one of eight Holme residents who sailed to America as followers of Ezekiel Rogers, the Puritan rector of Rowley, and in the 1660s Sebastian Ellithorpe suffered imprisonment in York Castle for his faith as a Quaker.[9]

Compton's census of 1676 records 387 inhabitants of communicant age (taken to be sixteen and over) of which twenty-one were 'popish recusants' and thirty-two 'other dissenters'. Records in the BIHR show that although there was only one recusant recorded in Holme in 1633 there were over twenty by 1663. This expansion of Catholicism took place with the return from exile on the continent in 1661 of the Catholic squire, Marmaduke, Lord Langdale. His son, who succeeded that same year, established Holme Hall as one of the chief centres of Catholicism in the East Riding. From the 1670s the Langdales had a Catholic chaplain who with an itinerant missioner priest, working in the Howdenshire and Holme Beacon divisions, provided for the increasing number of Catholics in the parish. A 'secret' chapel was created in the south garret of Holme Hall and here the Catholic parishioners, still subject to periodic persecution, regularly heard Mass. In 1743 there were over fifty Catholics attending the garret chapel. The Benedictine Dom John Fisher, who served Holme 1743-88, was responsible for beginning the surviving Catholic registers and he also compiled a *Liber status animarum* — a statement on the spiritual condition of the parish — in 1743 and 1766. At the latter date Marmaduke Langdale erected a new chapel attached to the Hall, the first post-Reformation chapel in the East Riding to be built on the ground floor expressly for Catholic worship. The chapel, designed by the fashionable York architect John Carr, still survives. A decline in the fortunes of the local Catholics took place with the death of the fifth and last Lord Langdale in 1778 and the eventual abandonment of the house by his successors the Stourtons. In 1794 the Hall became a refuge for the English Canonesses Regular from Liège who had fled from the continent in the wake of the French Revolution. The arrival of the nuns and their party of over fifty persons alarmed the villagers at first but soon many were attending the chapel out of curiosity to see the nuns and hear the singing. The Reverend Mother died in June 1796 and surprisingly she was buried the same evening in the chancel of the Anglican parish church. The nuns left that year and it became once more the home of the Catholic squire until the death of the last male heir, Henry Stourton, in 1896. In 1825 Charles Langdale built a Catholic school at Moor End which survived until 1968. The Catholic presence in the parish was greatly increased in 1846 when a training college for Roman Catholic schoolmasters was built two miles east of the village. In 1856 it became Weighton Catholic Reformatory School, and is now St. William's School.[10]

The value of the Anglican living, the patrons of which were St. John's College, Cambridge, and its position in what the Duchess of Devonshire described in 1773 as 'the dirtiest and I believe ugliest part of Yorkshire' encouraged non-residency on the part of the incumbents in the eighteenth century. John Savage, vicar 1703-33, chose to reside at Moorcot in Rutland and his successor Samuel Drake, vicar 1733-53, lived at his rectory in Treeton, near Sheffield. He in turn was succeeded by Christopher Anstey, vicar 1753-83, who in 1764 was residing in Rotterdam! In 1777 he became the holder of 1300 acres awarded to St. John's College at enclosure in lieu of tithes and glebe. Anstey was also a pluralist holding the rectory of Armthorpe and a prebendal stall at Lincoln Cathedral, but his pluralism was exceeded by the next and possibly most celebrated vicar of Holme, Dr. Thomas Kipling. Kipling, who had the living for almost forty years (1783-1822), also held the positions of rector of Fiskerton near Lincoln, Deputy Regius Professor of Divinity at Cambridge, Master of the Temple, and Dean of Peterborough during part of the same period. Surprisingly Kipling generally resided at Holme. The old vicarage house, built partly of brick and partly of daub and roofed thatch, had been rebuilt in 1778, and enlarged by the addition of wings in 1785-6. Kipling's role in the local community was secular rather than religious for he was one of the most active magistrates in the East Riding. With such non-residency, pluralism, profit from tithes, and the exercise of magisterial power on the part of the established church it is not surprising to discover that dissent had a strong following in Holme in the later eighteenth and nineteenth century.[11]

In 1743 the curate, John Fawcett, reported that there were no protestant dissenters present in the parish; however, twenty-one years later a successor noted that there were six Methodist families and a Methodist meeting house. Holme was one of the first parishes in the East Riding to have an established Methodist society and by 1770 its quarterly contribution to York Circuit funds was only exceeded by those from the Hull and York societies. The following year the house of Richard Blackburn was licensed as a meeting house, as was the barn of Thomas Johnson in 1776, the barn of George Goode in 1781 and the house of Nicholas Smart in 1783. Then in 1787 comes the first reference to a chapel — a new chapel is licensed in Thomas Smart's yard and in the same year we know there were twenty-seven full members of the society in Holme. Membership reached a peak of sixty-eight in 1795. The Methodists had the support of one of the leading families of the parish, the Clarksons of Holme House. The Clarksons, who as well as farming were bankers at Howden and Selby, had entertained John Wesley at Foggathorpe Manor House in July 1776. They paid for the building of a number of local chapels including a new one at Holme opened in 1827. This action may have been in response to the arrival of the Primitive Methodists in the area. They built their first recorded chapel in Holme in 1850 when they had fifteen members. Ten years later they had sixty-four members and an average Sunday attendance of 130. A new chapel was built in 1880.[12]

Five places of worship were recorded at Holme in the returns of the census of religious worship in 1851, the parish church, the Roman Catholic chapel, Wesleyan chapels at Holme and Bursea and the Primitive Methodist chapel. A total of 992 attendances were made at places of worship on Sunday 30 March 1851 — 209 (21%) at the church, 280 (28%) at the Catholic chapel and 503 (51%) at the three Methodist chapels. By this time there were also three day schools run by the Anglicans, Catholics and Wesleyans.[13] Comments made in 1843 by the vicar, Charles Yate, illustrate the polarisation of the community. He recorded only some twenty communicants and remarked: 'The small number of communicants, considering the population (1500), is out of all proportion, and much to be lamented. It is mainly to be attributed to the prevalence of Methodism here, actuated by a spirit of great hostility to the Church. There are also about 100 Romanists. Very few *staunch* Methodists attend Church at all. Some *moderate* ones do'.[14]

Yate, like his predecessors and successors, had been a Fellow of St. John's College, Cambridge, and he was the first of the new breed of active resident clergy. He kept an interesting record of his activities at Holme and the opposition he faced in a memorandum book which has survived with the parish records. On arriving in the parish he found the church in a sorry state and he began at once to make moves for its restoration. In March 1842 a vestry meeting was held 'for the purpose of adopting measures for the repairs of the Church'. A rate of 4d in the pound was proposed but as Yate recorded: 'This motion was opposed by the Hon. Philip Stourton, R.C. Squire, who was supported by other Papists and also some Chartists and low fellows ill affected to religion . . . The respectable Farmers and Wesleyans supported the Church'. On a division the rate was carried by thirty-three to twenty-nine and the restoration implemented.[15]

In 1865 a later vicar, William Sharpe, who had been Professor of Mathematics at Sandhurst, reported to the archbishop that his ministry at Holme was impeded by the presence of a Roman Catholic squire and family at the Hall, the strong clanship and personal canvassing of the Wesleyans, and 'the great distance of many of my people's houses from church'. To remedy the last he planned the building of an Anglican chapel of ease at Bursea but died before he could implement his scheme. The new vicar, George Gorham Holmes, took over the scheme with the support of T. H. S. Sotheron Estcourt of Estcourt, Gloucestershire, a former Home Secretary and the chief landowner at Bursea. In 1867 the vicar invited the celebrated architect William Butterfield to design the chapel. It was a far more laborious task than Butterfield supposed and amongst the parish records are 180 letters concerning the building, seventy-five of them being from Butterfield to the vicar. The chapel was not finally completed and opened until August 1872 because of numerous disagreements between architect, builder and Sotheron Estcourt (see figure 19). For eleven years a Sunday service was taken at Bursea by Holmes or his curate but by 1883 the agricultural depression had so far eroded the vicar's income that he could not afford a curate and the chapel was closed and remained so until 1903.[16]

The activities of the Anglican clergy did little to increase support for the church. During the decade 1880-89 the average number of communicants at the monthly and chief feast day services was only eight while there were around fifty names on the communicant list and during the same period over seventy villagers were confirmed. In 1903 a new vicar commented in the parish magazine: 'It is to be wondered whether the parishioners of the

84

large and ancient parish of Holme-on-Spalding Moor thoroughly appreciate the very old and beautiful building on the top of Beacon Hill'. He goes on to describe it as a 'dilapidated, neglected church' with old crumbling walls and a tower which 'was never intended to be used as a coal-shed, ash-heap, timber yard, and general receptacle for rubbish'.[17]

Today the church is well cared for, as is Bursea chapel, and the varied religious life of the parish continues with the Catholic church and two Methodist chapels still in use. In many ways Holme is not a typical East Riding parish but the sources available for the study of its religious history are not untypical.

Figure 17: Post-Reformation Catholicism: Everingham Hall (1764) and Roman Catholic Chapel (1839)

Figure 18: Quaker graves: late seventeenth century gravestones to members of Acklam family in garden of White House, Southgate, Hornsea

Figure 19: Bursea Chapel of Ease, 1870-72, designed by William Butterfield

Figure 20: Zion Primitive Methodist Chapel (1880), Runner End, Holme-on-Spalding Moor

87

Notes for chapter 5

1. D. M. Smith, *A guide to the archive collections in the Borthwick Institute of Historical Research* (York, 1973) and *A supplementary guide . . .* (York, 1980); W. J. Shiels, 'Sources for the history of dissent and Catholicism at the Borthwick Institute', *Borthwick Institute bulletin*, 3 (1983), pp.11-28

2. Bodleian Library, Tanner MS.150

3. VCH ER 1, pp.95-98; *Northern history*, 18 (1982), pp.230-238 and D. Baker, ed., *The church in town and countryside* (Oxford, 1979), pp.269-78

4. S. L. Ollard and P. C. Walker, eds, *Archbishop Herring's visitation returns 1743*, YAS record series, 71-2, 75, 77, 79, 5 vols (Leeds, 1928-31)

5. BIHR Bp.V.1764/Ret.

6. See N. Curnock, ed., *The journal of John Wesley*, 8 vols (London, 1938)

7. See also VCH ER 1, pp.311-30

8. D. Neave, *Notes on the history of the church and parish of Holme-on-Spalding Moor Yorkshire* (Privately printed, 1970)

9. K. M. Longley, *Heir of two traditions: the Catholic church of St. John the Baptist, Holme-on-Spalding Moor, 1766-1966* (Privately printed, 1966), p.3; BIHR York wills; Holme parish records: lists of followers of Ezekiel Rogers who went to America; HCRO DDQR [Quaker Records] Elloughton Monthly Meeting sufferings book

10. BIHR, Microfilm of Holme Catholic Parish Records; 'The Catholic registers of Holme-on-Spalding Moor, E.R. of York', *Catholic Record Society publications*, 4 (1907), pp.272-318; K. M. Longley, *Heir of two traditions*; H. Aveling, *Post-Reformation Catholicism in East Yorkshire 1558-1790*, EYLHS 11 (York, 1960)

11. D. Neave, *Londesborough: history of an East Yorkshire estate village* (Londesborough, 1977), p.19; details of clergy from J. Venn, *Alumi Cantabrigienses*, 10 vols (Cambridge, 1922-54), biographical information on Cambridge graduates; HCRO RD AX/357 Holme enclosure award 1777; BIHR Ter. Holme glebe terriers; HCRO Quarter Sessions records

12. *Archbishop Herring's Visitation returns 1743*, 72, p.72; BIHR Bp.V. 1764 Visitation returns; J. Lyth, *Glimpses of early Methodism in York* (York, 1885), p.302; BIHR DMH Meeting-house certificates; HCRO MRP Pocklington Methodist Circuit Membership Book and Pocklington Primitive Methodist Circuit Reports 1860-69; T. E. Laverack, *Holme, Selby Road Methodist Church 1827-1977* (Holme, 1977)

13. HCRO Microfilm of Census of Religious Worship 1851; D. Neave, *Notes on the history of . . . Holme-on-Spalding Moor*, pp.16-17

14. BIHR PR. Market Weighton Rural Deanery Book

15. BIHR PR. Holme-on-Spalding Moor Parish memoranda book

16. BIHR V.1865 Holme-on-Spalding Moor; Holme parish records: Bursea Box; P. Thompson, *William Butterfield and the building of Bursea Chapel: centenary booklet* (Privately printed, 1972)

17. BIHR PR. Holme-on-Spalding Moor Preachers Book 1879-98; Holme parish magazine January and March 1903

6

FAMILY HISTORY

Leslie Powell

The growing interest in history in general has led to an exceptional increase in the number of people tracing their ancestors. During the past twenty years, many groups of like-minded family historians have formed societies and had become sufficiently numerous by 1974 to promote the establishment of a Federation of Family History Societies (FFHS). The Federation has helped with the formation of new societies and co-ordinated their work. The East Yorkshire Family History Society (EYFHS) was founded in 1978 and by 1985 had more than four hundred members, and its own newsletter, *The Banyan tree.*

Many family historians have become absorbed in their study, a study which can be compiled at a pace to suit each individual, can be made as simple or as detailed as desired and need cost only as much as one is prepared to spend. It is now generally the case that most family historians are not content just to draw a pedigree chart but become so interested that a study of the ancestral village community is an essential part of building a picture of the historical background.

This rapid growth of interest and research has its advantages and disadvantages. Amongst the advantages can be included the provision of much helpful information to assist study and the willingness of public librarians to stock relevant material. The disadvantages must include the pressure that numbers of readers have placed on archive departments and library resources. It is, for example, essential to make an appointment to consult archive records and to give prior notice of the type of material required. Similarly, although reference library facilities can usually cater for the reader, it can often save a wasted journey if a microfilm reader is requested in advance.

The starting point for the family historian interested in his or her own lineage will normally be to make a collection of birth, marriage and death certificates from family sources. Elderly relatives have long memories and are usually willing to lend family photographs and documents to copy. Most families have old photograph albums, press cuttings relating to the family, and if one is very fortunate a family bible which may contain lists of names and dates. The method of recording information as investigations proceed is a personal choice but a loose-leaf binder with a page for each person researched is as good a way as any. From these private sources a history of the family traced back to the grandparents of the interested party can be recorded with special reference to places of birth.

Directories

The study of town and county directories can be the next useful source of information. East Yorkshire is well covered by directories, the first for the county being that of Edward Baines for 1822-23. The first for Hull (including Beverley) appeared in 1791. These early publications were trade directories and only included gentry, clergy, publicans and tradespeople in general but broadened their coverage as the nineteenth century progressed. By 1892, Bulmer's *History, topography and directory of East Yorkshire* had become what is now a valuable source of local and family history.[1] The best collection of directories is held by the Hull Local Studies Library (HLSL), but most libraries have some. When using early directories it is important not to waste a lot of time on a surname which has no connection with one's own surname. Always work backwards in time — from grandparents, to great grandparents, and so on. It is equally important to record each source carefully as it is searched whether the results prove to be positive or negative. Each generation doubles the number of names to look for — four grandparents, eight great grandparents, sixteen great great grandparents and so on.

Civil Registration

Genealogical research can easily be placed into a time scale with the advent of Civil Registration. The Registration and Marriage Acts came into force on 1 July 1837. From this date the country was divided into registration districts controlled by a Superintendent Registrar. The districts were further divided into sub-districts. East Yorkshire has District Register Offices in Hull, Beverley, Bridlington and Pocklington. The national indexes for these records are kept in London and are separated into indexes of births, marriages and deaths. Because of the time allowed to register births, the registration may not appear until the following quarter. These index volumes can be inspected at St. Catherine's House, London, without any appointment or charge.

Having found the appropriate entry it is then possible to obtain a certificate. These may be obtained in three ways. Firstly, by post: the staff will make a five year search of the index volumes and then post on the details. Secondly, by finding the details in London and then applying to the appropriate District Register Office for the certificate. Thirdly, after searching the index and completing an application form the certificate can then be posted on. The certificates give the family historian a wealth of information. A birth certificate will include the date and place a child was born, its name and sex, name and occupation of the father, name and maiden name of the mother and the description and residence of the informant. A marriage certificate gives the date of the marriage, names and surnames of each party, their ages, previous marital status and the full names and profession of the fathers of both bride and groom. It should be noted here that occasionally the stated ages of the bride and groom may not be accurate. A death certificate tells us where and when the death took place, name, sex, age, occupation, cause of death, the signature, description and residence of the informant and when the death was registered. Again the age on a death certificate can only be to the best knowledge of the informant.

Census returns

These are usually studied in conjunction with Civil Registration information. A census of the population has been taken from 1801 at ten-yearly intervals, the latest being 1981, but excluding 1941. The first return of value to the family historian is that for 1841. Census information is, of course, confidential, and is not made available to the public until one hundred years have elapsed. The latest census available for inspection is 1881. However, direct descendants can apply for written details of the 1891 and 1901 census returns provided the information is not used for litigation purposes. The cost of this service is high.

The 1841 census has little detail and the ages are rounded down to the nearest five years (except in the case of children under fifteen) so that a person aged twenty-nine would be classed as twenty-five. The returns for 1851, 1861, 1871 and 1881 contain the names, addresses, a list of people present on census night, the relationship of each person to the head of the household, matrimonial status, age and sex, birth place and whether blind, deaf or dumb. From 1871 is included whether the person is an imbecile, idiot or lunatic.

A complete set of these returns for East Yorkshire can be viewed on microfilm at the HLSL. A similar set but omitting Hull can be seen at the Beverley Reference Library. To help with the complexities of the Hull districts, streets and terraces, an index of streets and terraces has been prepared for each census by the staff of the library in Hull for the speedier location of addresses. The EYFHS, in conjunction with the FFHS, is compiling an index of names and information from the 1851 census returns for the region. Each entry in the index shows surname, forename, age, place of birth and a folio number. The folio number is then used to identify the township where the person was living on the night of 31 March 1851. The areas of Holme-on-Spalding Moor, Bubwith and Aughton now have published indexes and others are in preparation. A complete set is also held by the Church of Jesus Christ of Latter Day Saints, Anlaby.

Parish registers

Having studied some of the available records for the Civil Registration period, i.e. from 1837, the largest and possibly the most valuable archive must now be investigated. Parish records[2] and especially parish registers still remain the chief source of information for the family historian for a period of over three hundred years. Parish registers were introduced following an injunction issued on 5 September 1538. This gave instructions that every parson, vicar, or curate was to enter into a book every wedding, christening and burial in his parish with the names of the parties. The entries were to be made each Sunday after service in the presence of one of the churchwardens. The instructions were repeated by Elizabeth I in 1598, who ordered that parchment registers should be purchased by each parish and that the old registers should be copied from the beginning 'but especially since the first year of her Majesty's reign'. In some registers the whole of the records were transcribed from 1538 but in others the registers were only copied from 1558. These early registers which recorded

91

baptisms, marriages and burials continued to be used until 1755. It must be emphasised that the data in early parish registers differs from the period of Civil Registration in that it records date of baptism and not the date of birth, and the date of burial and not of death. These early parish registers must be treated with the greatest care and respect until they can all be available on microfilm. They are of great interest to historians. Often the baptisms are recorded at the front of the register, the marriages in the centre pages and the burials at the end. Others have intermixed entries and many contain copies of glebe terriers and lists of fees payable.

It is unfortunate that only a few registers have survived which commence in 1538. A large number start in 1653. An Act of that year concerned the registering of marriages and directed that an 'able and honest person' should be elected to keep the register. The next important date for parish registers was 1754 when 'Hardwicke's Marriage Act', which was an attempt to prevent clandestine marriages, laid down that marriages should be kept in a separate register on a printed form. Registers of banns were introduced at the same time and these are sometimes combined with the marriage register. The register of banns is extremely important to the family historian because it records cases of grooms marrying brides from a different parish and makes it possible to trace distant marriages. Also, it is not unknown for marriages not to take place after the banns have been read in church.

The next date of importance for parish registers is an Act of 1812, known as 'Rose's Act' after which a separate register was to be kept for both baptisms and burials. From this date, in the case of baptisms, are recorded the names of parents, their place of residence and the occupation of the father. Prior to this time the mother's name was often omitted.

The parish registers for East Yorkshire are deposited either at the Borthwick Institute of Historical Research (BIHR) or the Humberside County Record Office (HCRO). To understand the reasons for their location it should be explained that the Diocese of York, under the direction of the Archbishop, is divided into portions, each entrusted to a Suffragen Bishop. East Yorkshire is in two parts: the eastern part is the Archdeaconry of the East Riding, whilst the western part of the East Riding is in the Archdeaconry of York.[3] Additionally, the Archdeaconry of the East Riding includes in the north a few parishes which are actually in the North Riding, including Scarborough. The boundary of the two archdeaconries is irregular, but the Archdeaconry of the East Riding includes Wressle, Howden, Eastrington, Hotham, Sancton, Cherry Burton, Etton, Middleton-on-the-Wolds, North Dalton, Kirkburn, Fridaythorpe, Sledmere, Cowlam, Langtoft, Butterwick, Ganton, Seamer, Hackness and Harwood Dale and all parishes to the east of these. The Archdeaconry of York includes Hemingbrough, Bubwith, Holme-on-Spalding Moor, Market Weighton, Goodmanham, Londesborough, Warter, Huggate, Wharram Percy, Wharram Le Street, Kirby Grindalythe, Helperthorpe, Weaverthorpe, Sherburn and all parishes to the west.

Since 1978, parish registers and records more than a hundred years old have to be deposited in a record office unless the parish can fulfil conditions relating to their safety and preservation. The HCRO is recognised by the Diocese of York as the repository for the Archdeaconry of the East Riding.[4] Similarly, the records for the Archdeaconry of York are deposited in the BIHR.[5] Both record offices have extensive lists of each other's holdings. If there is a need to consult more recent registers it is necessary to contact the incumbent of the parish. Some of the more recent registers have been photocopied by the respective record offices, but for information concerning the clergy, the annual Diocese of York *Year book and clergy list* is available in most reference libraries.[6]

Many of the registers are being transcribed, typed, or photocopied and some are printed. The Parish Register Section of the Yorkshire Archaeological Society (YAS) has to date printed 148 volumes of Yorkshire parish registers. These volumes have the added advantage of containing an alphabetical list of names which makes it so much easier to find a family name, and also being printed are easier to read. However, it is always advisable to check the original register as a confirmation of a printed source. Full sets of the printed registers are held by the libraries in Hull, Beverley and York and the BIHR. It is important to note that the original registers should never be used until all printed or microfilm sources have been checked.

Parish register transcripts

To be used in conjunction with the parish registers are the parish register transcripts which are more generally known as the Bishops transcripts.[7] These copies of the registers for the previous year were meant to be sent to York annually but as with most records some parishes were more diligent than others. They are important because they often contain entries which were omitted from the parish registers and frequently survive for parishes where a register is lost. The earliest of the transcripts date from c.1600. There are none for the period of the Civil War and the Commonwealth. They are mostly complete between the Restoration in 1660 and the commencement of Civil Registration in 1837. All the transcripts are available on microfilm at the BIHR. Some of the East Riding transcripts are available on microfilm in the HCRO. The parish records of the Archdeaconry of the East Riding were surveyed in detail by a Commission instigated by the Archbishop of York in 1935. This extremely useful survey was published in 1939, and is to be found in most record offices and libraries.[8] The great majority of the parish records recorded in this survey are now in the HCRO.

Marriage by licence

It has previously been mentioned, in connection with the registers of banns, that difficulties occur when a groom marries in a parish other than his own. An alternative to the reading of the banns was marriage by licence, which could also be used when neither party lived in the parish where the proposed wedding was to take place. To obtain a licence, it was necessary to enter a marriage bond and allegation, both designed to prevent an illegal marriage. The bond is a financial penalty and the allegation states that there are no legal impediments, and that the consent of parent or guardian has been given if either party is aged under twenty-one years. The licence was then issued to the groom, who handed it to the clergy before the marriage. Some of these survive amongst the parish records. These bonds and allegations are available for the Diocese of York at the BIHR from 1660. Although the earlier bonds and allegations have been lost, they were indexed by William Paver in the nineteenth century and these index volumes are now in the British Library. They have been published by the YAS for the period 1567-1630. There is a consolidated index, also published by the YAS, entitled *Index to Paver's marriage licences 1567-1630*, YAS extra series volume 2 (Leeds, 1912). Indexes for 1630-1645, 1660-1674 and 1674-1714 have also been published by the YAS.

The compilation of a marriage index is a continuing project with many family history societies, and the EYFHS is no exception. Transcripts of marriages have been published for Routh, Holmpton, Skipsea and Welwick (all c.1750-1837) and an index to marriages for Sculcoates (1813-1817). Just as the reading of banns did not always result in a marriage ceremony, the obtaining of a licence is no guarantee that a marriage took place. An entry in Paver's *Index* must always (if possible) be checked against the original parish register or transcript.

Nonconformist records

Nonconformity has always been very strong in East Yorkshire. The whereabouts of many of the registers of the numerous nonconformist churches is not known and a lot are probably still in private hands. A commission of 1837 resulted in many registers being deposited with the Registrar General. These are now held at the Public Record Office (PRO). An important register of births was kept by Dr. Williams' Library in London between the years 1742 and 1837. This combined register of Presbyterian, Baptist and Congregational births was surrendered to the Registrar General in 1838 and is now in the PRO. A large number of registers are held by the HCRO[9] and are supplemented by microfilm copies of registers held by the PRO. For the numerous nonconformist churches in Hull, many of the registers of baptisms and marriages are in the Kingston upon Hull Record Office (KHRO). Since 1977, the Methodist archives have been kept at the John Rylands University Library of Manchester. Methodists have extensive knowledge of the whereabouts of baptismal and marriage registers for their church through a system of District Archivists.[10] Methodist periodicals are an important source of information and exist from 1778 (*The Arminian Magazine*), and are useful for their obituaries and biographies in particular.[11]

Wills and inventories

Until the Probate Act of 1857 the responsibility for probate records belonged to the Church. From 1858, all wills are to be found at the Principal Probate Registry, Somerset House, London. The Diocese of York had many courts which could grant probate but the main series are those of the Exchequer and Prerogative Courts. These courts had no jurisdiction during

94

the Commonwealth and wills for the period 1649-1660 are at Somerset House. The very first volume of the YAS record series published in 1885 is a catalogue of the Yorkshire wills at Somerset House for the years 1649-1660.[12] A further fifteen volumes in the same series contain the index of wills in York and cover the period 1389-1688.[13] Most reference libraries hold this series. They can also be used at the HCRO, where there is also available, on microfilm, the index which covers the period 1688-1857. The BIHR, which holds all the wills and indexes, will supply a photocopy of the original will, and the wills at Somerset House can also be copied.

In the late seventeenth century and until the mid-eighteenth century, many wills have probate inventories. This inventory gives the details of the deceased's goods with their value, often detailed room by room, thereby providing a picture of the life of the period as well as indicating the relative prosperity of the family.[14] Wills often name many members of the family (and their relationships) which can confirm knowledge from the parish registers or provide information which is no longer available when registers have not survived. A will can also be of help where families of the same surname lived in the parish and two people or more have the same forename. Most record offices have wills amongst their collections, many of these having been deposited with documents from solicitors' offices in connection with the title deeds of property. The HCRO has a card index of such wills deposited.

The International Genealogical Index
The International Genealogical Index (IGI) is a useful recent development in the study of family history. It is a comprehensive index of baptisms and marriages for this and many other countries prepared by the Church of Jesus Christ of Latter Day Saints (the Mormon Church). It has been compiled with the aid of computer facilities in Salt Lake City and microfiche copies and extracts are available on a county basis. The Index continues to grow, and the microfiche copies are frequently updated. The information held is obtained from a variety of sources: parish registers, parish register transcripts and individuals. Because of the wide range of sources the information should always be checked against the original source whenever possible. The information covers a wide period from the sixteenth to the early nineteenth centuries and is listed under the surname, which may have variant spellings. Details of parentage, marital status, sex, christenings, marriages (and the date of such events) are given. Then comes the town or parish (in the case of a town the church or nonconformist chapel is usually named). The source of the information is also included and this can be verified with the compilers in Salt Lake City in case of difficulty. The IGI is a useful source but it can be very confusing. It contains several million names for Yorkshire and if a surname is fairly common the mass of information can be daunting. However, it is of great value when tracing families who have moved to distant parishes. Copies of the microfiche are held by the EYFHS, the BIHR and the largest collection, covering the whole country, at the Church of Jesus Christ of Latter Day Saints, Anlaby.

Enclosure Acts and awards

The Parliamentary enclosure of the open fields and commons which took place mainly in the eighteenth and nineteenth centuries provides the researcher with much information concerning the inhabitants of the period. Enclosure plans are in many cases the earliest available for a township and still have some legal use. Many plans show buildings but others show boundaries and roads. The awards were mostly enrolled in the Registry of Deeds in Beverley, now part of the HCRO. Copies were usually kept with the parish records and further copies held by the major landowners. A large proportion of these copies can be found in the HCRO. The awards have been the subject of considerable study by historians. An excellent handlist listing the location of awards is available.[15] In addition to the awards and usually pre-dating them are the correspondence files concerning the enclosure. The Acts of Parliament necessary for the award rarely contain information of use to the family historian.

Land tax

A valuable collection of land tax assessments and payments for most of the townships in the East Riding can be seen in the HCRO.[16] These assessments cover most of the period 1782-1832 and are annual. They give details of land ownership and of the occupier or tenant as well as the tax assessment. The information is often repeated over the years but changes of ownership can be traced. The results of using land tax assessments in conjunction with the enclosure awards and parish registers can be very rewarding.

Maps

Maps will have to be consulted at all stages of family research. Most libraries have map collections but the most comprehensive are held by the HLSL and HCRO.

Newspapers

Apart from the general interest in newspapers, the information from obituary notices can often solve a mystery of a family member for whom one has found a notice of baptism or marriage but no record of burial. Good coverage of the area can be found in the *York courant* and this can be seen for the period 1728-1805 on microfilm at Beverley Reference Library. York Reference Library has an index of births, marriages and deaths recorded in York newspapers until 1885. A large collection of newspapers is held at HLSL including the *Hull advertiser*. This fine newspaper has an index to important local history information 1794-1825[17] and a separate card index of obituaries is a continuing project which now covers more than half of the collection. The *Beverley guardian* (1856 to date) can be seen at the Beverley Reference Library, mostly on microfilm.

Registry of Deeds

The registration of deeds of title to property commenced with the establishment, by Act of Parliament, in the West Riding of Yorkshire of a

Registry of Deeds in 1704. In addition to deeds were registered conveyances and wills where a will concerned land or property. A similar registry was established in Beverley in 1708. This scheme for registration was never compulsory but the custom of registering freehold land was observed as a protection against fraud and was managed by a Registrar. The Registry operated from 1708 until 1974 and comprises a vast archive of information which is now held at the PRO. A second copy was held by the Diocese and is now part of the HCRO. The large bound volumes of memorials of deeds and often wills were copied from the original deeds and index volumes were compiled. The indexes are of vendors, grantees and townships. From 1882, a combined personal name index continues until 1974. The wills which were registered have a separate index from 1828 to 1882. The memorials of the wills in the Registry are mostly abbreviations of the full will and the original should always be consulted when possible. The major difficulty with the registration of deeds is the exception of copyhold land. The transfer of property which was copyhold was a matter for the Manorial Court and registered in the Manorial Court Rolls, a system which was only finally superseded in 1926 by the various Law of Property Acts.

A search of the index volumes can reveal the memorial, which is an abbreviated version of the deed, copied into a large volume, not strictly chronologically because they were entered as received, and if it was relevant, a memorial of a will was also copied. The original memorials are still kept but can only be used in extreme circumstances, e.g. to check a doubtful entry. It is very unusual to find a plan of the property deposited before 1885.

Tithe awards and maps
Tithes, or payments in kind, were intended for the support of the clergy and church. Various attempts were made to commute the tithes for a sum of money instead of goods. In some cases, parliamentary enclosure removed the obligation to pay tithes, sometimes by the allotment of land instead or by a financial arrangement (corn rent). The payment of tithes was much resented. The Royal Assent for the Tithe Commutation Act was granted on 13 August 1836. Each parish or township then began the process of listing each landowner or occupier whose lands were subject to tithe and producing a map showing the whereabouts of the land. Three copies of the awards and maps were made. One copy was sent to the Tithe Commissioners which is now held at the PRO. A second copy was held by the Diocese and is now at the BIHR. The third copy was held by the parish and has usually been deposited with the parish records. Those of the Archdeaconry of the East Riding are now in the HCRO. Those for the parishes or townships within the Archdeaconry of York are held at the BIHR. These tithe awards and maps, with the earlier land tax documents and records of enclosure, combine to give valuable details of the owners and occupiers of land for the latter part of the eighteenth century and the first half of the nineteenth century.

Monumental inscriptions

The location of families by the above sources will enable the family historian to discover any surviving memorial inscriptions in churches, churchyards or cemeteries. The older memorial stones are now being removed in many churchyards to help reduce maintenance costs. In this process much valuable evidence of family relationships can be lost. A systematic recording of churchyards prior to clearance is being undertaken by the EYFHS.[18] The aim is eventually to publish all the surveys but before publication, all the information is checked against existing records. The surviving memorials in churchyards are mostly nineteenth century and a few are late eighteenth century. Memorials inside churches have a higher survival rate except for those in aisles which become badly worn. Many memorials were lost in the nineteenth century when church restoration was in progress. Thomas Gent (1735) records many inscriptions for St. Mary's and Holy Trinity churches in Hull as well as some for Bridlington, Scarborough and Whitby.[19] A series of monumental inscription booklets is being produced by the EYFHS; to date these are for North Frodingham, Skerne, Lowthorpe, Lockington, Lund, Middleton on the Wolds and Easington. The surviving memorial inscriptions can provide a lot of detail on family relationships, and family memorials should be carefully recorded and photographed. It is important that a minimum disturbance of ivy and lichen takes place during such a search. Ancient churchyards are often the refuge of wildlife and plant life.

Other sources

Poll books, burgess rolls and registers of electors are all of value. The poll books at the Beverley Reference Library exist from 1727, and the HLSL has Hull poll books from 1747. Poll books for Yorkshire can be seen at the York Reference Library from 1741 and the York City poll books from 1758. From 1832, registers of electors in Hull are kept at the KHRO and a similar set for the East Riding is available at the HCRO. These volumes are all well worth the search but it must be remembered that the franchise was extremely limited until comparatively recently.

Not to be overlooked are the various parish records, often associated with the parish registers in the parish chest and now usually deposited in the appropriate record office.[20] Churchwardens' accounts (was your ancestor a churchwarden?) contain details of expenditure to maintain the church and the assessments of the church rate. Most of the parish officers were elected annually and an important member of the community was the parish constable. Amongst his numerous duties was the transport of criminals to the Quarter Sessions, moving on vagrants and collecting stray animals. Poor Law records can be informative — the elected overseers of the poor were responsible for payments to the poor and the collecting of the necessary rate to maintain the payments.

Manor court rolls

The available manor court rolls are the only source by which the transfer of copyhold land can be traced. The usual method of transfer when a copyholder died was for the manor court to admit his next of kin or heir as the new copyholder on the payment of a 'fine'. The manor courts also dealt with larceny and felony cases. The other important function of the court was to enforce the manorial bye-laws which regulated the communal system of open-field farming. The value of these records to the family historian is obvious. They usually contain a list of the jury and the names of those presented to the court as well as the details of copyhold transfers. Court rolls of manors which were held by the crown are now held at the PRO (Chancery Lane). Some few manorial records are now in the BIHR but the major source for the East Riding are those in the HCRO. A register of the whereabouts of all known manorial records is maintained by the Royal Commission on Historical Manuscripts.

Quarter Sessions records

The courts of Quarter Sessions not only dealt with misdemeanours of the population, but were also responsible for orders relating to roads, bridges, paupers, ale-house licences and the licensing of dissenters' meeting houses as well as many other functions. An example of the use of these records is well illustrated by a publication on transportation which examined the Quarter Sessions records of Hull (1707-1846), the Beverley Quarter Sessions records (1759-1836), and the East Riding Quarter Sessions records (1735-1856).[21] The Hedon Quarter Sessions had no transportations. The resulting publication with its alphabetical list of persons transported (to America and Australia) can often account for the sudden disappearance of a family member. A detailed calendar of such records is available at the HCRO covering the period 1706-1799 and lists minutes, indictments, recognizances, orders and petitions.[22] These records also contain insolvent debtors' papers 1729-1829.

Estate records

Perhaps the greatest collection of estate records are those deposited at the HCRO by the Chichester Constable family of Burton Constable.[23] These estate records include many manorial court rolls and records. The main areas covered by these deeds and records is of course Holderness, but the estate records have much information relating to all parts of the East Riding and beyond. Although some topographical indexing has been achieved for these estate records, the researcher will probably find it most useful (and educational) to scan systematically the detailed calendars which are available for most of them. These estate collections often contain early plans of estates and villages which can add greatly to one's knowledge of a family to supplement the information gleaned from registers and wills.[24]

CASE STUDY: THE WITTY FAMILY OF MIDDLETON ON THE WOLDS[25]

There was a family tradition that the Witty family had lived in Middleton until 1935 and for the previous 400 years. County directories listed Wittys as farmers until 1933 and a family bible contains birth dates of Wittys from 1799. Gravestones in the churchyard at Middleton included grandfather, great grandfather and great great grandfather. These details were all checked with the census returns and the parish registers. No record could be found of the marriage of the great grandparents, but this was found in the Civil Registration records at St. Catherine's House and had taken place at Hemingbrough. During the nineteenth century two members of the family had emigrated to Canada and one to Australia.

The land tax returns showed the Wittys as a family at Middleton (1782-1832) and the 1795 return was especially interesting because William Witty was an assessor for the land tax. The enclosure award and map of 1803 showed the Witty land allocation. For the eighteenth century, the parish registers were used in conjunction with the wills at York. The hearth tax returns in the 1670 period revealed that Manor House Farm had three hearths and the 1672 return showed Philip Witty was the parish constable for that return. The parish registers for Middleton only commence from 1678, but the parish register transcripts survive from 1602. The family supported the Royalist cause in the Civil War — Phillipp Wittie of Middleton, a husbandman, had his goods assessed at £45 6s 8d and was fined £14 in 1645 for assisting the enemy when Queen Henrietta Maria was in the area. Two wills of this period, Phillipp Witty of 1715 and Mathew Witty of 1683 both had accompanied probate inventories. The most informative will was that of John Witty: his will of 1609 mentions thirty-two different people and they were mostly related to him. There are also those of Phillippe Wytte of Middleton (1583), and that of his widow (1588) in which she leaves her best gown to her eldest daughter, her second best gown to her second daughter and an old white petticoat to her daughter-in-law. John Witty in 1543 mentions his sons John and Phillippe. The two earliest wills so far discovered are for Peter and Emmote Wittye. Peter Wittye (1534) left goods to his wife and son but Emmote in her will of 1540 mentions a son and three daughters, all married.

This very abbreviated history of the Witty family is an example of what can be achieved. The parish of Middleton is difficult in that there is a shortage of early registers and almost no parish records but it does show how a variety of sources can be used for the compilation of a family tree. The search for information continues — no manorial records have yet been used and a wealth of estate records remains to be searched.

100

Notes for chapter 6

1. T. Bulmer, *History, topography and directory of East Yorkshire* (Preston, 1892; reprinted 1985)
2. For further reading see W. E. Tate, *The parish chest*, 3rd ed. (Chichester, 1983)
3. See Map of the ancient parishes and chapelries of Yorkshire, published by the YAS; also the East Yorkshire family history map (1982)
4. List of parish registers on deposit at the County Record Office, Beverley. Humberside County Archive publications, 1
5. D. M. Smith, *A guide to the archive collections in the Borthwick Institute of Historical Research* (York, 1973); D. M. Smith, *A supplementary guide . . .* (York, 1980)
6. Diocese of York, *Year book and clergy list*
7. N. K. M. Gurney, *A handlist of parish register transcripts in the Borthwick Institute of Historical Research* (York, 1976)
8. M. W. Barley, ed., *Parochial documents of the Archdeaconry of the East Riding: an inventory*, YAS record series, 99 (Leeds, 1939)
9. Brief list of non-Anglican church records on deposit, HCRO
10. W. Leary, *My ancestor was a Methodist . . .* (London, 1982)
11. Methodist Archives and Research Centre Information Folder available from the Connexional Archivist, c/o The Property Division, Central Hall, Oldham Street, Manchester M1 1OQ
12. *Catalogue of Yorkshire wills at Somerset House, 1649-60*, YAS record series, 1 part 2 (Leeds, 1885)
13. YAS record series volumes 4, 6, 11, 14, 19, 22, 24, 26, 28, 32, 35, 49, 60, 68, 89 (Leeds, 1888-1934) for the period 1389-1688
14. S. Needham, *A glossary for East Yorkshire and North Lincolnshire probate inventories*, University of Hull Department of Adult Education studies in regional and local history, 3 (Hull, 1984)
15. V. Neave, *Handlist of East Riding enclosure awards* (Beverley, 1971)
16. HCRO QDE/1
17. K. A. MacMahon, ed., *An index to the more important local historical information contained in the files of the 'Hull Advertiser and Exchange Gazette'* (Hull, 1955)
18. For guidelines see J. L. Rayment, *Notes on the recording of monumental inscriptions*, 2nd ed. (Plymouth, 1978)
19. T. Gent, *Anales Regioduni Hullini; or, The history of the Royal and beautiful town of Kingston-upon-Hull . . .* (York, 1735; reprinted 1869)
20. See W. E. Tate above
21. D. Mount, ed., *Transportation from Hull and the East Riding to America and Australia* (Hull?, 1984)
22. HCRO QSF
23. HCRO DDCC
24. *Brief guide to the contents of the East Riding County Record Office . . .*, 3rd ed. (Beverley, 1966)
25. Family study compiled by Mrs. A. Cawley

7

URBAN SETTLEMENT

Margaret Noble

In studying urban settlement in any region the student of local history is faced with questions of definition: what is a town; and how does it differ from a large rural village? It is generally accepted that towns are distinguished from villages by their size, economic structure and physical character. The simplest definition is perhaps indicated by the right to hold a market on a regular basis. Settlements possessing markets performed distinctly urban functions as they became more important distribution centres, attracting buyers and sellers from surrounding villages whilst also acquiring an important social role.[1] It should, however, be noted that the right to hold a market was not necessarily exercised and not all market centres were towns.

The major period of town formation in England and Wales occurred in the centuries following Domesday. East Yorkshire participated in this trend. According to the Calendar of Charter Rolls a total of thirty-three settlements in East Yorkshire had been granted market and fair charters by the start of the fifteenth century (figure 21). In the following four centuries more than half of these centres appear to have lost their weekly markets and at the start of the eighteenth century just fourteen remained in East Yorkshire.[2] Furthermore, by this time several of the remaining towns, namely Kilham, North Frodingham, Hornsea and Hunmanby, were on the margins of urban status and there were signs that they might have difficulty surviving as market centres.

At the start of the eighteenth century the towns of the region were not highly differentiated in terms of size, economic function or social structure. Hull apart, they were small country towns with populations of less than 1500 whose primary role was as service centres for their hinterlands. In the following century and a half, however, population growth, transportation developments and economic and social change brought a new competitive element to the urban system and by the mid-nineteenth century the region's towns were much more differentiated than before. Population growth over this period varied from six-fold increases in Great Driffield and Hull to the trebling of numbers in Market Weighton and Pocklington, while some places, among them Hedon, South Cave and Hornsea, only just managed to double in size. The towns experiencing the most marked increases had either a coastal, river or canal location, suggesting a strong connection between navigational links and growth.

Increased occupational diversity and a wider range of economic activity were characteristic of all towns. Employment in agriculture declined, while manufacturing crafts and trades and retail and professional services showed a corresponding increase. Social functions also developed in East Yorkshire towns in the period after 1700. At the time of the hearth tax most were of low social status, with very small social elites and few well-hearthed

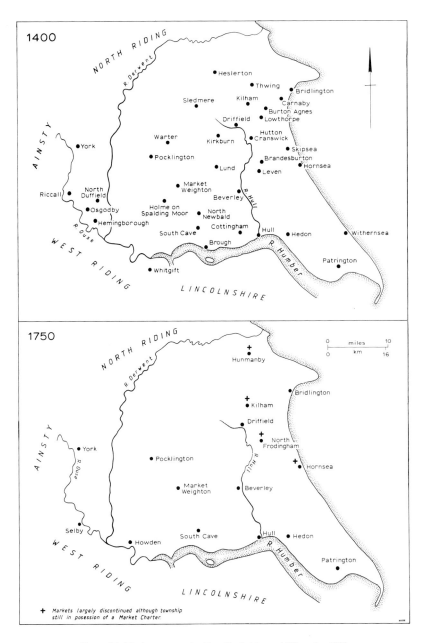

Figure 21: Market centres in East Yorkshire, c.1400 and c.1750

103

houses. Only in Hull and Beverley were significant numbers of peers, esquires, gentry and larger houses found.[3] From the middle of the eighteenth century the social standing of several towns increased as service and leisure facilities designed to cater for the growing upper and middle classes of urban society appeared, although many of the smallest centres saw little alteration to their social role.

SOURCES AND METHODOLOGY

In studying settlement, either rural or urban, analysis can take place at two levels: firstly, the aggregate approach, whereby a number of settlements comprising a region are studied in a comparative context; secondly, the study of individual towns. The choice of approach must inevitably belong to the individual.

Numerous sources are available for studying towns and in the space of this chapter it is impossible to mention them all. The discussion will focus primarily on eighteenth and nineteenth century sources for these present fewest constraints to the researcher. The study of smaller urban communities, which formed the mass of the urban settlement system in East Yorkshire, presents more problems to the student than the study of larger towns and cities. Many of the sources commonly employed in the study of large towns are seldom available for smaller urban centres while coverage of small towns in widely available sources is frequently less informative or detailed.

The sources available to the urban student are determined largely by the topic under investigation and numerous such topics suggest themselves. Everitt specifically mentions topography, building, population structure, patterns of landownership, structure of occupation and society, and family, religious and cultural life as areas worthy of investigation.[4] Before embarking on the use of primary source material the researcher should first acquaint himself with the considerable body of secondary published material that exists for East Yorkshire towns.

PUBLISHED MATERIAL

A standard reference work for any student of local history is the *Victoria County History* (VCH). The first volumes, published in the early years of this century, are relatively general but nevertheless contain important references to the region's towns. The more recently published volumes are topographical in nature and provide detailed insight into the history of individual settlements. Although not all of East Yorkshire is yet covered, Bridlington, York, Hull, Patrington and Cottingham are some of the larger settlements dealt with so far.[5] Comparative studies of the region's towns are few: Unwin has examined religious and social change in market centres of the Vale of York and Noble has looked at demographic, economic and social change in a number of East Yorkshire country towns.[6] Studies of individual towns are, however, more numerous, and some are listed in the bibliography at the end of this book. A number of other works are devoted to the study of individual aspects of urban growth and demonstrate the application of specific sources. Topics covered here include transport, trade and shipping, population and physical development and, again, examples of these studies are to be found in the bibliography.

A significant number of contemporary town histories have also been published, most of which are stocked by Hull and Beverley local history libraries. Town guidebooks and handbooks, topographical dictionaries, diaries and the descriptions of contemporary travellers provide additional information on urban development. The larger towns of Hull and Beverley are usually best covered by these works but many also mention smaller urban settlements. A note of warning should perhaps be made to the user of these contemporary accounts: while their comments and descriptions of events may be taken as fairly reliable, attempts to recount history for other than contemporary periods are frequently less so. Great care must be taken in the use and interpretation of such works with facts being checked wherever possible.[7]

UNPUBLISHED MATERIAL

Population structure

In tracing urban development some of the first questions asked will be: what size was the community in the past, has it grown or declined, and what are the reasons for the increase or decrease? The analysis of population history is covered in detail in chapter eight.

Economy, trade and industry

From an early date one of the most important functions of towns was the trade conducted through their weekly markets and less frequent fairs. Over time many of these institutions came to specialise in the marketing of particular products, rendering the towns in which they were held important distribution points within the region and even the country as a whole.[9] Details of the products regularly traded can be gleaned from a number of sources. Of particular importance are Best's farming book of 1642 and Owen's book of fairs of 1770. Many details of the character and volume of trade conducted at markets and fairs are given in a number of agricultural reports of the late eighteenth and nineteenth century, while the description of towns in commercial directories and travellers' accounts provide additional evidence.[10] Searching local newspapers published on market days and on fair dates can provide a mass of detailed information. Accounts of Howden's horse fair, for example, are to be found in the *Hull advertiser* in the first half of the nineteenth century, giving evidence that trade was conducted on an international basis with traders coming from as far as Russia. The Royal Commission on Market Rights and Tolls of 1888 gives valuable contemporary and historical details of markets and fairs throughout the country, especially through statements made by witnesses.[11] Further information concerning the fortunes of individual markets may be discovered in local records, particularly borough records and Quarter Sessions. Hedon corporation manuscripts, for example, contain details of the town's fortnightly cattle market.[12]

For the eighteenth century and earlier, details of a town's labour force can be investigated from a number of sources. For the corporate towns of Hull and Beverley apprentice registers provide information concerning the boy apprenticed, the residence of his parents and the master's trade, while their registers of freemen record details of the name and occupation of the person admitted.[13] Parish registers can also be employed to analyse occupational structure. Occupational recordings in the Anglican church parish registers generally began in the first quarter of the eighteenth century and continued, except in the case of burials, into the twentieth century. The recording of occupational details was, however, at the discretion of the incumbent. Thus there is considerable variation in occupational information recorded in registers both within and between East Yorkshire towns.

Occupations of the male parent recorded in baptism registers have been the most widely employed entries in the analysis of occupational structure: studies by Wrigley in Colyton, Pickles in Wharfedale and Noble in East Yorkshire demonstrate their usefulness.[14] It must be remembered, though, that due to differences in fertility among occupational groups and the possibility of double counting of individuals, this information does not enable us to quantify the number of persons employed in any given trade or economic sector. If recordings are collated over a number of years and percentages calculated the information does, however, provide an indication of the changing balance of the economy and the appearance of new trades and services within towns.

The availability of local directories from the end of the eighteenth century and census returns from 1801 enable a more comprehensive analysis of economic structure to be made. The *Universal British Directory* (published in six volumes between 1791-98) is the first commercial directory to give widespread coverage of East Yorkshire towns and was followed by the publication of numerous county directories in the nineteenth century. A full list of those for East Yorkshire can be found in Norton's guide to directories.[15] The use of directories must be approached with a degree of caution for many contain only a partial coverage of the range of crafts and trades within a town. Before embarking on an analysis of occupational structure from trade directories reference should be made to studies by Davies, West, Shaw and Chilton, among others, concerning their use. However, despite limitations in their data content they are a major source for the urban historian providing information about commercial life, the rise and decline of craft and industry, and the acquisition of new functions by towns.[16]

The early census returns of 1801-21 only provide information concerning the economic structure of communities in general terms. They identify the numbers employed in agriculture, in trade, manufacture and handicrafts, and other occupations. In 1831 a more comprehensive classification scheme was introduced but restricted to men over the age of twenty. From

1841 the detailed household schedules compiled by local enumerators became available and the column recording descriptions of individual occupations is invaluable to the local historian. This information, combined with other details contained within the schedules, enables us not only to investigate the detailed balance of the economy within any settlement but also to analyse the relationship between individual occupations and a person's age, place of birth and residence. Numerous studies have utilised census enumerators' notebooks to analyse the occupational structure of towns.[17]

One major problem facing the researcher investigating the occupational structure of a settlement concerns which occupational classification to employ, for there is no widely accepted scheme. Studies by Patten and Rogers discuss the issue at some length and should be consulted before determining one's classificatory scheme.[18]

Urban society

This is a large topic which covers a wide range of areas for study, three of which — wealth and social structure, the problem of the poor, and cultural and leisure provision — will be examined here.

Wealth and social structure

In investigating the social structure of settlements three sources are of particular importance: the hearth tax returns of the late seventeenth century, probate inventories and the census enumerators' notebooks, while the commercial directories can provide additional information concerning the number of resident gentry and persons of social standing.

The records of the short-lived hearth tax of the 1660s and 1670s list householders in a manner determined by their social position and this, combined with details of the number of hearths in individual households and of houses too poor to be charged, provides an important indication of wealth and social structure. Labouring classes, tradesmen and husbandmen were listed by their surname while upper social classes are recorded with the addition of a title. The number of hearths per household can be roughly equated to social groups: houses with one or two hearths belonged principally to labourers and small artisans; houses with three to five hearths belonged principally to yeomen and more prosperous craftsmen and traders; houses with six to nine hearths were owned largely by the gentry and more substantial merchants and manufacturers, and houses with more than nine by squires, manorial lords and the commercial aristocracy. The hearth tax returns for East Yorkshire are now available on microfilm in the Humberside County Record Office (HCRO), and an invaluable thesis by Purdy has extracted and analysed information for all settlements within Yorkshire and also provides a useful introduction to the history and use of the documents.[19]

Between about 1560 and 1800 the probate of a will required that a detailed inventory of the property and goods of the deceased be produced and because these cover all classes of society they are of great value in illustrating the distribution of wealth and domestic history in settlements.

Neave's study of Pocklington makes use of inventories and a recent publication for Winteringham, South Humberside, demonstrates their value. Reference should also be made to West's *Village records*, where a major section is devoted to the use and application of inventories.[20]

The census enumerators' notebooks, currently available for the period 1841 to 1881, are perhaps the most valuable documents for studying a settlement's social structure for they contain numerous details concerning the structure of both households and communities. The information content of the 1841 notebooks is restricted but from 1851 a comprehensive range of information is included. The schedules contain columns detailing street name and house number (if any), occupants' names, relationship to the head of the household, whether married or single, age, occupation and place of birth. The possibilities for analysis are numerous and a large number of studies demonstrate clearly the potential application of these records.[21] It would be impossible to detail all the topics that present themselves for possible investigation in the space of a few lines but several may be mentioned. The size and structure of the family can be examined and inferences made about migratory paths through evidence relating to the birth place of parents and children, while the number of servants employed may provide a good indication of the social status of households. Information concerning occupation may be employed both to analyse the economic structure of the settlement and to identify the distribution of social classes. The identification of individual household locations in the notebooks may enable us to repopulate our houses and streets and to answer a number of questions: to what extent was society intermixed, were there clearly defined economic areas within the settlement, were there areas of streets of distinct social status, did ethnic minorities cluster in certain locations?

The task of analysing the mass of statistical information contained in the notebooks may be onerous, particularly if a sizeable community is being investigated, and access to a main frame computer may not always be possible. Recently, however, a range of software has been developed for analysing census data on microprocessors, capable of handling well over one million persons. The Open University has been to the fore in pioneering this work and Mills has produced two packages for use on a microcomputer to analyse rural and urban communities.[22]

The poor

From the establishment of the office of overseer of the poor in 1597 records left by these officers and the churchwardens furnish details of the problem of the poor and policies adopted for their relief. Local rates were collected and expended on those applying for relief and the associated rate books provide insight into persons rated and amounts paid, and indirectly to the value of houses within the settlement. Much town business was, in the period 1662 to 1850, devoted to enforcing the laws of settlement which sought to restrict paupers, or potential paupers, to their own parish. Settlement certificates and copies of examinations of vagrants are of great value for they are in effect biographies of persons for whom little information is otherwise found. They frequently detail a person's movements since apprenticeship, lengths of residence, employment history, rental values of properties held and family structure. Most records relating to the poor in the period before the Poor Law Amendment Act of 1834 are found with parish records and Tate's *Parish chest* is an invaluable source of information on these documents. For East Yorkshire Mitchelson's study also provides a good introduction to the system of relief.[23]

Changes in the Poor Law in the first half of the nineteenth century resulted in a number of parliamentary papers containing evidence on the operation of the poor relief system. Of major importance is the report of the 1834 Royal Commission on the Poor Law which contains accounts for settlements within Yorkshire, while reports of the Poor Law Board published annually from 1835 also contain useful information.[24] Under the Act of 1834 responsibility for the poor became vested in boards of local guardians and it is their minute and account books, workhouse records, records of out-relief, settlement papers and bastardy orders that provide the most detailed insight into the operation of the social welfare system in the nineteenth century.[25]

As well as official relief, private charity played an important part in most settlements. The source material in this area is on the whole thin but churchwardens and parish accounts frequently contain references to private charities as do the commercial directories. The VCH also details local charities and much information can be obtained from the records of the Charity Commissioners and Friendly Societies contained in a number of parliamentary papers.[26]

Leisure and cultural provision
Considerable difficulty faces any attempt to investigate leisure activities for the eighteenth century and earlier. In corporate towns, such as Hedon, Beverley and Hull, borough records often indicate the presence of theatres and assemblies, but for the mass of unincorporated towns references are far fewer. Occasionally, reference to leisure activities can be found in parish records, letters and estate papers. The Grimston papers, for example, contain references to gambling, card playing, cockfighting and shooting at Pocklington inns and in the neighbouring settlement of Nunburnholme in the 1770s.[27] Indeed, most leisure activity was centred around inns and it is for these places that most records survive. Records of the Quarter Sessions contain registers of alehouses and enable us to build up a picture of provision in the region's towns. In 1775, for example, Pocklington contained thirty licensed premises — one for every thirty inhabitants — and in 1780 Patrington had eleven — or one for every fifty-six inhabitants.[28]

From the turn of the eighteenth century it is possible to investigate leisure and cultural provision with greater ease. The commercial directories frequently contain details of societies and clubs in towns whilst also providing information on the number of licensed premises and brewers. Of major importance are local newspapers which are a mine of information on events and activities in towns. Even when smaller places did not have their own newspapers, those of the nearest large town usually contained sections devoted to outlying towns and villages, as in the case of the *Hull advertiser*. The *Hull advertiser* is indexed from 1794 to 1825 but most newspapers are not. Several studies discuss the use of newspapers to the local historian and West's *Town records* contains a gazetteer of English and Welsh newspapers.[29]

Town histories may also contain contemporary references to cultural activities. Sheppard's history of drama in Hull and East Yorkshire contains information on the growth of theatrical provision.[30]

Physical development

The changing fortunes of a settlement over time are clearly reflected in the pattern of building and physical growth. There are numerous aspects of a town's physical growth worthy of investigation, many of which are discussed at length by Hoskins.[31] Vernacular architecture is one such aspect, and this is covered in chapter twelve, while housing and topographical change are two others.

The nature of housing provision in any settlement is difficult to investigate before about 1800 for information is scattered amongst a number of sources. Surveys made at the time of enclosure or commissioned by local land and estate owners, may provide a good indication of the number of houses in the community. Poor rate returns found in parish records may also provide details on the number of houses and their yearly rental values. Where, as in the case of Howden, these returns are made by streets investigation can be made of spatial differences in the value of housing.[32] Records of individual houses are perhaps more numerous and mortgages, leases and the East Riding Registry of Deeds in the HCRO enables the changing ownership and characteristics of properties to be traced in some detail, while probate inventories are also of significance.[33]

From the nineteenth century far more information is available concerning housing through the decennial census returns and parliamentary papers. The printed census abstracts record the number of inhabited and uninhabited houses, the number being built and the total of households in all settlements, enabling us to infer something of possible degrees of housing shortage and overcrowding. The later land tax assessments are also important since from c.1825 it was normal for property descriptions to be included, whilst these documents also provide details of tenure.[34] The condition of housing in towns is frequently mentioned in parliamentary papers. The 1833 Report on the State of the Municipal Corporations contains details for the region's corporate towns, and Chadwick's report on the sanitary condition of the labouring population contains details for Hull. Small towns are mentioned less frequently in such documents, but the report on the House Accommodation of Rural Labourers and the seventh report of the Medical Officer of the Privy Council, both from 1864, contain useful references.[35] The census enumerators' returns are of course invaluable for investigating household composition, multiple occupancy, house size and location.

Maps and plans are a major source for investigating topography. It was in the sixteenth and seventeenth centuries that maps and plans of individual towns first appeared and in the following centuries they were produced with increasing frequency, especially for larger centres; two good local examples are Watson's maps of Market Weighton and Pocklington.[36] Enclosure maps and tithe plans frequently detailed information on ownership and occupation of the built areas in towns not large enough to be independently surveyed. Ordnance Survey maps, produced from the start of the nineteenth century, tell us a good deal about urban expansion and the location of commercial and industrial premises. Of particular value are the large scale maps and plans produced from mid-century onwards. West's *Town records* provides examples of the potential usefulness of maps and contains a gazetteer for borough towns; Harley's works are an invaluable guide to the local historian and a Yorkshire Archaeological Society (YAS) publication lists the availability of maps for settlements within Yorkshire.[37]

Transport

The nature of town growth in the eighteenth and nineteenth centuries depended to a large extent on the relationship with the surrounding region. Any study of urban settlement would be incomplete without investigation of the role played by transport on change within and between towns. In investigating the role that transport and communications played in urban change concern is best focussed on a limited range of questions. These might include: the volume and type of traffic and trade using rivers and canals, roads and railways serving the town; the condition of the communications (silting and lack of maintenance of Patrington and Hedon havens, for example, seriously affected the trading potential of both towns); support for the communications through investigating subscription levels, and the balance between town subscribers and those from other settlements and areas, and the nature of improvements. A large number of sources are available for studying transport and there are several well known studies dealing with the development of roads, navigable waterways and railways in East Yorkshire.

Relatively little information is available concerning the early development of roads and it is maps, which in the sixteenth and seventeenth centuries were largely focussed on routeways, that provide the main source. Vestry minutes and records of the surveyors of the highways can, however, provide details of both traffic and the state of the roads. From the turnpike age much more information becomes available and MacMahon's book on the turnpike trusts of East Yorkshire provides a valuable introduction to the development of the road network in the region. Additional material can be found in records of local turnpike trusts in the HCRO and from a number of parliamentary papers which contain accounts and returns of trusts for the whole country.[38] The commercial directories are a further importance source on the relationship of roads to towns. Their details of carriers' carts visiting various towns and villages and of stage coach services provide an indication of town trade and of the relative importance of settlements within the region.

A good deal has already been written concerning the region's canals and navigable waterways that is of great value to the student of urban settlement and several of these studies are listed in the bibliography. Additional material can be obtained from records of the individual navigation companies found at the HCRO and the Public Record Office, while those of navigations concerning corporate towns are found among borough records. For two of the region's waterways some records are still in private hands: Hedon Haven Commissioner records are deposited with Andrew M. Jackson and Sons, solicitors, of Hull, and some of the Market Weighton canal are at Market Weighton Drainage and Navigation Board in Pocklington. Parliamentary papers also cover canals, the most important report for any local study being that of the Royal Commission on Canals, 1906-1911.[39]

The impact of railways on town growth is a large topic and the records of railway companies are too extensive to be discussed here. For East Yorkshire two studies by Foulkes and MacMahon are important introductions to the early development of railways and sources for their investigation in the region. Numerous parliamentary papers and reports deal with railways as do returns made to the Board of Trade and the student will need to consult indexes to identify the appropriate documents.[40] Local newspapers may also provide a source of information on meetings of shareholders, public opinion and the opening and use of railways, as well as for roads and canals.

The preceding discussion is by no means a comprehensive coverage of all primary source material and all topics of study available to the student of local history. No mention for example has been made of local government and politics, and crime and health and disease are other aspects of town life that could be investigated (see chapter thirteen). The following section is a case study of the town of Great Driffield, the fastest growing country town in East Yorkshire in the eighteenth and nineteenth centuries.

CASE STUDY: THE GROWTH AND DEVELOPMENT OF GREAT DRIFFIELD, c.1700-1850

Within the urban system of East Yorkshire Driffield grew faster than any other centre, save Hull. Over the period 1700 to 1850, the town's population increased from 660 to 3963. Much of this growth was fuelled by immigration and in 1851 more than 41% of the inhabitants came from other East Yorkshire settlements. The demographic experience of Driffield was paralleled by economic and social expansion and physical growth which rendered the town one of the most important trading centres in East Yorkshire by the mid-nineteenth century.

Much of the explanation for the dynamic growth of Driffield during this period rests with the town's access to the region's transportation system (figure 22). The turnpiking and improvement of roads in the vicinity of Driffield and the acquisition of a canal link in 1767 enabled the town to become a trading centre of more than local importance, usurping the

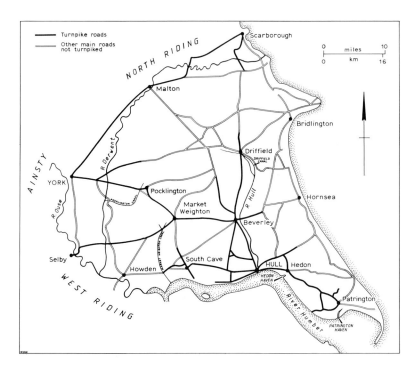

Figure 22: The transportation system in East Yorkshire c.1840

position of many smaller centres whose failure to attract a canal or local investment in a turnpike led to a stifling of growth.

In the early eighteenth century Driffield had only one market, devoted largely to the sale of general retail goods.[41] In an era of improving agriculture and communications, however, only those centres that specialised in the marketing of particular products could survive and enjoy economic fortunes above the regional average. Agricultural improvement, the turnpiking of the road northward from Beverley and the cutting of the Driffield canal just three years later gave the necessary fillip to the town's economy bringing it a degree of trading specialisation unrivalled in the northern part of East Yorkshire. In the hundred years between 1750 and 1850 Driffield became increasingly important as a specialised centre for trade in grain and livestock within the region. In the period after 1767 the town drew much corn trade away from Bridlington and some also from Malton, and Bridlington market was accounted to be largely controlled by Driffield factors.[42] According to the *Universal British Directory* of 1798 over 20,000 quarters of grain were exported from the town annually and the weekly corn market was said to be frequented by more agriculturalists than any other corn market in East Yorkshire. William Marshall, writing in

113

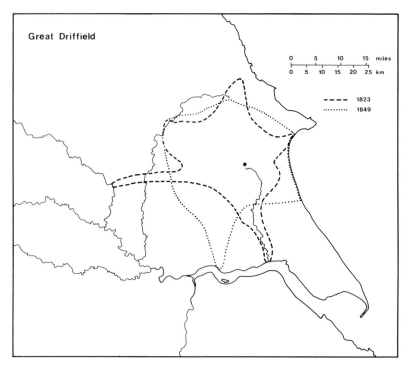

Figure 23: The market area of Great Driffield, 1823-1849 (based on journeys of carriers' carts)

1788, attested that Driffield corn factors received an annual income of between £300 and £400, striking evidence of both the large quantities of grain produced on the Wolds and the volume of trade conducted in the town. By the time the corn exchange was built in 1841 more than 70,000 quarters were annually exported and by 1860 about 100,000, while large quantities of corn were also converted to flour in the mills of the town and neighbourhood.[43]

In the first half of the nineteenth century livestock trade also developed. The Royal Commission on Market Rights and Tolls of 1888 and local newspapers provide details of the somewhat precarious existence of the town's livestock trade in the early years of establishment. In 1833 both livestock and pig markets were started in the town although the former appears to have lasted for only a few months. However, attempts to establish a permanent and diverse livestock trade were maintained and in 1846 William Jarratt, a local hotelier, established a new market which was described in a newspaper report of 1850 as 'the best for cattle and pigs in the East Riding'.[44]

Further evidence of the importance of Driffield as a trading centre is provided by the increasing number of carriers' carts, listed in commercial directories, connecting the town to other centres within East Yorkshire. Between 1791 and 1849 the number of places served increased from three to forty-five, whilst the number of services per week rose from eight to ninety. The evidence of carriers suggests that the market area of Driffield was, by 1850, extensive, encompassing places both within and beyond the region (figure 23). The town's canal served to extend trade over a far wider area. At the close of the eighteenth century twenty-seven vessels regularly traded between the town and the West Riding, and Legard, in his prize essay on farming, noted the considerable body of trade that occurred between Driffield and Wakefield. Exports via Driffield canal stood at more than 46,500 tons in 1830 and imports at over 32,500 tons, more than double the tonnages handled on the Market Weighton and Pocklington canals.[45]

The development of Driffield's marketing function was paralleled by new levels of specialisation and diversity in other economic activities. Analysis of occupational entries in the town's baptism and burial registers, in the period for which they are available after 1770, of entries in trade directories and of information contained in printed census abstracts and the census enumerators' returns enables a detailed picture of the changing nature of economic history in Driffield to be established.[46]

Economic development in Driffield remained closely tied to the agricultural basis of the regional economy throughout the eighteenth and nineteenth centuries but became more specialised and more industrialised. In the agricultural sector farmers, yeomen and husbandmen came to constitute a smaller percentage of the workforce while market gardeners, nurserymen and seedsmen registered a corresponding increase. Parish register analysis indicates that over the period 1771 to 1840 the former group declined from 89% to 59% of all agricultural entries while the latter increased from 5% to 36%.

Manufacturing and craft industry was an important sector of the town economy accounting for about one third of the entries in each of the data sources. A wide range of trades and crafts were practised from milling and brewing to iron founding and textile working. Most of this manufacturing industry remained on a small scale but by 1851 thirty-six manufacturers employed labour and from the close of the eighteenth century several attempts were made to mechanise traditional craft industries. The availability of water power resources in the vicinity of the town made Driffield the focus of attempts to industrialise textile working in the region although the town had little previous involvement.[47] Several mills were either built or converted to manufacture textiles and carpets from the 1770s onwards but in the event none of these ventures proved really successful and in time each mill reverted to the agricultural basis of town economy and became corn, flour or bone mills.[48]

The eleven retailers and professionals listed as employing labour in the census enumerators' returns of 1851 are indicative of the growing importance of Driffield as a service centre for East Yorkshire. By the early nineteenth century both parish registers and directories indicate that the town had acquired many specialist services such as confectioners, fishmongers and fruiterers. By the middle of the nineteenth century approximately 50% of all directory entries and 25% of all employment was found in retail and professional occupations.

At the time of the hearth tax returns the social profile of Driffield was poorly developed. Only two inhabitants were accorded a title (one esquire and one mistress) and the hearth structure differed little from that of surrounding villages. More than half of the town's houses were too poor to be taxed and of those charged about 91.5% contained only one or two hearths, 5.6% three to five hearths and only 2.6% with more than this number. In the ensuing centuries this situation was transformed as the town became one of the most socially important centres within the region. In the eighteenth century the number of persons of social standing steadily increased. Driffield's parish registers suggest that about one in every ten persons were of professional or upper social status, while the trade directories indicate that by the early nineteenth century this proportion may have been as high as one in five. Clearly, from the late eighteenth century the town began to emerge as a place of fashionable residence. Just seven resident gentry are recorded in the *Universal British Directory* of 1798, but forty in 1823 and fifty by mid-century. The clearest picture of the social structure of the town is provided by analysis of the 1851 census enumerators' returns.

The five tier socio-economic classification developed by Armstrong in his study of York, based on the General Register Office's classification of occupations, has been the most widely used schema in studies of urban social structure.[49] In this scheme class I comprises professional occupations and all persons employing twenty-five or more people; class II intermediate occupations and tradesmen employing one or more persons; class III skilled occupations; class IV semi-skilled occupations; and class V unskilled occupations. Although this scheme was formulated for studies of large towns it can also be employed in the study of smaller urban centres.

Adopting this scheme for Driffield we find that in 1851 4.7% of the town's population were of social class I, 22.2% class II, 38.2% class III, 20.8% class IV and 14.1% class V suggesting that the town had a well balanced social structure, although the fairly high proportion in class V was more akin to levels found in industrial towns than in other market towns. A further indication of the changing social status of the town is provided by figures relating to the employment of domestic servants. At mid-century almost one-fifth of all employment in the town was found in domestic service and one-fifth of households also employed domestic servants: over 60% of class I households employed domestic help and almost 40% of class II.

The developing social standing of Driffield within the region is further evidenced by a 'sophistication' of urban life and urban improvements. This took three distinct forms: the improvement of the appearance of the town through the provision of lighting, paving and sanitation; the building of public amenities such as market halls and corn exchanges; and the provision of leisure facilities such as theatres, assembly rooms and sports facilities to meet the demands of the new urban elite. As an important trading town Driffield was quick to follow Beverley in the development of

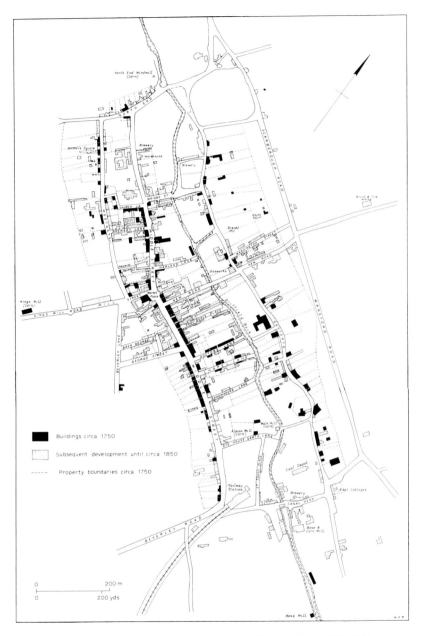

Figure 24: The expansion of the built area in Great Driffield c.1750-1850

117

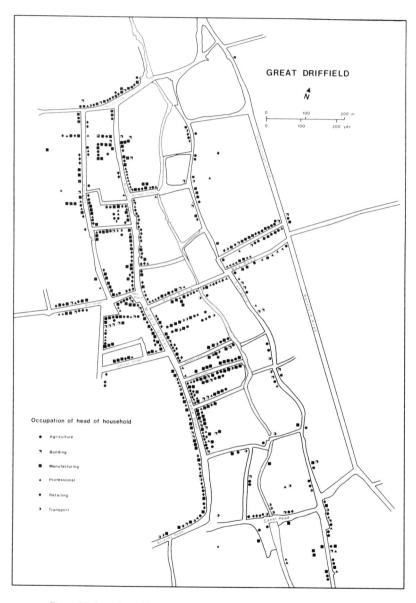

Figure 25: Location of households engaged in selected economic activities
in Great Driffield, 1851

118

leisure facilities, institutions and societies. The known dates at which the town acquired various improvements include the hunt and horse racing in about 1770, the theatre in c.1775, gas lighting in 1835 and a law court in 1844.

At the other end of the social spectrum was the problem of the poor. The eighteenth century workhouse in Driffield was ill-suited to meet demand: it housed just three inmates in 1795 for the town found it cheaper to pay the paupers relief or farm them out than keep them in care. Following the Poor Law Amendment Act of 1834 a new and larger workhouse was built with accommodation for 200. There is evidence to suggest, however, that this may in some measure have increased social problems in the town. Following its construction the number of illegitimate births rose sharply: out of 1131 baptisms recorded in the parish registers for the period 1841 to 1851, 135 were illegitimate, and in the period March 1847 to March 1848 more than 2000 vagrants were received at the workhouse, a 100% increase over the previous year.[50]

Population growth and economic and social development were manifested in physical and spatial changes within the town. Between 1750 and 1850 the town underwent a considerable degree of physical restructuring and expansion (figure 24) through the demolition and rebuilding of existing properties, infilling of vacant plots and the subdivision of plots of land to provide additional building space. To the long established pattern of three main streets within the town were added numerous new roads, lanes, alleys, courts and yards. Between 1801 and 1841 the printed census abstracts indicate that the number of dwelling houses within the town rose from 320 to 646. Over the period 1830 to 1850 twenty-seven houses with shops, five industrial premises, forty-seven medium to large dwelling houses and 180 workers' cottages were built in the town.[51]

The expansion of Driffield involved considerable change in the nature of the urban fabric as low one-storey houses of mud and thatch were replaced by brick and tile houses. A contemporary account attests that between 1800 and 1840 all the houses in Middle Street (between the Market Place and the railway station) and in New Road, Mill Street and George Street were either refurbished or newly built. In this period it is estimated that only about one dozen houses in the town remained unaltered.[52]

The restyling of much of the urban fabric led to new levels of socio-economic segregation within the town. By the first quarter of the nineteenth century certain parts were becoming established as areas for industry and trade, while others were assuming a more residential character. Analysis of the location of tradesmen and professions recorded in Baine's *Directory* of 1823 suggests something of the socio-economic structure of the town. The Market Place and surrounding streets were the focus of retail and service trades, although a large number of craft industries, particularly producer retailers, also occupied the central areas. The area around the canal head had become an important subsidiary manufacturing area and the centre of much of the town's wholesale trade on account of the merchants, factors and dealers who leased or built warehouses there. The wealthier inhabitants and professions resided principally to the east and south of the town. Information contained in the census enumerators' notebooks demonstrates more clearly the developing nature of social and economic segregation in the town.

If we plot the street locations of the occupations of all household heads in Driffield for 1851, it is evident that a commercial core existed stretching along the east side of Middle Street from Bandmakers Lane to Bridge Street (figure 25). Almost 50% of retail activity was located in Middle Street, the remainder being widely dispersed. Few professionals resided in this area, most lived at the northern or southern end of Middle Street or to the east in Bridge Street and New Road. Manufacturers and craftsmen were found in large numbers in the streets and lanes to the east and west of Middle Street, and in alleys, courts and yards built to infill the town centre. Not surprisingly, agricultural households were predominantly located on the edge of the built area, particularly in Eastgate, and clearly the developing commercial importance of Driffield left little room for agricultural activity in the central area. Within this broad pattern of economic location there were specific functional concentrations of householders. Leather workers, for example, dominated craft industry in Bandmakers Lane and wood and metal workers Chapel Lane and Doctors Lane.

Spatial differences in the location of economic activity were closely linked to social structure. High status residential areas showed a close association with professional service, low status residences with agricultural and labouring activity and middle class residences with manufacturing and retail trades. Within the town there was a marked social distinction between residents living on the main streets and those living in small back lanes and yards of inferior housing. Figure 26 plots the residential location of household heads of social classes I and II and figure 27 the location of household heads in groups IV and V. The former were virtually absent from locations other than the main streets while the latter predominated in the small lanes to the east of Middle Street, and in the north west of the town on Westgate and the surrounding streets, one being aptly named Dossers Place.

Space precludes any further analysis of the usefulness of the census enumerators' notebooks or of other sources and aspects of the town's development. Studies similar to this brief survey of Driffield's development in the eighteenth and nineteenth centuries could be undertaken for other towns, or indeed for villages, while individual aspects of development touched upon in this case study could be investigated in much greater depth.

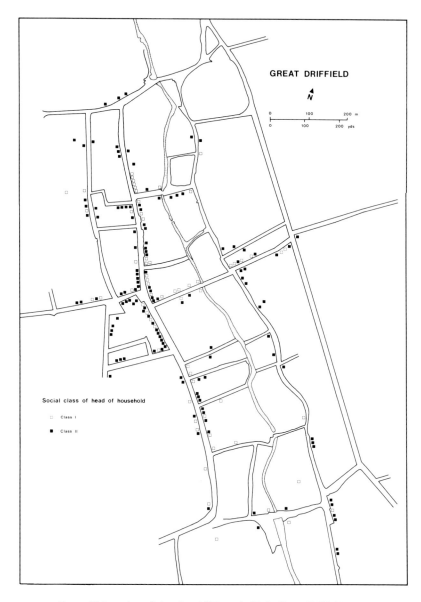

Figure 26: Location of class I and II households in Great Driffield, 1851

121

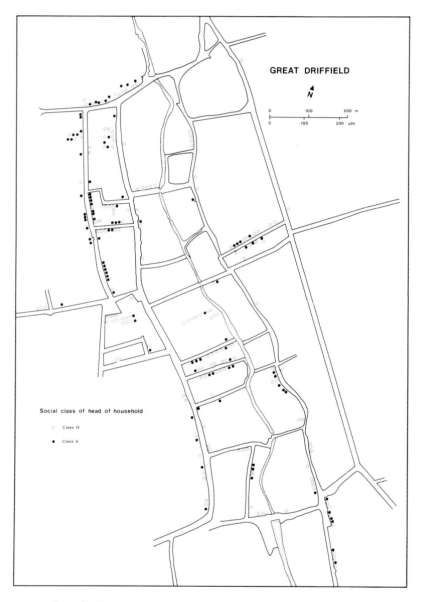

GREAT DRIFFIELD

Figure 27: Location of class IV and V households in Great Driffield, 1851

122

1. A. Everitt, 'The marketing of agricultural produce', in *The agrarian history of England and Wales, 1500-1640*, vol. 4, edited by J. Thirsk (Cambridge, 1967), pp. 466-592

2. Information drawn from K. L. McCutcheon, *Yorkshire fairs and markets*, Thoresby Society publications, 34 (Leeds, 1940); A. Everitt, 'The market town', in *The early modern town*, edited by P. Clark (London, 1976), p. 170; J. Adams, *Index Villaries; or, An alphabetical list of all cities, market towns, parishes, villages and private seats in England and Wales* (London, 1680); W. Owen, *Book of fairs*, 6th ed. (London, 1770)

3. J. Purdy, 'Hearth tax returns for Yorkshire' (unpublished M.Phil. thesis, University of Leeds, 1975)

4. A. Everitt, *Ways and means in local history* (London, 1971); A. Everitt, *New avenues in English local history* (Leicester, 1970)

5. VCH ER vols 1 to 5 (Oxford, 1969-1984)

6. R. W. Unwin, 'Tradition and transition: market towns of the Vale of York', *Northern history*, 17 (1981), pp. 72-116; M. Noble, *Change in the small towns of the East Riding of Yorkshire, c.1750-1850*, Hedon local history series, 5 (Hull, 1979); M. Noble, 'Growth and development of country towns: the case of eastern Yorkshire 1700-1850' (unpublished Ph.D. thesis, University of Hull, 1982)

7. A. de la Pryme, *The diary of Abraham de la Pryme*, Surtees society publications, 54 (Durham, 1870); D. Defoe, *A tour through the whole island of Great Britain*, 2 vols (London, 1928; first published in 3 vols, 1724-27); C. Fiennes, *Journeys of Celia Fiennes*, edited by C. Morris, 2nd ed. (London, 1949); W. Camden, *Britannia*, edited with revisions by E. Gibson (London, 1695)

8. Many guides to the sources and study of local history deal with population and other topics discussed in the following pages. Of especial value are A. Rodgers, *Approaches to local history*, 2nd ed. (London, 1977); W. B. Stephens, *Sources for English local history* (Manchester, 1973); J. West, *Village records,* 2nd ed. (Chichester, 1982); J. West, *Town records* (Chichester, 1983); D. Iredale, *Enjoying archives*, 2nd ed. (Newton Abbot, 1985); W. G. Hoskins, *Local history in England*, 3rd ed. (London, 1984); J. E. Exwood and R. W. Unwin, *Yorkshire topography: a guide to historical sources and their uses* (Leeds, 1974)

9. Everitt, 'Marketing of agricultural produce'; D. Alexander, *Retailing in England during the Industrial Revolution* (London, 1970); D. Davis, *A history of shopping* (London, 1966)

10. D. M. Woodward, ed., *The farming and memorandum books of Henry Best of Elmswell, 1642* (London, 1984); Owen; H. E. Strickland, *A general view of the agriculture of the East Riding of Yorkshire*, 2 vols (London, 1788); I. Leatham, *A general view of the agriculture of the East Riding of Yorkshire* (London, 1794)

11. *Hull advertiser*, 28 October 1803, 1 October 1841, 3 October 1834, 6 October 1843; Royal Commission on Market Rights and Tolls H. C. 1888-91 C.5550 I-LLI and C.6268 xxxvii-xxxviii

12. HCRO DDIV 33/3

13. D. M. Woodward, 'Freemens Rolls', *The local historian*, 9 (1970), pp. 89-95

14. E. A. Wrigley, 'The changing occupational structure of Colyton over two centuries', *Local population studies*, 18 (1977), pp. 9-21; M. F. Pickles, 'Mid-Wharfedale, 1721-1812: economic and demographic change in a Pennine Dale', *Local population studies*, 16 (1976), pp. 12-45; Noble, *Change in the small town*

15. J. E. Norton, ed., *A guide to national and provincial directories of England and Wales, excluding London, published before 1856* (London, 1950)

16. W. K. D. Davies, J. A. Giggs and D. T. Herbert, 'Directories, rate books and the commercial structure of towns', *Geography*, 53 (1968), pp. 41-54; West, *Village records*, pp. 162-173; West, *Town records*, pp. 206-223; G. Shaw, 'The content and reliability of nineteenth century trade directories', *The local historian*, 13 (1978), pp. 205-9; C. W. Chilton, 'The Universal British Directory: a warning', *The local historian*, 15 (1982), pp. 144-6

17. R. Lawton, *The census and social structure: an interpretive guide to the nineteenth*

century censuses for England and Wales (London, 1978); A. Armstrong, 'The interpretation of census enumerators' books for Victorian towns', in *The study of urban history*, edited by H. J. Dyos (London, 1966), pp. 67-86; J. A. Patmore, *An atlas of Harrogate* (Harrogate, 1963); J. A. Patmore, 'The spa towns of Britain', in *Urbanization and its problems*, edited by R. P. Beckinsale (Oxford, 1968), pp. 47-69

18.   Rodgers, pp. 99-102; J. Patten, 'Urban occupations in pre-industrial England', *Transactions of the Institute of British Geographers*, New series, 2 (1977), pp. 296-313

19.   Purdy, *Hearth tax returns*; D. Foster, 'The hearth tax and settlement studies', *The local historian*, 11 (1975), pp. 385-389

20.   D. Neave, *Pocklington: a small East Riding market town 1600-1914* (Beverley, 1970); D. Neave, ed., *Winteringham 1650-1760* (Winteringham, 1984); West, *Village records*, pp. 92-131

21.   E. A. Wrigley, ed., *Nineteenth century society* (London, 1972); Ashbourne Local History Society, *Early Victorian county town: a portrait of Ashbourne in the mid nineteenth century* (Ashbourne, 1978); see also note 17

22.   These can be obtained from Mills Historical and Computing, Cat Lane House, Bridge Street, Thornborough, Buckingham, MK18 2DN

23.   W. E. Tate, *The parish chest*, 3rd ed. (Chichester, 1983); N. Mitchelson, *The Old Poor Law in East Yorkshire*, EYLHS, 2 (York, 1953); C. P. Ketchley, 'Settlement and its legal definition', *Amateur historian*, 2 (1956), pp. 268-70

24.   Reports of the Select Committee . . . on the Poor Law Amendment Act, 1837-38, H.C. 1834 xvii-xviii; see W. R. Powell, *Local History from Blue Books: a select list of the sessional papers of the House of Commons* (London, 1962)

25.   Many of these are found in the HCRO, while parliamentary papers also contain returns for unions and parishes

26.   See D. Owen, *English philanthropy 1660-1969* (Oxford, 1965); P. Godsen, *The friendly societies of England, 1815-75* (Manchester, 1960); and Powell for a list of parliamentary papers

27.   HCRO DDGR 42/43 1775

28.   HCRO QDT 1, 9, 12, 15

29.   West, *Town records*, pp. 237-271; P. Lucas, 'Sources for urban history (9): Local newspapers', *The local historian*, 11 (1975), pp. 321-6; K. A. MacMahon, 'Local history and the newspaper', *Amateur historian*, 5 (1963), pp. 212-217

30.   T. Sheppard, *The evolution of drama in Hull and district* (Hull, 1927)

31.   Hoskins, *Local history*, pp. 96-129, 140-163; W. G. Hoskins, *Fieldwork in local history*, 2nd ed. (London, 1982); W. G. Hoskins, *Provincial England* (London, 1963)

32.   HCRO PR 847

33.   See note 20; J. H. Harvey, *Sources for the history of houses* (London, 1974)

34.   D. Grigg, 'A source on landownership: the land tax returns', *Amateur historian*, 6 (1964), pp. 152-6; J. Gibson and D. Mills, eds., *Land tax assessments c.1690-1930* (Plymouth, 1983)

35.   Powell, *Blue books*; Chadwick's report is now published as M. W. Flinn, ed., *Report on the sanitary condition of the labouring population of Great Britain* (Edinburgh, 1965); Privy Council, *Seventh report of the Medical Officer of the Privy Council* (London, 1864)

36.   A. Harris, 'An East Yorkshire land surveyor: William Watson of Seaton Ross', YAJ, 45 (1973), pp.149-57; copies of the maps are available at HCRO DDPY 19/4, DDEV 7/13

37.   West, *Town records*, pp. 131-165; H. Whitaker, ed., *A descriptive list of the printed maps of Yorkshire and its Ridings 1577-1900*, YAS record series, 86 (Leeds, 1933); J. B. Harley, *Maps for the local historian: a guide to the British sources* (London, 1972); J. B. Harley, 'The maps of England and Wales at the 6 inch and 25 inch scales', *Amateur historian*, 5 (1963), pp. 161-90

38.   K. A. MacMahon, *Roads and turnpike trusts in East Yorkshire*, EYLHS, 18 (York, 1964); Rodgers, *Approaches*, pp. 103-125

39.   C. Hadfield, 'Sources for the history of British canals', *Journal of transport*

history, 2 (1955-56), pp. 80-89; H. C. Cd.3183 etc. xxxii etc. (1906 etc.)

40. E. H. Fowkes, *Railway history and the local historian,* EYLHS, 16 (York, 1963); K. A. MacMahon, *The beginnings of East Yorkshire railways,* EYLHS, 3 (York, 1953); see D. B. Wardle, 'Sources for the history of railways at the Public Record Office', *Journal of transport history,* 7 (1955-56), pp. 141-48; P. and G. Ford, *A guide to parliamentary papers* (Oxford, 1955)

41. HUL DDCV 42/12

42. HCRO DDX 17/15

43. P. Barfoot and J. Wilkes, *The Universal British Directory of trade and commerce* (London, 1791-98) vol. 6; W. Marshall, *The rural economy of Yorkshire* (London, 1788), p.248; HCRO DDX 17/15

44. *Yorkshire gazetteer* 21 March 1833, 30 March 1833; *Hull advertiser* 31 May 1833, 7 June 1850

45. B. F. Duckham, *The inland waterways of East Yorkshire, 1700-1900,* EYLHS, 29 (York, 1972), p.13; G. Legard, 'Farming of the East Riding of Yorkshire', *Journal of the Royal Agricultural Society of England,* 9 (1848), p.108; HCRO DDIV 1, 2; M. Noble, 'Inland navigations and country towns', in *Ports and resorts in the regions,* edited by E. M. Sigsworth (Hull, 1981), p.98

46. For a discussion on the choice of occupational classification see Noble, *Growth and development,* pp. 134-36

47. Some textile working may have been pursued in the eighteenth century as the manorial records make some mention of hemp and linen, HUL DDCY 42/10. Parish registers record few textile occupations

48. M. W. Barley, *The history of Great and Little Driffield* (Hull, 1938); K. J. Allison, *East Riding water mills,* EYLHS, 26 (York, 1970), pp. 20-21; HCRO DDX 17/15

49. A. Armstrong, *Stability and change in an English country town: a social study of York, 1801-51* (London, 1974); A. Armstrong, 'The use of information about occupation', in *Nineteenth century society,* edited by E. A. Wrigley (London, 1972), pp. 191-310; see also Lawton, *Census and social structure*

50. Mitchelson, *The Old Poor Law;* HCRO PR 947; *Hull advertiser* 24 March 1848

51. HCRO DDX 17/15

52. HCRO DDX 17/15

8

POPULATION

David Foster

The study of population is fundamental to any study of local history. Its ebb and flow may reflect the availability and fertility of land, the opportunity for employment and the availability of housing; it may point to the environmental conditions in which people lived and their consequent life expectancy; and it will raise questions about social practices and customs such as age-at-marriage and birth control. In short, it may well be the most fruitful introduction to the study of economic and social history, particularly at the parochial and regional levels. This chapter surveys the principal sources for the study of population, briefly indicates the main trends in the population of East Yorkshire and offers an illustrative case study, in some detail, based on Driffield.

Sources for population studies

The introduction of the decennial census and the system of Civil Registration in 1801 and 1837 respectively enable the demographic history of the nineteenth and twentieth centuries to be studied with confidence at all levels from the nation as a whole to the smallest township. In contrast, the study of population behaviour prior to 1801 is fraught with uncertainty, principally because few if any records of enumeration were taken before the first national census. However, it is far from impossible to study population history before 1801 provided that any statistical results produced are recognised as estimates rather than reality and treated with a healthy scepticism.

Pre-censal sources for population estimates are chiefly a range of ecclesiastical and administrative records made for a variety of non-demographic purposes.[1] Thus, in addition to assessing the general reliability of the records, even for their initial purposes, the historian must devise ways of exploiting them for the study of population. The records with potential can be classified into two groups, the first a somewhat random set, specific in both time and intent, the second the ubiquitous and generally extensive parish registers of the established church. From the sixteenth to the eighteenth centuries, a range of returns were made to both lay and ecclesiastical authorities in particular years which allow estimates for population to be made, often at the parochial level. The principal administrative returns include the lay subsidies of 1524-25 which enable the total number of households to be calculated; the hearth tax returns of the later seventeenth century which list the names of all householders, and their hearths, who paid the tax and who were exempt, the total of which again provides a base from which to work; and the Muster Rolls and Books which were made at periods of national crisis from the early sixteenth to the mid-eighteenth centuries. The chief ecclesiastical sources are the chantry certificates of 1547 which give an estimate of the total number of communicants in a parish; the 1563 Bishop's Returns to the Privy Council listed the number of families in each parish while those of 1630 give the totals of communicants, nonconformists and Catholics; the 1642 Protestation Returns list all who signed or refused to sign an undertaking to support the rights of Parliament; the 1676 Compton census provides the same information as the 1603 returns; and a range of diocesan visitation records whose survival is random and whose value is even more varied.

However, it is rather unusual to find many parishes represented in all these documents and the survival rate is mixed; for example, neither the Bishops' Returns for 1563 and 1603 nor the 1642 Protestation Returns have survived for the diocese of York. Still, sufficient have withstood the ravages of time and some are quite accessible to the local historian within the county. For the sixteenth century, the lay subsidies and the Muster Rolls exist in considerable numbers in the Public Record Office (PRO) in London, and but one of the latter, for 1584, has been published by the Yorkshire Archaeological Society (YAS);[2] for the seventeenth century the hearth tax returns, of which the one of Michaelmas 1672 is the most comprehensive, are on microfilm in the Humberside County Record Office (HCRO). The eighteenth century has a good diocesan visitation by Archbishop Herring in 1743 which gives the number of families in each parish which replied and which is also published by the YAS;[3] the published Muster Roll for the sixteenth century also contains summaries by wapentake of further levies in 1757 and 1762, but these are of little value at the parochial level.

Since the information in these documents is given in a variety of forms, the essential problem for the historian is to convert any statistics into an estimate of population. Where the information is given in the form of families or households, it is normal to use a multiplier of four or five; in the case of able-bodied men and labourers in the Muster Rolls, historians have suggested multipliers as far apart as four and six or seven; and where the information relates to communicants, they are usually assumed to represent 60% of the population.[4] Using this approach, it is possible to produce sets of population estimates which allow the formulation of hypotheses concerning long-term trends.

To obtain more detailed information on population trends prior to the nineteenth century, we turn to parish registers which provide some insights into the scale and rate of changes in baptisms, marriages and burials. The keeping of registers became compulsory in 1538, though many date from 1558 or 1598. In addition to the question of survival, the reliability of parish registers is very varied; in particular, their comprehensiveness must be questioned for any particular parish, though they tend to be more reliable for the sixteenth and seventeeth centuries than for the eighteenth which saw the spread of legal nonconformity. Those nonconformist registers which have survived are at Somerset House in London and every local historian will need to check their existence for his own parish.

It is widely acknowledged that parish registers are not very helpful in trying to arrive at actual populations, an elusive and probably impossible task before 1801, though some historians have made an attempt. Professor

Hoskins has suggested that if we take the total baptisms for a decade, find the average number per annum and multiply that figure by thirty, we shall arrive at a fairly close estimate of the population for that period; the average of a ten-year period is necessary to smooth out any fluctuations caused by exceptional years, and baptisms are used because marriages tend to be too few and burials too volatile. However, this is an extremely rough-and-ready approach and much greater use is made of parish registers to assess population trends through the aggregative analysis method which involves calculating the natural increase or decrease from the difference between baptisms and burials thus indicating whether the trend was upwards, downwards or stable. Recording the number of burials per annum will also allow the identification of years in which the deaths seem to have been abnormally high, and a note of the monthly profile may even allow some hypothesis as to the nature of the mortality problem. If a suspect year has twice the number of deaths as the average of eleven years of which it forms the midpoint, then the suspect year experienced crisis mortality; a peak of burials in high summer may point to an epidemic killer such as bubonic plague whilst a winter high may suggest a severe outbreak of endemic disease such as influenza. Occasionally, and normally in the later eighteenth century, burial registers give cause of death, though the accuracy of many and the meaning of some diagnoses is far from clear. A more sophisticated, though time-consuming and less popular method of exploiting parish registers is that of family reconstruction which involves the painstaking recreation of whole families from the entries in the registers. Such work yields far more explanatory information, such as age-at-marriage, family size, gap between marriage and parenthood and infant mortality, but the labour is immense and such work is not normally undertaken by individuals.[5]

Most parish registers will be found in the parish chest or, more likely now, in appropriate repositories. In the East Riding there is a large collection at the HCRO and others are at the Borthwick Institute of Historical Research (BIHR). In addition, the Yorkshire Parish Register Society have published the registers of more than a dozen East Riding parishes.

The student of parish registers must be aware of two problems in their use for population research. First, the methodology outlined above takes no account of population mobility, though it is clearly incorrect to suggest that mobility is a feature only of modern society. However, the marriage registers can be exploited to throw some light on this topic by a study of the place of origin of marriage partners, and all the registers, along with other nominal documents, can be used to yield some material by comparing the continuity or replacement of surnames in two decades separated by perhaps as much as a century. Second, many rural parishes were so small as to be statistically unreliable and it is often recommended that groups of parishes should be studied in preference to single ones. However, those who wish to confine their investigations to one parish will doubtless take this into account when assessing the validity of their findings.

Nineteenth and twentieth century population studies are dominated by the decennial census returns, though it was not until 1851 that very detailed information was first collected. The first three censuses were little more than counts of the population and the housing stock, though by 1831 information was given about occupations under the broad headings of 'agriculture' and 'manufacture, trade or commerce'. There are two main types of source available for the local historian, the printed summary volumes and the detailed enumerators' books for each community.[6]

The printed census reports cover the whole country, providing a variety of information at different levels. For the 1851 census, the country was divided into superintendent registrars' districts, normally a large area centred on a town, reaching out into the surrounding countryside and often coterminous with the new Poor Law unions; examples of such districts in the East Riding were Driffield, Beverley, Pocklington and Sculcoates. These units divided into sub-districts — Driffield consisting of Bainton, Foston, Langtoft and Driffield — which themselves contained every parish and township within the sub-district. The 1851 report is particularly valuable as it recasts all the information for 1801-41 into these categories; subsequent volumes for the nineteenth and early twentieth century follow this pattern, but the presentation of material in the twentieth century volumes conforms to the major local government changes of the 1890s which introduced urban and rural district councils. This indicates the need for care when tracing one community through the centuries, but the researcher must also be alive to smaller boundary changes which are noted in the appropriate decennial volume. The printed reports for the nineteenth century give population and number of houses for every separate community, no matter how small; at the district and sub-district levels, there is information on age-sex structure also, and at county level details of the occupational structure and the birthplaces of all people. Similar details are given in the twentieth century reports, though, outside the large towns, summary material is grouped under urban districts, thus defeating any attempt to isolate one particular community for anything other than enumeration. From these volumes, it is a simple matter to note the growth, decline or stability of a specific community, thus opening up a whole range of questions which can only be approached through a wider study of economic and social history.

The enumerators' books are vitally important sources for the detailed study of a local community. They record the names, residence, age, marital status, occupation and place of birth of everyone resident within a community on census day, and allow the historian to recreate a community at one point in time. Subject to the hundred year rule, the enumerators' books are only available for 1841 to 1881, and the first does not contain quite as much information as its successors, but no local historian can avoid confronting these books. Most small villages would consist of one enumeration district, but even quite small towns such as Beverley were divided into more than twenty districts. Beverley Reference Library has copies for the East Riding on microfilm for 1851 to 1881 and the Hull Local Studies Library covers the city.

The establishment of Civil Registration in 1837 eventually led to the production of annual reports on births, marriages and deaths which are important in helping to explain the behaviour of population. As with the census, this information is given at sub-district level and above, a recognition of the fact that the parish and township is too small for such information to be meaningful. Unlike the census, these returns were published annually in parliamentary papers, though decennial summaries were produced for some periods in the nineteenth century; the published indexes to parliamentary papers are essential to locate the returns, but they are vital sources from which to collect or calculate birth rates, death rates and migration totals, the essential mechanisms of population behaviour. Additional descriptive material on a localised scale can be found in the quarterly reports for all sub-districts; these sources are part of a separate collection housed in the British Library in London.

Population trends in the East Riding

Given the uncertainty surrounding the pre-1801 sources, an estimate of specific population totals is impossible, and the poor survival rate of national sources, as far as this country is concerned, render reliable comment on general trends extremely hazardous. Consequently, the following suggestions are very tentative and should be treated with appropriate scepticism.

On the evidence of the 1584 Muster Roll, the population of the county must have been at least 57,000 to 67,000 using the multiplier of six or seven suggested by Hoskins, although a smaller multiplier would inevitably produce a much lower figure. A rather more secure estimate can be made on the basis of the 1672 hearth tax return which suggests, using a multiplier of 4.5, that the county's population was around 70,000. Depending on which figure is more acceptable for 1584, the county's population may have remained static or almost doubled in the century between our two sources. There are two reasons for suggesting that the higher figure for 1584 may well be an underestimate and that the population therefore may well have declined during most of the seventeenth century. First, the Muster Roll does not list any labourers for the wapentakes of Dickering, Buckrose and Ouse and Derwent which seems a most unlikely situation, and second, detailed study of the Driffield parish register suggests that there was approximately a 20% loss of population during the period from c.1580 to c.1680. Only much painstaking work on numerous parish registers will shed more light on the problem, but it does seem that the population of the county towards the end of the sixteenth century was in excess of 75,000.

Although the East Riding possesses the detailed visitation by Archbishop Herring in 1743, it does not facilitate an estimate of the population of the whole county because certain parishes did not make a return, but it does provide some picture of the distribution of population. In the early eighteenth century, the Wolds was the most sparsely populated area followed closely by the Vale of York, with Holderness more thickly populated, though very few parishes had more than a hundred families outside the market towns of Beverley, Bridlington, Hedon and Patrington, and the port of Hull which would soon expand outside its old walls and attract more people from the surrounding countryside. Faced with such deficient sources for the eighteenth century, historians have fallen back on the techniques of, firstly, backward projection, where natural increases derived from parish register abstracts are subtracted from known population in 1801, and, secondly, the ratio method whereby the ratio of baptisms per annum for 1796-1800 to the known population of 1801 is applied to other years in the century. The results of such estimates are shown in table 1 and suggest that whilst the county barely maintained its population during the first sixty years of the eighteenth century, it doubled during the final forty years; within the broad picture, Hull seems to have acted as a magnet for population throughout the century, with particularly spectacular growth in the last four decades.

Table 1
Population estimates and population figures for the East Riding 1700-1931

	East Riding (inc. Hull)	Hull and Sculcoates/ Hull Municipal Borough
1700	60,100	7,500
1730	57,500	9,500
1760	59,000	12,700
1801	111,192	22,161
1831	168,891	32,958
1861	233,508	97,661
1901	327,400	240,259*
1931	482,936	300,880

* Some of this large increase was the result of an extension in the municipal boundaries in 1882 and 1897.

In the nineteenth and early twentieth centuries, the whole county experienced population growth, though there was a marked difference between the rural and urban experience. At the centre of growth was the explosion of population in Hull, which experienced an eightfold increase between 1801 and 1911, though even here, the expansion was differential with the centre eventually losing population while the suburbs developed. The other, smaller urban centres in the county also experienced population expansion throughout the period, though the actual numbers and the rates of growth were much less than in Hull. In contrast the rural areas of the county experienced steady if unspectacular growth during the first half of the nineteenth century, but suffered serious depopulation from 1861, particularly on the Wolds, as a result of agricultural depression and unemployment; the earlier part of the twentieth century saw a continuation of that trend.

CASE STUDY: POPULATION CHANGE IN GREAT DRIFFIELD

Given the inadequacies of the national sources for estimating population, study of any one parish is heavily dependent on parish registers before 1801. The registers of Driffield are housed in the HCRO and, at first sight, appear to be complete from 1556.[7] However, closer inspection reveals a number of problems. The earliest entries are sufficiently thin as to be suspect and may well reflect the fact that a statute of 1598 reiterated the earlier requirement of 1539 to keep registers. Secondly, the registers are rather deficient in the occasional years and some are missing, necessitating recourse to averaging to provide a running series, and some entries are illegible, leading to the same practice. Thirdly, whilst it is normally possible to count the number of entries, it is not always possible to allocate them to precise months with confidence. Within these limitations, it is possible to obtain a picture of the trends in population in the parish of Driffield from the late sixteenth century to the end of the eighteenth century. The broad picture can be seen in figure 28, which indicates a number of trends. If, in common with national trends, the parish's population was rising during the sixteenth century, its increase began to slow down markedly towards the end of the century whence it embarked on a century of decline, interrupted only by a slight rise in the 1640s. From the late seventeenth century there was a period of slow population growth until the 1770s, though the second and third decades recorded small losses. In the final three decades of the eighteenth century, growth was rapid and consistent, but it was only during these years that the pre-1600 population was actually achieved. Using the 1672 hearth tax return as a reference point, we may hazard an estimate of the parish population at specific points within the trends outlined above, and these are represented in table 2.

Table 2
Population estimates for Great Driffield

1560	930	1730	840
1590	1,000	1760	930
1672	770 (hearth tax)	1800	1,380
1700	830	1801	1,483 (census return)

The statistics are too imprecise to produce birth and death rates, but study of the distribution of burials suggests interesting lines of further inquiry. Seven of the first eight decades of the seventeenth century experienced nett population loss, with the 1650s and 1660s being the ones with highest mortality. However, the crisis and near-crisis years occur almost at random throughout the pre-1801 period. There were four actual crisis years — 1591, 1624, 1707 and 1770 — and a further five — 1638, 1658, 1667, 1716 and 1728 — when mortality almost reached crisis proportions. Some of these years coincide with mortality crises in other parishes in different parts of the country, notably in 1624 when there was a serious problem associated with plague and food shortages in the north of

England, and 1728 when there was a widespread influenza epidemic; the others may well have been more localised, though the mid-seventeenth century were problem years in many places.

In the printed census reports 'Driffield' refers to a number of different communities. Great and Little Driffield were parishes in their own right which merged to form the Driffield urban district after 1894; Driffield is one of the sub-districts in the larger superintendent registrar's district which also included the parishes of Hutton Cranswick, Nafferton, Ruston Parva and Skerne; the main district was made up of the four sub-districts of Driffield, Foston, Bainton and Langtoft; and finally, the twentieth century reports classify the local communities into urban and rural districts. In this case study, the material has been reordered where necessary to ensure that the same units are being described throughout.[8]

The accompanying graph (figure 28) indicates that the general trend of population in the Driffield area during the nineteenth and twentieth centuries was of steady if unspectacular growth during the first eighty years of the period, followed by a slight but permanent decline thereafter. However, the experience was differential within the area. First, while all districts grew during this period, the more urbanised district of Driffield increased more rapidly and for a greater length of time than the predominantly rural districts. Within the overall superintendent's district growth continued until 1881 at a decennial rate of 15.7%, but this masks the fact that the Driffield sub-district also increased until 1881 with an average decennial growth rate of 23.7% whereas Foston peaked in 1851 (14.4% per decade), Bainton and Langtoft in 1861 (18.2% and 19.7% respectively). The importance of urbanisation within the Driffield sub-district is emphasised by comparing the experience within that town unit: the township of Great Driffield grew continually until 1881 whilst Hutton Cranswick and Nafferton peaked in 1861, Ruston Parva in 1851 and Skerne as early as 1821. Second, the experience of decline was equally differential, with the rural districts suffering much more heavily as well as beginning to lose people earlier. Although the principal district lost population after 1881, it was at 1.4% per decade in comparison to Foston's 4.5%, Bainton's 3.0% and Langtoft's 4.7% over the same period. Within the Driffield sub-district, the importance of urbanisation is evident with the township remaining stable after its losses of the 1880s and undertaking a slow recovery in the second quarter of the twentieth century, but the incipient stages of village development in close proximity to urban centres is suggested by both Nafferton and Skerne being able to hold their own and Hutton Cranswick's good recovery after 1931.

In the search for explanations of these trends, demographic historians turn to rates of change in the vital events of births and deaths and to the question of natural increase versus migration. Figures available for the study of birth and death rates (per thousand of population) are presented in Tables 3 and 4.[9]

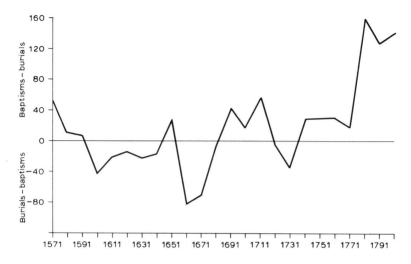

Figure 28: Natural increase/decrease in population of Great Driffield, 1571-1801

Table 3
Birth rates and death rates in Driffield S.R.D. 1851-1910

	Birth rate	*Death rate*
1851-60	36.2	20.0
1861-70	35.2	21.0
1871-80	35.7	19.3
1881-90	30.2	17.0
1891-1900	26.8	15.8
1901-1910	23.2	14.3

Table 4
Birth rates and death rates in Driffield S.R.D. Sub-Districts 1851-90

	Foston		*Driffield*		*Bainton*		*Langtoft*	
	B.R.	*D.R.*	*B.R.*	*D.R.*	*B.R.*	*D.R.*	*B.R.*	*D.R.*
1851-60	34.4	18.1	38.3	23.3	34.3	17.6	35.8	19.0
1861-70	32.3	18.7	39.4	25.3	32.4	16.8	35.6	18.8
1871-80	33.7	19.6	38.7	21.5	31.4	16.3	34.8	18.0
1881-90	32.5	15.4	29.6	17.2	30.1	15.1	30.9	15.9

At the principal level, the birth rate declined more rapidly than the death rate with particularly noticeable falls in the decades after 1881 when the area experienced an overall loss of population. Up to this date, although both birth and death rates were in decline, the latter had fallen more sharply, thus allowing total population to increase, but in the last two decades for which figures are available, the fall in the birth rate was more dramatic than that in the death rate, thus leading to a decrease in overall population. Similarly, each sub-district experienced a marked decline in both birth and death rates in the 1880s, though in most cases the reduction in the latter was greater than the former. A second notable feature is the consistency of the death rate from 1851 to 1881, a contributory factor to which would be the outbreaks of epidemics of typhus in Driffield in 1862 and outbreaks of diphtheria and measles in Langtoft during 1863, together with the generally insanitary state of housing which was sufficiently bad in Langtoft to be worthy of mention in the quarterly reports of the superintendent registrar in the early 1860s.

The second important explanatory mechanism of population behaviour is migration which can be shown by comparing the natural increase with the actual change in population over a specific period. Table 5 reveals that the whole area of Driffield was losing population from the middle of the nineteenth century, including those decades when there was a registered increase, with the greatest losses coming in those decades which also experienced nett loss. Table 6 shows that no sub-district retained its natural increase in any one decade between 1850 and 1890, suggesting that whilst the town of Driffield might have held some attraction for the population after 1851, it was more than counteracted by the pull of more distant centres. As early as 1871, population from Beeford and North Frodingham was emigrating overseas as well as to the mining districts in Cleveland, agricultural labourers from Butterwick, Cowlam, Langtoft, Nafferton and Sledmere had left in search of higher wages, and young people had left Garton to become servants in other districts.[10]

Table 5
Out-migration from Driffield S.R.D. 1851-1910

	Natural increase	Population change	Out-migration
1851-60	+2926	+992	—1934
1861-70	+2874	+8	—2866
1871-80	+3083	+802	—2281
1881-90	+2761	—1224	—3985
1891-1900	+2130	—1089	—3219
1901-1910	+1595	+31	—1564

Table 6
Out-migration from Driffield S.R.D. Sub-districts 1851-1890

	Foston			Driffield		
	Natural increase	Population change	Out-migration	Natural increase	Population change	Out-migration
1851-60	+524	—29	—553	+1073	+648	—425
1861-70	+431	—262	—693	+1101	+579	—522
1871-80	+417	—53	—470	+1440	+787	—653
1881-90	+488	—214	—702	+1127	—435	—1562
	Bainton			Langtoft		
1851-60	+635	+213	—422	+694	+125	—569
1861-70	+624	—146	—770	+718	—132	—850
1871-80	+584	—43	—627	+697	—111	—808
1881-90	+571	—110	—681	+636	—465	—1101

In general, the out-migration as a proportion of the population was much higher in the predominantly rural areas, reflecting the national trend of rural depopulation, particularly after 1871, though the loss in the Driffield sub-district is quite startling during the 1880s. The study of such mechanisms goes some way towards explaining the trends in population at the local level, but often raises as many questions as answers, and the picture can only be completed by an examination of wider economic and social topics.

Notes for chapter 8

1. A valuable introduction to the range available is W. Stephens, *Sources for English local history*, rev. ed. (Cambridge, 1981), chapter 2; for a general survey of their value, see A. Rogers, *Approaches to local history*, 2nd ed. (London, 1977); and for a classic example of specific use see W. G. Hoskins, *Provincial England* (London, 1963) chapter 10

2. *Miscellania V*, YAS record series, 106 (Leeds, 1951)

3. S. L. Ollard and P. C. Walker, eds, *Archbishop Herring's visitation returns 1743*, YAS record series, 71-2, 75, 77, 79, 5 vols (Leeds, 1928-31)

4. These problems are discussed in W. G. Hoskins, *Local history in England*, 3rd ed. (London, 1984), ch. 10

5. A valuable discussion of the various methods referred to is E. A. Wrigley, ed., *An introduction to English historical demography* ... (London, 1966); see also R. Schofield, 'Crisis mortality', *Local population studies*, 9 (1972), pp. 10-21, and M. Drake, ed., *Population studies from parish registers* ... (Matlock, 1982). Researchers would be well advised also to consult the volumes of *Local population studies*

6. The works by Rogers and Wrigley noted above contain good introductions to the census. See also R. Lawton, ed., *The Census and social structure: an interpretative guide to nineteenth century censuses for England and Wales* (London, 1978)

7. I am grateful to my colleague Dr Margaret Noble who allowed me to use her material from the Great Driffield register for part of the eighteenth century

8. This section is based on the decennial census returns from 1851 to 1931

9. Figures are derived from the annual reports of the Registrar General, published as parliamentary papers, and the references to the conditions will be found in the quarterly reports of the same office

10. 1871 Census report, area housing and population, vol. II, *Parliamentary papers* 1872, C.676, lxvi, pt II, pp. 456-7

9

AGRICULTURE

Jan Crowther

The East Riding has been, and largely still is, an agricultural region, with little industry save in the vicinity of Hull. It lacks the dramatic scenery of the other two Ridings, but its landscape is nevertheless quite varied. It may be divided into three broad geographical districts: the Wolds, the Vale of York, and Holderness with the Hull valley. The chalk Wolds are the only hills, sweeping in a broad crescent from the cliffs of Flamborough Head in the north east, to the Humber in the south. Before the changes in cropping and techniques introduced during the parliamentary enclosure period — mid-eighteenth to mid-nineteenth centuries — the Wolds were principally devoted to sheep-corn husbandry. Most open-field villages had extensive sheep walks, and sheep were essential to the farming economy, being folded on the arable fields after harvest and providing almost the only manure. Some Wolds townships, often those which were the sites of deserted medieval villages, were kept entirely under grass. Here sheep frequently shared the land with rabbits, which were farmed commercially for their fur and flesh.

Parliamentary enclosure transformed the Wolds into the more familiar landscape of today. Rectangular closes replaced the large open fields, broad straight roads were laid down, brick-built farmhouses, often surrounded by shelter belts, appeared away from the villages, and new crops and rotations (still with sheep as an essential element) were introduced. The Wolds may certainly be said to have experienced an agricultural revolution during these years.

In the lowlands the changes were less dramatic. Much enclosure took place in the Vale of York before the parliamentary enclosure period. However, at the beginning of the eighteenth century there were many areas of rough, unimproved, common pastures, such as Wallingfen and Spalding Moor. During the eighteenth and nineteenth centuries these commons were enclosed, drained, and in many cases converted to productive arable land. The remaining open fields and meadows were also enclosed by Act of Parliament. The light sandy soils benefited from the introduction of the Norfolk four-course rotation, but the heavy clay soils were unsuitable for root crops. Nevertheless, drainage and enclosure had a significant effect upon the productive capacity of these heavier lands. Holderness and the Hull valley were in a similar position to the Vale. Much enclosure had already taken place. In many parts of Holderness the soil was heavy clay, and turnips, an essential constituent of the Norfolk rotation, could not be grown. Drainage and enclosure of the remaining open fields and commons still brought considerable improvement: even the substitution of a three- or a four-yearly fallow for a two-yearly one was a forward step.

Between 1700 and 1850 the East Riding landscape underwent changes which have had little parallel since. Present-day farmers have enlarged some fields by ploughing up hedgerows, but the landscape we see today, especially on the Wolds, is largely the creation of the parliamentary enclosure commissioners and surveyors.

Sources for the agricultural historian

The most useful and instructive task for the agricultural historian is a visit to the village or district which is being studied. There is no substitute for walking the ground: a fieldworker can discover ridge and furrow (suggesting that the land was part of the open fields), detect differences in shape between old-enclosed and parliamentary-enclosed fields, and contrast the narrow winding lanes of the old-enclosed landscape with the broad straight roads of the enclosure commissioners.

The documentary sources available are numerous, and have the advantage that most are available locally. At the beginning of the early modern period the East Riding was primarily a region of open fields, commons and meadows. Various sources allow an assessment of the extent of such land and an investigation of the communal arrangements made by its cultivators. Among the most useful and easily available are glebe terriers, which recorded each church's endowment of land and property for the benefit of the ecclesiastical authorities in York.[1] They have been much used by historians, for they often include detailed descriptions of parsonage houses as well as of the land belonging to the living. Assuming that glebe land was representative of the whole township one can assess whether a parish was in open fields or enclosed, and when a series of glebe terriers is available the enclosure history may sometimes be revealed. Glebe terriers are available in the Borthwick Institute of Historical Research (BIHR), and a number may also be found among parish records held at the Humberside County Record Office (HCRO).[2]

Glebe terriers do not normally throw light upon the way the land was cultivated. Fortunately, manorial bye-laws or pains (penalties) often survive. The cultivation of open fields was dependent upon co-operation between farmers whose plots were much dispersed. Moreover, at certain times arable land was thrown open to the stock of all farmers, meadows after mowing were also opened for pasture, and more marginal land was available as common pasture at all times. To ensure the smooth running of the system a list of rules was agreed to by the whole community. The manor, often though not always coincidental with the township, was the most appropriate institution to oversee them, and the manorial court provided the place for their enforcement. Bye-laws constitute a useful source on the management of common land.[3] They may be found in the HCRO and in Hull University Library (HUL).

Another source which can provide useful information on the agricultural arrangements in a township is the probate inventory. In this document, drawn up at the time of a person's death, and usually kept with the will, his property is listed: contents of the house and barns, livestock, crops, farming implements, and so forth. If several inventories are available for the same district at the same period useful comparisons may be made. Inventories vary considerably in the amount of information they contain, however, and general conclusions are difficult. Nevertheless when used in conjunction with other sources they can provide illuminating detail.[4] Many are available at the BIHR.

During the eighteenth and nineteenth centuries the East Riding experienced much parliamentary enclosure. Although there were some townships where all the open fields, commons and meadows had already been enclosed by agreement, in most places much common land remained at about 1730. By means of separate private Acts of Parliament such land was re-allotted, and enclosed by hedges, many of which remain. It is relatively easy to identify such villages by the rectangular fields, straight wide roads, and isolated farmhouses.

Parliamentary enclosure has left some excellent primary source material. Enclosure Acts usually include a description of the land to be allotted, together with the names of the principal landowners and tithe owners.[5] Enclosure awards are frequently the earliest general records of landownership in a township, and they enable the historian to analyse the distribution of landholdings at one point in time. Awards also give information on boundaries, roads, ditches, stone pits and buildings. The enclosure plan, often the earliest map available, gives the same information. Most enclosure documents for the East Riding may be found in the HCRO, but some are deposited with landowners' papers in the HUL and BIHR.[6]

Enclosure awards naturally do not record any subdivision of the fields which may have taken place afterwards, but another source fills this gap. In 1853-4 the Ordnance Survey (OS) six inch maps were published for the East Riding. They provide detailed topograpical information of considerable value, including parish and township boundaries, woodlands and plantations, buildings, drains and field boundaries. By using the OS maps in conjunction with enclosure plans the historian can readily reconstruct the physical appearance of a township.

Whilst OS maps provide the first detailed records there are several county maps from an earlier period which give much useful information. Those produced before the eighteenth century tend to be large in scale and therefore of limited use, but those of later periods may be valuable.[7]

Where they are available tithe awards and maps may also cover the whole township. In many parishes, in the East Riding as elsewhere, enclosure offered landowners an opportunity to rid themselves of an unpopular burden by combining the re-allotment of land with the commutation of tithes. Accordingly either land or a tithe rent charge was allotted to the tithe owner in lieu of tithes. However, in some parishes the tithes were not commuted at enclosure; in others the land had been enclosed at an earlier date when there had been no opportunity for commutation. Thus in the 1830s tithes were still being collected in kind in many places.[8] In 1836 an Act was passed setting up commissioners to oversee the commutation of the tithes in those parishes that remained. It provided for both voluntary and compulsory commutation: voluntary agreements involved the concurrence of the owners of at least two thirds of the land; compulsory commutation was set in hand after 1838.

The records of tithe commutation are awards and maps, which were both produced in triplicate. They indicate the extent and use of land, the names of owners, occupiers, and fields, and the existence of plantations and buildings. Many awards and maps are available, despite the fact that much commutation took place at enclosure. The most accessible depository for tithe material is the BIHR. Copies are also held at the Public Record Office (PRO), and a number may be found with parish records in the HCRO.[9]

Parochial records often include other material relevant to agriculture. Some incumbents noted local events and weather in their parish registers. Deeds and land valuations are useful records sometimes found with parish records. The minutes of the parish vestry can also provide interesting material. Parish records are kept at the HCRO and the BIHR.

The distribution of landownership is of considerable interest to the agricultural historian and a most valuable series of documents is available on this subject — the land tax returns. First imposed in the late seventeeth century, this tax on land was an important source of government revenue. From about 1780 until 1832 records of its payment were deposited for election purposes with the local Clerk of the Peace, and they are now in the HCRO. The returns give the names of owners and occupiers, and the tax paid for each year. Although they do not give acreages, the amount of tax paid gives a broad indication of property size. It is, of course, possible to use them to trace land ownership change in individual parishes.[10] Land tax returns apart, the historian concerned with landownership is not well served with source material. A survey of 1873 names all landowners in England, but they are listed only by county, and the property is not identified.[11]

The Registry of Deeds (RDB) is an institution which is found only in the three Ridings of Yorkshire and the county of Middlesex.[12] That for the East Riding is located at Beverley and is now part of the HCRO. From 1707, when the Registry was established, transactions involving freehold property were registered there. Two indexes, one of townships and one of surnames, were compiled making individual transactions quite easy to locate. Sales and mortgages of copyhold land were recorded in manorial court rolls. Those rolls which have survived are often found with the lord of the manor's estate papers. Many are deposited in the HCRO and HUL.

In 1801 crop returns were made to provide the government with information on the agricultural resources of the kingdom during a wartime emergency. They exist for many East Riding parishes, and include the acreage of various crops grown that year. They were compiled by parish incumbents, some of whom included notes with the figures. The originals are held at the PRO, but fortunately they have now been transcribed and published.[13]

The regular collection of agricultural returns began in 1866 when after a severe outbreak of cattle plague it was decided to ask farmers for annual returns of their livestock. The following year they were asked to add acreages of crops. The returns themselves have been destroyed, but parish summaries have been preserved and are available in London.[14]

In 1801 the first census was taken of the population of Great Britain, and

140

thereafter one was made every decade. Information on the occupational structure of rural communities may be gathered from the enumerators' returns. They list all the inhabitants of a community by name, and give their ages, occupations and places of birth. The East Riding returns are available for the years 1841 to 1881 on microfilm in local record offices and local history libraries.

Another source originating from central government is the proceedings of select committees of the House of Commons. In the nineteenth century, at a time of agricultural depression, several such committees were set up. Their brief was to call in farming experts — often farmers or land agents — and question them on various aspects of farming in their locality. The reports make interesting reading and as long as the possibility of bias and exaggeration is taken into account they can provide the historian with valuable information.[15]

Local newspapers can be a useful source.[16] In the eighteenth century the *York courant* and the *York packet* seem to have had the widest circulation in the East Riding, but in 1794 the *Hull advertiser* began regular publication,[17] and other Hull newspapers followed. They often include details of property sales, advertisements for farming implements and crops and notices of enclosure meetings. Files of newspapers are available in many libraries, either in the original or on microfilm.

Collections of estate records often include maps, surveys, court rolls, title deeds, tenancy agreements and correspondence. Many East Riding families held land in several townships and their records contain information on farming practice, topography, landownership, and improvements such as enclosure. Many of these collections are deposited at HCRO, with some at HUL. Excellent summaries of their contents are available.

Most people find contemporary accounts more interesting than statistical surveys. A detailed contemporary account of farming on the Wolds in the seventeenth century is the farming book of Henry Best of Elmswell, which is of immense interest to the historian.[18] Also from the seventeenth century is a report to the Royal Society on Farming — the so-called Georgical report — a photocopy of which may be found in HUL.[19]

In 1769 Arthur Young, the agricultural writer, visited the East Riding. In an account of his travels he wrote in detail on the farming of the districts he visited.[20] Young tended to notice innovations rather than general practice. A more balanced view may be found in the work of Young's contemporary, William Marshall.[21]

A semi-private body, the Board of Agriculture, was established in 1793, and it recruited a number of specialists to report on agriculture in the English counties. Two reports were published for the East Riding, in 1794 and 1812. The second, by H. E. Strickland, is the more informative, but the first by Isaac Leatham is also useful.[22] There are two other reports on farming, in 1848 by George Legard and in 1861 by William Wright.[23]

This is by no means an exhaustive list of the primary sources available to the agricultural historian. The footnotes of the economic history sections of the relevant *Victoria County History* (VCH) articles will supply many more, as will other secondary works. A number of works on East Riding agriculture are listed in the bibliography at the end of this book. What follows is a case study of one parish, Cherry Burton, in the first half of the nineteenth century, demonstrating how some of the primary sources mentioned above may be used. Parliamentary enclosure took place there between 1823 and 1829, and the Act, award and plan have been used, in conjunction with a survey of the open fields, the land tax returns, manorial records, the registered deeds, and the tithe apportionment and map.

THE AGRICULTURAL HISTORY OF CHERRY BURTON, 1800-1850: A CASE STUDY

Cherry Burton is situated on the eastern slopes of the Wolds, some four miles from Beverley. In recent times it has become something of a dormitory village serving Beverley and Hull, but in the nineteenth century it was a small agricultural community. Like many in this district the parish is long and narrow, covering a variety of soil types. In the west the Wolds rise to over 400 feet above sea level and the land gradually descends eastwards towards the Hull valley. The village itself is in the east of the parish, and there were three depopulated hamlets, Gardham, Newton, and Raventhorpe (figure 29). The open fields of Gardham (if they ever existed) were enclosed at an early date, whilst those of Raventhorpe may have been added to Cherry Burton's fields.[24]

In 1803, when a survey was made for the lord of the manor, Cherry Burton was still an open-field township, and there were 1,974 acres of unenclosed land. The farmers' holdings were in strips divided between several fields, described in the survey as the clay lands, apparently comprising parts of Long Field, with Middle West Field, East Field, West Field, plus Routice and Crakes, and the wold lands, comprising parts of Long Field, with Middle Field, South West Field and Etton Field.[25] By the 1820s the names of these fields appear to have been changed (figure 29).

Twenty people owned open-field land in 1803 with their holdings varying from the substantial manorial estate of 980 acres to a holding of half an acre. Ten of these owners cultivated their land and there were six tenant farmers. Twenty-nine per cent of the open fields was owner-occupied, which by East Riding standards was a high proportion.

It was evidently customary to leave one third of the open fields fallow in Cherry Burton, for the 1801 crop returns show that 1,222 acres were being cropped in that year, with wheat growing on 450 acres, beans on 400 acres, and smaller acreages of barley, oats, peas and turnips or rape.[26]

The 1803 survey only relates to open-field land, which formed about sixty per cent of the parish. The remainder comprised the garths around the village, the whole of Gardham township, a large area on the eastern boundary of the parish near the site of Raventhorpe, and a small piece of land towards Etton (figure 29). The land tax returns of 1803 show that thirty-nine people paid tax that year; many of them were very small property owners, paying three or four shillings a year, which suggests that they owned only a house and garth.[27] Some of the tax payers were

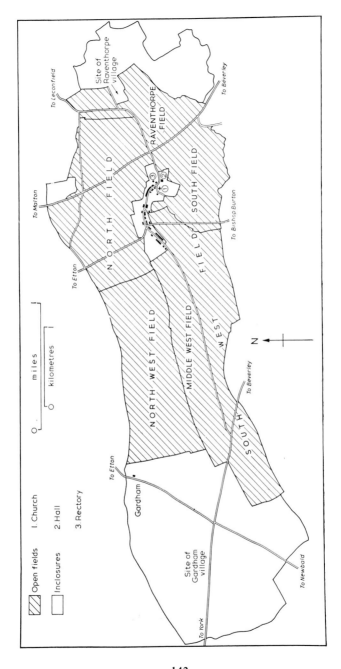

Figure 29: Cherry Burton in 1823 (from VCH ER 4)

landlords, and probably lived away from the village, others were owner-occupiers. Some men owned small properties in the village, but rented additional open-field land from others.

Many East Riding townships were enclosed in the eighteenth century, but no trace has been found of attempts to enclose the open fields of Cherry Burton then. Bishop Burton, a neighbouring parish, was enclosed between 1767 and 1773; one can only speculate upon why the landowners of Cherry Burton waited another half century for their enclosure. Were some of the farmers unimpressed by the results of enclosure in Bishop Burton and elsewhere? Were the tithe owners opposed to enclosure? Subsequent events suggest that these may have been some of the reasons. The first documentary evidence comes in September 1812, when a notice was placed on the door of the parish church informing interested parties that an enclosure was in prospect. Between December 1812 and March 1815 three petitions for enclosure Acts were presented to Parliament, but counter-petitions were also presented and there was evidently sufficient opposition to prevent enclosure going ahead at this stage. Over two hundred pounds was spent in legal fees, apparently by the lord of the manor, David Burton Fowler, one of the principal proprietors.[28]

The matter was allowed to rest until 1822, when a meeting was held in the village.[29] A fourth petition to Parliament was presented in February 1823. A counter-petition showed that there was still opposition, but it was insufficient to prevent the Bill going through. At the report stage it was recorded that there were 227½ oxgangs in the open fields, that the owners of thirty-seven and a half oxgangs refused to consent to their enclosure, and that the owner of five oxgangs was 'neuter'. There were forty-eight common rights over the open land, the owners of ten refusing their consent and the owner of one being neutral.[30] It is not known how many people were involved in this opposition. Their landowning was quite extensive but not sufficiently so to prevent an enclosure.

Once the Bill became law matters were speedily put in hand. The commissioners, all local men, had been chosen by the promoters before the petition was presented to parliament. They were John Hall of Scorborough, John Lee of Leconfield, and Cornelius Collett of Beverley. Hall was land agent for Lord Hotham, who lived at South Dalton, and owned property in several nearby parishes, including Cherry Burton and Etton. By a ruling of the House of Commons made in 1801 it was forbidden for the owner or agent of the land being enclosed to serve as a commissioner. However in the East Riding this ruling was often ignored, and Hall was also commissioner for Etton and South Dalton.

The commissioners were paid three guineas a day for their work and were authorised to appoint a clerk and one or more surveyors. Their meetings were to be advertised in the *Hull advertiser* and the *Yorkshire gazette* and held no more than eight miles from Cherry Burton. Whilst they were engaged upon the enclosure the commissioners were empowered to 'direct the course of husbandry', a necessary step to prevent farmers from 'milking' their land of all they could get before it was re-allotted.[31]

The enclosure Act received the Royal Assent on 12 May 1823 and the commissioners met on 28 and 29 May. They chose as surveyors Edward Page of Beverley and James Bulmer of York.[32] It is not known how often they met thereafter. Having taken the oath and selected the surveyors their next meeting was probably the occasion for an inspection of the land to be enclosed. They would then call for all owners and interested parties to submit claims to their property. When the claims were all in the clerk could draw up a list which would be made available for owners to make objections. The commissioners could then judge the validity of the claims. They might ask for written evidence, or, if the rights were small, such as cottagers' claims of rights of common, they might ask elderly villagers for corroboration. Meanwhile the surveyors would be engaged upon the survey. John Hall frequently wrote to his employer Lord Hotham, and the correspondence shows that the commissioners began valuing the land on 25 November 1823. The next step was the 'division' of the land, when, armed with the survey and valuation, the commissioners re-allotted the open fields. The allotment of Cherry Burton began in January 1824. John Hall wrote that he expected the matter to occupy ten days 'if we go along pleasantly'.

If the tithes were being commuted, as was usually the case, the commissioners would settle the tithe allotments first. However, at Cherry Burton the tithes were left alone. John Hall wrote in March 1823 that the principal proprietors:

> will never agree to commute the tithes on any terms (this may appear extraordinary) but so it is . . . The incumbent Dr Waddilove is a Dog in a Manger. He has been applied to again and again to consent to an inclosure and always said he would not consent on any terms.[33]

The commissioners therefore probably began with the manorial allotments. The lord of the manor of Cherry Burton was David Burton Fowler, the largest proprietor, and the lord of the manor of Beverley Chapter, which included land in the parish, was William Beverley. Each received about five acres for his rights to the soil.

The commissioners also had to decide the course of roads, which were often realigned at enclosure. Two turnpike roads passed through Cherry Burton: both the Beverley to Market Weighton and the Beverley to Malton roads were sixty feet wide. Other public roads were to be thirty or forty feet wide. A local farmer was often appointed as Surveyor of Roads, and Buttle Stephenson of Cherry Burton was so appointed in March 1824. In October 1825 he affirmed that the roads were 'in good and sufficient repair and fit for the carriage of travellers and carriages'.[34]

It was usual at enclosure to set out gravel or stone pits to provide material for road making, and three pits were allotted in Cherry Burton. An item from the 1799 parish register shows that these were not the first stone pits in the parish: in that year William Watson of Cherry Burton and Thomas Stork of Etton were drowned whilst bathing 'in the limestone quarry in Cherry Burton Field'.[35]

By February the allotments were settled, and the surveyors set about staking out the plots. Shortly after this the owners were allowed to take over their land. Although the enclosure award is dated 1829 it is clear that most of the work was complete by the spring of 1824. Usually the commissioners arranged for the land to be taken over in early spring, and it is known that people were buying and selling the new plots early in 1824.[36] It seems strange that the award was delayed for five years, but a delay was common. It may be that commissioners and solicitors tended to drag out the proceedings in order to increase their fees.

The award records that twenty-one people received allotments ranging from 1,080 acres awarded to David Burton Fowler to three acres awarded to Benjamin Everingham, cordwainer.[37] Had the award been drawn up early in 1824 it might have shown a different picture: several owners, possibly because they were unable to afford the enclosure costs, sold their allotments in that year. They would have experienced no difficulty in finding buyers. Lord Hotham for one was interested in increasing his estate and Hall wrote to him in 1821 that he would 'never omit any opportunity' of buying land in Cherry Burton. In the event Hotham's purchases were modest: two common rights at £160 each, one bought from a shoemaker and the other from a labourer who was already encumbered with a mortgage to a tallow chandler and was probably unable to pay enclosure costs. Hall considered the common rights to be cheap:

> and they will make our allotment much more handsome . . . and wont cost or take any more fencing. I hope these two rights will be above 16 acres but I cant exactly say.[38]

This illustrates the injustice of a system where a commissioner, as agent of a principal proprietor, could make an offer for property knowing its value better than the owner did himself.

On Hotham's behalf Hall turned down several properties, considering them too dear. The Reverend Henry Ramsden was not so cautious. He built up an estate in the village by buying various properties, large and small, in 1824. They varied from three roods of open-field land and a common right bought from a cordwainer for £217 10s, to six oxgangs and a common right bought from a yeoman for £2,600.[39] Ramsden became rector in 1828 and appears to have combined his own allotment of eighty-nine acres and the glebe allotment of twenty-five acres into a single farm.

Enclosure was both disruptive and expensive. All land owners paid costs according to the value of their allotments, as well as the cost of fencing. John Hall calculated that an estate of sixty-five acres would cost up to £200 in enclosure expenses and up to £100 to fence. One owner-occupier, Buttle Stephenson, sold his estate of twenty-four oxgangs (about 192 acres) in 1823-4, to Henry John Shepherd, a Beverley solicitor.[40] According to Hall's figures Stephenson would have had to pay almost £900 for enclosure and fencing and this may have been the reason for the sale. The owners of the eight acre common right holdings sold to Hotham would have had expenses of almost £40, a considerable sum for people of small means, whilst the £160 they were offered if they sold up must have seemed riches indeed. The land tax returns, the court rolls, and the registered deeds show that some common right holdings were sold in 1824. Twenty-three of the original thirty-one land tax payers of 1821 remained in 1830, but no fewer than six had sold part of their property, usually a common right. Of eight people who disappeared completely from the returns some, like Buttle Stephenson, sold their property in 1824 to newcomers such as Henry John Shepherd.[41] Some people's names appear in all the returns but the sum they pay increased as they bought more property. Such was Henry Ramsden: in 1821 he paid £1 2s but in 1830 over £25.[42] David Burton Fowler bought nothing in the decade in which enclosure took place, but he was old and probably had lost interest. Hall recorded in February 1828:

> Old Burton Fowler died on Thursday suddenly. He was 94, a remarkable old gentleman . . . the old Dean the Rector I believe is also 94 — a very extraordinary instance in one village.[43]

Waddilove, the rector, died the same year and Ramsden took his place.

The enclosure plan (figure 30) shows that the commissioners placed the smaller allotments near the village where they would be more convenient. The new owners were usually responsible for fencing and hedging two sides of their allotments, and the work had to be completed within a few months of taking over the land. It was a lucrative time for nurserymen: many thousands of hawthorn quicksets were sold during the enclosure period. The subdivision of larger holdings could be completed at the owner's convenience, and that process may be seen in the six inch OS map or the tithe map (figure 31).

In 1837 a calculation was made of the value of Cherry Burton tithes. This shows that the parish contained 3,439 acres, of which forty-eight acres were roads, fifty acres plantations, two acres drains and two acres stone pits. The major part of the parish — 2,504 acres — was arable, requiring 126 draught horses, each horse cultivating about twenty acres and eating the grass of one and a half acres annually. The tithes were commuted in 1841: twenty-five people were listed as tithe payers and many of the names were identical with those in the land tax returns of the 1820s.[44]

The tithe plan provides an interesting contrast with the enclosure plan: by 1841 a number of farms had been built in the former open fields away from the village; plantations had appeared, notably on the manorial land south of the village, and on the glebe land; and the large allotments had been subdivided (figures 30 and 31).

The effects of enclosure in Cherry Burton are difficult to quantify. After enclosure enterprising farmers could introduce new crops and rotations without the need to consult their neighbours and their land was more convenient to farm. Clearly some people sold their land at enclosure. Possibly they could not pay the enclosure costs, though in the case of the common right owners they may have been delighted to receive substantial sums for rights which they had not made full use of in the past. When the land had been enclosed there was no longer a need for regular meetings of the villagers to make decisions on the commencement of ploughing,

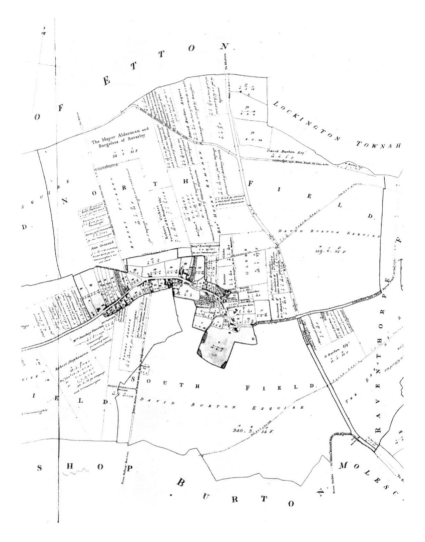

Figure 30: Cherry Burton: part of the enclosure plan (HUL DDHO/16/57)

sowing, harvesting, and when the stock could be turned onto the stubble. There are dangers of romanticising the community spirit in an open-field village, but something must have been lost at enclosure when each farmer began to farm his own separate plot of land, for the first time wholly independent of his neighbours.

148

Figure 31: Cherry Burton: part of the tithe map (HUL DDCB/4/341)

149

Notes for chapter 9

1. D. M. Barratt, 'Glebe terriers', *History*, 51 (1966), pp.35-8
2. A useful study of Yorkshire glebe terriers is M. W. Beresford, 'Glebe terriers and open-field Yorkshire', YAJ, 37 (1951), pp.325-68
3. M. W. Barley, 'East Yorkshire manorial bye-laws', YAJ, 35 (1943), pp.35-60. A valuable study, but it underestimates the number of bye-laws now available
4. For a study using probate inventories see A. Harris, 'The agriculture of the East Riding before the parliamentary enclosures', YAJ, 40 (1959), pp.119-28
5. Enclosure Acts to 1800 are listed in K. A. MacMahon, ed., *Acts of Parliament relating to the East Riding and Kingston upon Hull, 1707-1800* (Hull, 1961)
6. For information on enclosure awards, plans, and related material see B. A. English, ed., *Yorkshire enclosure awards*, University of Hull Department of Adult Education studies in regional and local history, 5 (Hull, 1985)
7. See H. Whitaker, ed., *A descriptive list of the printed maps of Yorkshire and its Ridings*, YAS record series, 86 (Leeds, 1933)
8. Although in some parishes a modus, or tithe rent, had been established
9. J. B. Harley, 'Maps for the local historian: a guide to British sources. 3: Enclosure and tithe maps', *Amateur historian*, 7 (1967), pp.265-74; R. J. P. Kain, 'Tithe surveys and landownership', *Journal of historical geography*, 1 (1975), pp.39-48
10. J. Gibson and D. Mills, eds., *Land tax assessments, c.1690 to 1930* (Plymouth, 1983)
11. Local Government Board, *Return of owners of land, 1873*, 2 vols (London, 1873)
12. F. Sheppard and V. Belcher, 'The deeds registries of Yorkshire and Middlesex', *Journal of the Society of Archivists*, 6 (1980), pp.274-86
13. Home Office, *Home Office acreage returns (HO 67): list and analysis, 1801. Part 3: Staffordshire - Yorkshire*, transcribed and edited by M. E. Turner, List and Index Society publications, 195 (London, 1983); See also P. Churley, 'The Yorkshire crop returns of 1801', *Yorkshire bulletin of economic and social research*, 5 (1953), pp.179-97
14. J. T. Coppock, 'The agricultural returns as a source of local history', *Amateur historian*, 4 (1958-9), pp.49-55
15. A number of these reports have been reprinted by the Irish University Press in *Irish University Press series of British parliamentary papers : agriculture* (Shannon, 1968)
16. P. Perry, 'Newspaper advertisements', *Local historian*, 9 (1970-1), pp.334-7; J. R. Walton, 'Newspaper advertisements: some further considerations', *Local historian*, 10 (1972-3), pp.271-6
17. K. A. MacMahon, ed., *An index to . . . the Hull advertiser and exchange gazette* (Hull, 1955)
18. D. M. Woodward, ed., *The farming and memorandum books of Henry Best of Elmswell, 1642*, British Academy records of social and economic history, new series, 8 (London, 1984)
19. See also R. Lennard, 'English agriculture under Charles II: the evidence of the Royal Society's "Enquiries"', *Economic history review*, 4 (1932-4), pp.23-45
20. A. Young, *A six months tour through the North of England . . .*, 4 vols (London, 1770)
21. W. Marshall, *The rural economy of Yorkshire*, 2 vols (London, 1788)
22. I. Leatham, *A general view of the agriculture of the East Riding of Yorkshire* (York, 1794); H. E. Strickland, *A general view of the agriculture of the East Riding of Yorkshire* (London, 1812)
23. G. Legard, 'Farming of the East Riding of Yorkshire', *Journal of the Royal Agricultural Society*, 9 (1848), pp.85-136; W. Wright, 'On the improvements of the farming of Yorkshire', *Journal of the Royal Agricultural Society*, 22 (1861), pp.87-131. See also J. Caird, *English agriculture in 1850-51*, 2nd ed. (London, 1968), pp.297-318
24. VCH ER 4, p.16
25. HUL DDCB/4/33
26. Home Office, *Home Office acreage returns*, pp.116 and 125. There is no separate heading for turnips in the returns

27. HCRO QDE 1

28. HUL DDCB/22/24 for the solicitors' papers; *House of Commons journals*, 67-70 (1812-15) for parliamentary business. Opposition from owners of one fifth of the property was needed to prevent the passage of an enclosure bill

29. *Hull advertiser*, 23 August 1822

30. *House of Commons journal*, 78 (1823)

31. HUL DDCB/4/161

32. RDB DQ/16/16

33. HUL DDHO/8/3

34. RDB DQ/16/16

35. HCRO PE/69/1

36. From property transactions recorded in the Registry of Deeds and in the two manorial court books: HUL DDCV/16/2 and DDCB/5/6-7

37. RDB DQ/16/16

38. HUL DDHO/8/3. A common right allotment allowed a person to put stock on open land at certain times of the year. At enclosure the right was converted into a small allotment

39. HUL DDCV/16/2 and DDCB/5/6-7

40. HUL DDHO/8/3

41. HUL DDCB/5/6

42. HCRO QDE 1

43. HUL DDHO/8/3

44. HUL DDCV/34/15

10

MARITIME HISTORY

Arthur G. Credland

This chapter will concentrate on Hull as the principal centre of maritime activity in the East Riding of Yorkshire and beyond over many centuries, and on shipping, fishing and whaling rather than trade. As what follows will show, there is a wealth of material for the student of local maritime history to be found within this region itself. However, a useful general source of addresses for libraries and miscellaneous bodies with maritime connections is *Marine transport: a guide to libraries and sources of information in Great Britain*, edited by R. V. Bolton and F. J. Bryan (London, 1983).

Initially overshadowed by the now vanished port of Ravenserodd at the mouth of the Humber, and at times in competition with Beverley and Hedon, Hull's pre-eminence was clearly established by 1299 when the citizens of 'Kingstown-upon-Hull' received a royal charter. Some notices of Hedon as a port can be found in the general histories of that town but materials for the study of maritime affairs in the other settlements of East Yorkshire are scattered and fragmentary. This is also true of the coastal towns of Holderness and of Bridlington Quay. Some of the more important histories and descriptions of Hedon and a few of the other fishing villages are listed in the general bibliography for this book. Most of these settlements were small fishing communities but in the eighteenth and early nineteenth centuries Bridlington was of some significance as a port trading both coastwise and to the continent. Bridlington was also the town of origin of Sir Samuel Standidge, mayor of Hull in 1795 and leader of the renewal in the whaling trade in the eighteenth century. The Bridlington shipping registers for 1786-1847 are preserved in the Kingston upon Hull Record Office (KHRO)[1] and a useful series of documents and printed material relating to the piers and harbour are to be found in the local studies section of Bridlington Public Library. The Library also contains a series of fifty-nine bound volumes of cuttings from the local newspaper entitled the 'Annals of Bridlington', which covers every kind of event in the town's history from 1867 to 1947, though unfortunately these are indexed only from 1905 onwards. The most useful description of Bridlington is to be found in volume two of the *Victoria County History, East Riding* (1974), which also includes an account of Filey; volume five (1984) embraces Withernsea. The first volume of the set, however, is devoted entirely to Hull.

The port and shipping of Hull

The town's Dock Company was established in 1774 and four years later Hull's first enclosed dock, later known as Queen's Dock, was opened.[2] The complete circuit of docks, built along the line of the old city walls, was finished in 1829 with the opening of the Junction (later Prince's) Dock.

Figure 32: The *Cape Trafalgar,* launched from Beverley shipyard in 1957 for Hudson Brothers of Hull

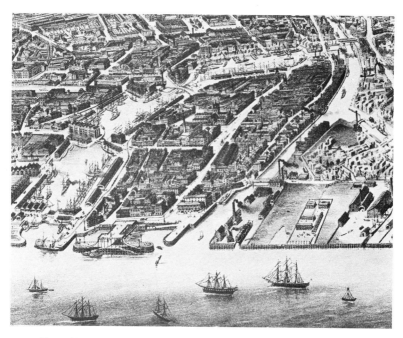

Figure 33: Part of Pettingell's *Birds eye view of Hull* (1881) showing the town docks system and the shipyards on the banks of the Humber, east of the river Hull

Other docks, located along the Humber itself, were built, the last being the Queen Elizabeth Dock, opened in 1969. Hull's growth as a port continued apace throughout the nineteenth century. One of the most useful accounts of Hull's trade and commerce at that time is the unpublished doctoral thesis by Joyce Bellamy entitled 'Some aspects of the economy of Hull in the nineteenth century with particular reference to business history' (Hull, 1965), copies of which may be consulted in the Hull University Library (HUL) or Hull Local Studies Library (HLSL).

The Corporation Bench Books, especially after the middle of the sixteenth century, are an important source regarding the use of the Haven and its wharves. These can be supplemented by the records of the water bailiffs, who were officers of the Corporation entitled to collect dues on shipping and certain goods being imported and exported. These records are to be found in the KHRO. They give a comprehensive picture of shipping using the port, the size of the vessels and the places with which they traded. The series WB/1-336 begins in 1569 but the most useful, because most complete, are the returns for 1770-1820 and 1840-74. The records of the Hull Dock Company are also to be found in the KHRO. These papers include bound transaction books (from 1791 onwards), reports and accounts, acts of Parliament relating to the development of the

154

Figure 34: A classic Arctic whaling scene by John Ward of Hull, c.1830

155

docks system, engineers' reports and miscellaneous correspondence.[3]

Shipbuilding was an important occupation on the Humber, well developed by the seventeenth century at Hull, Paull and Hessle Cliff. In the eighteenth century local yards were a major source of warships for the Royal Navy. A list of the vessels built at Paull, Hessle and Hull (also at Thorne) are contained in the scrapbook and journal of Samuel Standidge Walton along with details of all vessels built and repaired in the Walton Yard. This document is to be found in the Town Docks Museum (TDM) in Hull.[4] Pioneering efforts in the building of steam-powered vessels were made as early as 1774 but the first locally built steamship to enter regular service on the Humber was the PS *Kingston* in 1821. She was built by Pearsons of Thorne and that family's significant contribution to local shipping and trade can be gauged from F. H. Pearson, *The early history of Hull steam shipping* (Hull, 1896; reprinted 1984).

Important shipowners, like Joseph Gee (d.1860) and W. and C. L. Ringrose, have left very little record, though a large number of their ships were captured on canvas by Hull's marine artists. From the latter part of the eighteenth century Hull had a growing number of marine artists whose works are preserved in some quantity in the TDM and the Ferens Art Gallery, Hull. Their work provides a significant source of information for vessels built, owned or trading into and out of Hull. Robert Willoughby (1768-1843) painted a long series of canvasses depicting the Hull whalers; but John Ward (1798-1849) is the best known and he combined accurate and detailed recording of all kinds of vessel with a real artist's eye for composition (see figure 34). The works of these artists can be relied on for nautical accuracy even when flair may be lacking since the pictures were invariably commissioned either by the owner or master. The local tradition of marine painting is continued with Henry Redmore (1820-87), originally a marine engineer; and many Humber craft were captured by Reuben Chappell, a prolific artist from Goole. Joseph Arnold (fl.1900-1920) produced a large quantity of studies of fishing vessels, especially steam trawlers. Finally, Ernest Dade (1865-1935) sketched and painted many scenes of coble fishermen at work.

Thomas Wilson (1792-1869) founded a firm which later became the world's largest privately owned steamship company until it was purchased in 1916 by Sir John Ellerman. An important collection of records for the Wilson Line is to be found in the HUL archives department.[5] These records include accounts ledgers from as early as 1825, bills of sale for various vessels in the Wilson fleet, and details of personnel, as well as printed brochures and books of press cuttings. Also included are documents relating to Bailey and Leetham, the Wilson Line's greatest rivals until swallowed up by them in 1903[6] and the fleet of Brownlow Marsdin acquired in 1878.[7] A supplementary collection in the TDM contains general arrangement plans of vessels and photographs of ships and personnel, fleet lists and many artefacts.[8] It should always be remembered that in maritime history, museum collections of artefacts can be invaluable, and not just as illustrative material. A contemporary ship model or a painting may be the only surviving source of information for a particular vessel or may be a useful way of checking on the accuracy of the written sources.

In 1901 the Wilson Line purchased Earl's shipyard, so the archive collection in HUL also includes documentation on Hull's largest shipbuilding concern from the time of the takeover to the yard's closure in 1932.[9] Again, these records are supplemented by plans, photographs, ship specifications and comprehensive yard lists in the TDM, but here covering the whole history of the yard from the launch of the first ship in 1845. The TDM also has a bound volume of the builders' certificates for the vessels laid down at Martin Samuelson's shipyard, at the mouth of the River Hull, between 1854 and 1864.

An Act bringing in the general registration of British ships was introduced in 1786. This required that the owners of all vessels with a deck and carrying more than fifteen tons should register them with the customs officers of their home port. The Hull customs registers for 1804 to 1902 are now in the KHRO.[10] Unfortunately the first volume of the series which had vital information on Hull vessels of the eighteenth century was lost many years ago and the duplicate transcripts which were sent to the Custom House in London were subsequently destroyed in a fire in 1814. More recent volumes are still in the local customs house. Customs registers can provide a great deal of useful information, since under the name of each ship is recorded the date and place of building, the number of decks and masts, dimensions and tonnage, and the presence or otherwise of a gallery or figurehead. Names of owners are enhanced from 1825 with notice of the number of shares held by each person; also, until 1854 the registers usually have a list of changes in master.

There are sources of information regarding the personal and biographical details of seamen and masters additional to those normally used by genealogists. Seamen's discharge certificates and the continuous certificate of discharge which replaced them give the name of the vessel as well as the mariner's name, rank or status and place and date of birth. These may survive in family hands or in the local archive office, museum or local studies library; but if not, much of this information can be extracted from the records of the Registrar General of Shipping and Seamen in the Public Record Office (PRO) at Kew, organised under class numbers in the Board of Trade (BT) group. As well as the registry of individual seamen there are the crew lists, a vast corpus of documents which has now unfortunately been dispersed. The PRO retains a 10% sample, a batch was deposited at the National Maritime Museum (NMM) and local record offices were able to select material relevant to their regions. The remainder is now at the Memorial University, St Johns, Newfoundland, Canada, and is in the process of being computerised by the Maritime History Group.

As regards the captain and crew of merchant (and indeed all) vessels information can most easily be obtained if documentary fragments have been handed down in the family. However, from 1835 it was required by the Merchant Shipping Act that apprentice indentures be enrolled with the Registrar General and by the Merchant Marine Act of 1854 he was also made responsible for recording details of the certificates of competency of masters and mates. These provisions were extended to engineers in 1862

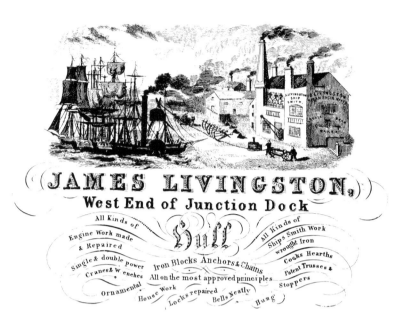

Figure 35: Trade card (c.1850) of James Livingston, shipsmith of Junction Dock (later Princes Dock), Hull

and skippers and mates of fishing vessels in 1883. Nicholas Cox provides a guide to what is at first sight a daunting series of records at Kew.[11] A useful case study based on an actual piece of research is to be found in C. T. and M. Watts, 'Unravelling merchant seamen's records', *Genealogists magazine* for March 1979. The search for naval personnel has now been made considerably easier by the recently published handlist compiled by N. A. M. Rodger, *Naval records for genealogists* (London, 1984). This also includes an explanation of the system of ranks and a directory of the reserve and auxiliary forces from 1798 to 1945, including the Coastguard.

The Hull Trinity House, with its origins in the Middle Ages, was for many years concerned with pilotage and the control of shipping movements in the Humber. F. W. Brooks has edited and transcribed some of the early judgements and orders of the House.[12] Arthur Storey has given us a general history in two volumes entitled *Trinity House of Kingston upon Hull* (Hull, 1967-69) and a special study in his *Hull Trinity House: history of pilotage and navigational aids of the river Humber, 1513-1908* (Driffield, 1971). In 1908 control of navigation was taken over by the Humber Conservancy and reference to documents in the KHRO yields details of the setting up of the Board and the appointment of commissioners, minutes of the buoyage and beaconage accounts, bye-laws and regula-

Figure 36: The offices of Ellerman's Wilson Line, Commercial Road, Hull. c.1925

159

tions, reports and publications and general administrative records.[13]

The Humber ferry was for many years the monopoly of the Hull Corporation but latterly was in the hands of a succession of railway companies until the cessation of the service in 1981 after a permanent link was established across the river by means of the Humber Bridge. Extensive documentation of the docks, ferries and related topics are tabulated in G. Oxley's guide to the KHRO's collections, *Transport by sea, rail and inland navigation* (Hull, 1983).

Hull as a fishing port

The story of Hull's large-scale fishing industry does not truly begin until the middle of the nineteenth century. Prior to that time any fish brought into the town was purely for local consumption. In 1840 the establishment of a rail link with Leeds opened up the markets created by the rapidly expanding populations of the industrial West Riding and fish could be transported in bulk having been packed in ice immediately upon landing in Hull. John Dyson's *Business in great waters* (London, 1977) gives a good general account of the evolution of the fishing industry. A useful study of the fishing industry in Hull is the Master's thesis by G. S. Clark, 'The location and development of the Hull fishing industry', presented to the University of Hull in 1957 and available for consultation in the HUL or HLSL.

One of the most important changes which ever took place in the fishing industry was the substitution of sail by steam power. The first purpose-built steam trawler, the *Zodiac*, built by Earles of Hull for the Grimsby and North Sea Fishing Company, was launched in 1882. New ideas were disseminated world-wide and it is significant that the most detailed contemporary assessment of the *Zodiac* comes in a report of the United States Fish Commission.[14] Within the space of ten years the sailing trawler had completely vanished from Hull. The International Fisheries Exhibition held at South Kensington in 1883 well illustrated the evolution of the modern fishing industry. The exhibition catalogue and associated literature give invaluable information on the growing range of tackle available at the time. Using this in conjunction with Olsen's *Fishing almanac*, an annual first published in 1877, the development of trawling methods and equipment can be followed in detail. Olsen's, as well as incorporating a yearly fleet list for every port in the United Kingdom, is filled with illustrated advertisements for the suppliers and retailers in the fish-related industries. The *Fishermen's handy billy* and its more recent successors coming down to the *Trawlerman's handbook* of 1975 add to this picture, as well as showing what skills were demanded of the fisherman both in handling his vessel and catching his prey. Finally, a collection of builders' plans and drawings of vessels constructed at the Beverley shipyard of Cook, Welton and Gemmell, and now in the TDM, are a vital source for anyone studying the evolution of the steam trawler and its eventual replacement by the modern motor-driven stern fishing vessel with its own fishing plant.[15]

The North Sea was exploited by means of the fleeting system in which large numbers of trawlers stayed at sea for up to twelve weeks at a stretch meanwhile transferring their catches to steam cutters for transporting to market. The dangers and abuses of this system led to an official investigation and the introduction of much tighter controls by the Board of Trade.[16] The dangers of the fisherman's life were further emphasised by the great storm of March 1883, when forty-seven vessels and 260 men were lost, leading to a further report[17] and the formation of the Royal National Mission to Deep Sea Fishermen, all of which together did much to alleviate the prevailing terrible conditions.

There is one particular event in the history of Hull fishing which has remained something of a mystery ever since it happened. In 1904 Hull trawlers came under fire from ships of the Russian Baltic fleet, a remarkable incident described by Richard Hough in *The fleet that had to die*, revised edition (London, 1975) and in the account of the official report, *Inquiry into the circumstances concerned with the North Sea incident, 21-22 October 1904; report for the commission appointed by the Board of Trade* (London, 1904). One vessel, the *Crane*, was sunk, and several others damaged by the Russians, who evidently believed themselves to be under attack from a squadron of Japanese torpedo boats!

A number of logs written by John Glanville, 'admiral' of the Gamecock fleet in the 1920s, are now in the TDM and may be compared with logs kept aboard the 'single boaters' fishing independently off Iceland, Greenland and Norway.[18] Some skippers have published their memoirs, including Jerome Willis, *The last adventurers* (London, 1937; reprinted in 1940 and 1947 as *Trawlerman's town: the story of the lives of trawlermen from Hull and Grimsby*), and F. D. Ommaney, *North Cape* (London, 1938). These memoirs show that though boats may have been bigger and more powerful, life aboard a trawler was still very tough. A sociologist's view is given in the highly readable account by Jeremy Tunstall, *The fishermen* (London, 1962).

In the two World Wars the British trawler fleets were requisitioned for convoy and minesweeping duties and the sturdy sea qualities of the ships and their men made a major contribution to the protection of this country. Useful descriptions of convoy protection duty and minesweeping are to be found in Taprell Darling, *Swept channels* (London, 1937) and Paul Lund and Henry Ludlum, *Out sweeps: minesweepers in World War Two* (London, 1971).

After World War Two a period of boom and expansion with the introduction of oil-fired steam trawlers and motor vessels was followed by glut and retrenchment. There were a number of disasters at sea due to heavy icing, particularly the loss in 1968 of the *Ross Cleveland, Kingston Peridot* and *St Romanus*, all in the space of ten days, which led to changes in trawler design.[19] More and larger freezer trawlers were introduced despite the ominous signs of depletion of fish stocks and fierce squabbles with Iceland over fishing limits. The series of disputes in 1958, 1972 and 1975 over access to fish in Icelandic waters is discussed by the former British ambassador in Reykjavik, Sir Andrew Gilchrist in *Cod wars and how to lose them* (London, 1978). The loss of the Icelandic fishing grounds, followed by British entry to the Common Market, resulted in the crash which has all but

161

destroyed fishing as an industry in Hull. The daily statistics of fish landings from 1946 to 1976 compiled by Russell's Services (to be found in the TDM) give an emphatic picture of the decline. Finally, William Warner gives an excellent survey of the modern stern trawlers and factory ships and the problems of overfishing which their activities have emphasised in *Distant water* (Harmondsworth, 1983).

Detailed information about individual fishing vessels can be gained from the pages of Olsen's *Fishing almanac*, and also by reference to Lloyd's *Register of merchant shipping*. An unpublished list in the TDM compiled by W. M. Dodds is a comprehensive record of all steam and motor trawlers built in Britain up till 1975; it is arranged alphabetically under the name of each shipyard. All Hull registered fishing vessels also appear in the Customs registers in the KHRO for all years to 1902.[20] Details of the skippers and crews of Hull fishing vessels between 1884 and 1914 can be found in the crew agreements, also held at the KHRO.[21]

Documentation of the individual trawler companies is patchy and many of the smaller firms of the nineteenth and early twentieth century are scarcely recorded at all. Hellyers (later British United Trawlers) were amongst the earliest pioneers of the Hull industry and a collection of documents, ledgers, cash books and material relating to associated and subsidiary companies can be found at the KHRO;[22] likewise the papers of Thomas Hamling and Company which include references to the Hull Ice Company, Hull Steam Trawler Mutual Insurance and Protecting Company, Kingston Steam Trawling Company and Loch Fishing.[23] Additional material on the last two companies and on Hellyers and other documents relating to Pickering and Haldane (1893-1956) are all in the TDM.

The Arctic whaling trade

The early days of the Hull whaling trade remain cloudy and it will require close investigation of the public records before a clearer picture emerges. There are glimpses of Hull's early involvement in the whaling trade in the Corporation Bench Books and these can be fitted into the broader picture of the national enterprise by reference to Gordon Jackson's *The British whaling trade* (London, 1978). Jackson gives us a useful economic history of the whale fishery both in the Arctic and the South Seas. Other works by Spence and Matthews are good illustrated accounts of all aspects of whaling up to the present;[24] the former includes reliable descriptions of the principal species of whale. Basil Lubbock, *The Arctic whalers* (Glasgow, 1937) is an invaluable season by season narrative of the progress of the Arctic fishery to its demise at the outbreak of the First World War when only the port of Dundee was still sending her fleet north.

It is known that local vessels were active off the North Cape of Norway before 1574 but apparently using Norwegian crews to capture whales and walrus. After a cessation of activities in the seventeenth century caused largely by the intrusion of the more successful Dutch, there was a revival largely associated with Sir Samuel Standidge (1725-1801) and the start of a continuous participation in Arctic whaling by

Hull shipowners which was to last over a hundred years. In 1819 the whale fleet reached its highest total in a single season of sixty-five vessels. An invaluable description of the whale fishery is given by William Scoresby in his classic work on the subject entitled *An account of the Arctic regions* (Edinburgh, 1820). Himself a whaling captain, he prefaces his account with an historical introduction and then proceeds with a description of the methods of fishing and the vessels and equipment employed. Scoresby persisted, very successfully, in fishing the waters of the east side of Greenland, but increasingly the British ships penetrated into Davis Strait and Baffin Bay on the west side in search of new and richer stocks. At the same time an unknown number of Hull vessels were occupied in seeking sperm whale in the South Seas. This undertaking is very poorly recorded but we know that the *Comet*, for most of its career active in the Arctic, made at least one voyage to the southern fishery which is recorded in her log (1812-15) preserved in Trinity House, Hull.

As the search for the Greenland right whale led the fleet further and further north, so the risk of being caught in the pack ice increased. Particularly disastrous seasons occurred in 1821, 1830, 1835 and 1836, with small catches and heavy losses of ships and men. A number of contemporary pamphlets written by eyewitnesses give a graphic account of the privations suffered by the whalers.[25] The year 1842 was an early low point for Hull whaling with only four vessels departing to the northern fishery.

Preserved in the HLSL is a manuscript volume compiled by William Coltish, ship's husband for Eggintons, whale shipowners of Hull. This includes a complete listing of all the whale ships leaving Hull for the Arctic for the period 1772-1842. From 1812 names of the masters, number of whales caught and tonnage of oil extracted are also included. Some idea of the organisation of the whaling trade at this time can be gained from reference to a manuscript volume in the TDM which records the minutes of the whale ship owners at the Hull Mansion House, 1813-25.

Logbooks represent a major information source for all vessels. The TDM has a series of logbooks including originals, photocopies and microfilms covering the period 1809-61. Other important collections are in the HLSL (for 1812-52) and the Scott Polar Research Institute, Cambridge (1817-55). The most important item of local (i.e. Hull) interest amongst the logbooks at the NMM, Greenwich, records the trials of the whaler *Swan* beset in the Arctic, 1836-37. Inevitably, these logbooks give a somewhat restricted picture owing to the laconic nature of the entries and the generally routine recording of course, weather and the numbers of whales caught. Very often, a more detailed and intimate view comes from private journals, the best and most informative usually being written by the ship's surgeon. The journal of John Sanderson was published as *A voyage from Hull to Greenland in the ship Samuel, 1789* (Hull, 1790), and John Laing's as *An account of a voyage to Spitzbergen* (London, 1815).

One of the most interesting journals is the personal record of William Eden Cass aboard the Hull whaler *Brunswick* in 1824. This little pocket book is now to be found in Goole Public Library. It details the story of a voyage in one of Hull's most famous whaling ships by a once notable but now largely forgotten surgeon. The career of the *Brunswick* is recorded season by season in the Coltish manuscript referred to above, usually under the command of Captain William Blyth. This is recorded in the customs register in the KHRO. Surgeon Cass himself became the first medical practitioner in Goole in the 1820s. His standing in the local community resulted in a very informative obituary notice in the *Goole times* and as so often it is the local newspapers which have to be carefully searched to provide information essential to studies in local history. The place of his burial was noted in the same source and the discovery of his headstone still intact in the cemetery at Airmyn, yielded yet more details of his family which would have otherwise taken a long search in the parish registers to uncover. Publication by Humberside Libraries of an edited version of this journal is pending.

After the low point of 1842 a revival ensued and, in 1857 the *Diana* became the world's first steam-powered whaler.[26] In 1866 she was trapped in the pack ice and forced to overwinter in Davis Strait. The events of this epic voyage are further detailed in the journal of her surgeon, Charles Edward Smith, now to be found in the TDM.[27] This record was published in an edited form as *From the deep of the sea* (London, 1922; reprinted 1977). The journal of Albert Johnson Whitehouse, boat steerer of the *Emma*, is a rare account of a whale ship deliberately overwintering in the Arctic in the season of 1859-60. In 1895 William Barron published his memoirs of a long career in the whaling trade as *Old whaling days*. More recently, Philip Hepton has published a season by season record of the Hull whaling fleet from 1843 to 1869, starting where the Coltish manuscript leaves off, entitled *Sailings of the Hull whaling fleet from the port of Hull 1843 to 1869* (Hull, 1985).[28]

Notes for chapter 10
1. KHRO DPC/1/41-2
2. B. B. Mason, *A brief history of the origin and progress of the Dock Co. at Kingston upon Hull* (Hull, 1885); E. P. Bates, *A note on the history of the Queen's Dock* (Hull, 1931)
3. KHRO DPD 12/1/29 etc.
4. TDM M3.3187
5. HUL DEW/1-12
6. See HUL DEW/4/31-47
7. HUL DEW/3/181-8
8. TDM 811.1980
9. HUL DEW/9-10/16-23
10. KHRO DPC/1/1-29
11. N. Cox, 'Sources of maritime history: the records of the Registrar General of Shipping and Seamen', *Maritime history*, 2 (1972), pp.168-188
12. F. W. Brooks, ed., *The first order book of the Hull Trinity House, 1632-65*, YAS record series, 105 (Leeds, 1942)
13. KHRO DPD/1-2
14. J. W. Collins, 'Suggestions for the employment of improved types of vessels in the market fisheries, with notes on British fishing steamers', *Bulletin of the United States Fish Commission*, 8 (1888), pp.175-191
15. TDM 264.1980
16. *Report of a Committee appointed under a minute of the Board of Trade to inquire and report whether and what legislation is desirable with a view to placing the relations between the owners, masters and crews of fishing vessels on a more satisfactory basis* (London, 1882)
17. *Report to the Board of Trade on the system of deep sea trawl fishing in the North Sea* (London, 1883)
18. TDM T3.274 to 284 etc.
19. *Trawler safety: final report of the Committee of Inquiry into Trawler Safety* (London, 1969)
20. KHRO DPC/1
21. KHRO DPF/1-31
22. KHRO DBHB/1-26
23. KHRO DBTH
24. B. Spence, *Harpooned: the story of whaling* (London, 1980); L. H. Matthews, *The whale* (London, 1968)
25. e.g. Anon., *Sufferings of the ice-bound whalers* (Edinburgh, 1836)
26. A. G. Credland, *The Diana of Hull*, Kingston upon Hull Museums bulletin, 15 (Hull, 1982)
27. TDM 30.52
28. P. Hepton, *Sailings of the Hull whaling fleet from the port of Hull 1843 to 1869*, Malet Lambert local history originals, 24 (Hull, 1985)

11

THE HISTORY OF EDUCATION

John Lawson

The history of education is concerned with educational agencies of all kinds, who provided them and why, and what was taught and how, and — more difficult — what their influence was on society, locally and generally. Its aim is to explain not only individual institutions but also education as it really was in particular areas in the past. To be intelligible education in any place has to be seen in its social setting and also in the context of national education. A general account with bibliographies is John Lawson and Harold Silver, *A social history of education in England* (London, 1973).

Although a start is best made with secondary works primary sources are eventually indispensable both in print and in manuscript and those for periods before about 1700 may require some elementary Latin and some practice in palaeography. Examples of manuscript material from the York diocesan archives, now in the Borthwick Institute of Historical Research (BIHR), can be found, with transcripts, in J. S. Purvis, *Educational records* (York, 1959). Samples of the multifarious primary printed sources, with bibliographical references, are reproduced in *Yorkshire schools and schooldays*, edited by R. W. Unwin and W. B. Stephens (Leeds, 1976). Many of these are from collections in the University of Leeds Museum of the History of Education.

The best general guide is W. B. Stephens, *Sources for English local history*, rev. ed. (Cambridge, 1981). This may be supplemented by R. B. Pugh, 'Sources for the history of English primary schools', *British journal of educational studies*, 1 (1952), and W. E. Tate, 'Some sources for the history of English grammar schools', *British journal of educational studies*, 1 (1953) and 2 (1954). These last two articles, though somewhat out-dated, have a wider usefulness than their title suggests.

To begin with secondary sources, lists of likely books and articles might be compiled from published bibliographies and the local collections in the larger public libraries. Robin Bateman, *Yorkshire school history: a bibliography* (York, 1969) eases this task. The older town and county histories sometimes include information about schools: the most important are given in R. F. Drewery, *A select list of books on Hull and district: a guide to the collections in the Local History Library* (Hull, 1968). After about 1800 local directories provide details not only about teachers and schools but also about the local communities which they served, and for their own time these are primary sources. Some are more reliable and informative than others. Lists up to 1856 are given in *A guide to national and provincial directories*, edited by Jane E. Norton (London, 1959).

The most systematic detailed and up-to-date survey of the region, still in progress, is being made by the *Victoria County History* (VCH). Volume one of *VCH Yorkshire* (1907) has articles, mainly on grammar schools, based on previous unexplored archive material, by A. F. Leach. More recent

East Riding volumes include, in the individual parish and town accounts, generally brief factual summaries of school history, but with valuable source references, which should be noted for further use. *VCH East Riding* 1 (1969) has a more extended survey of education in Hull and also articles on informal agencies of education such as libraries, museums and learned societies. Unpublished research studies on the region are catalogued in Victor F. Gilbert and Colin Holmes, *Theses and dissertations on the history of education presented to British and Irish universities between 1900 and 1976* (London, 1979) with subsequent annual supplements. These should not be missed, but their importance and reliability will vary, as with other secondary sources.

Of primary sources there are certain categories which have to be searched, but evidence may crop up in unlikely places. For example, the *State Papers Domestic* show the Sancton schoolmaster denied his £20 annuity in 1653 because the lands chargeable with it had been sequestered by reason of his patron's recusancy;[1] the parish registers at Rillington name schoolmasters not only there in 1727, 1781 and 1801, but also at Wetwang in 1790 and Garton in 1796;[2] and a parliamentary enquiry into the education of the poor in 1818 contains a long report on Pocklington school.[3]

Before the state-aided expansion of elementary education in the nineteenth century, schools were either private enterprises of uncertain duration and difficult to trace or supported by endowments that ensure a more permanent and documented existence. The essential source for endowed schools of all kinds are the reports of the Brougham Charity Commission.[4] The oldest charity schools, at Walkington, Burton Agnes and Halsham, were of Tudor foundation. Most were of eighteenth-century origin, and three of the earliest, Beverley Blue Coat School, Hull Charity Hall School and the Vicar's School, were aided by the Society for the Promotion of Christian Knowledge in whose correspondence files and annual *Account of charity schools* their beginnings are to be found.[5] The Charity Commissioners reported on twenty-one schools endowed or re-endowed, and fifty charities for education unconnected with particular schools, established in the East Riding during the eighteenth century.[6] Vocational training, implicit in many charity schools, was the express purpose of some, for example Bower's Knitting School at Bridlington,[7] Cogan's Girls' School at Hull[8] and the Hull Trinity House marine school.[9]

Until the school board era the church was the chief patron of education and its records, parochial and diocesan, are a major source. Parish registers of baptisms, marriages and burials, may provide the names of seventeenth- and eighteenth-century schoolmasters otherwise unknown; church-wardens' and overseers' accounts may also reveal a school. The parish chest or vestry was the common repository for these, and also for any documents specifically concerning the school, such as trust deeds, minutes and accounts. An out-dated but still useful inventory was published by the Yorkshire Archaeological Society (YAS) in 1939 and edited by M. W. Barley.[11] Most of the parish records of the East Riding archdeaconry, and many records of individual schools, are now in the Humberside County Record Office (HCRO); other East Riding parish records are in the BIHR. Some parish registers have been printed by the Yorkshire Parish Register Society. More are available in typescript.[12]

The York diocesan archives contain several categories of records bearing on education, chiefly concerned with ensuring the religious and political conformity of schoolmasters.[13] J. S. Purvis, *Tudor parish documents of the diocese of York* (Cambridge, 1948) gives examples of East Yorkshire schoolmasters examined soon after the Elizabethan settlement. After 1604 all were required to obtain the bishop's licence to teach; to procure this they had to subscribe to the royal supremacy and articles of religion; and to support their application some produced letters of nomination or testimonials. Nomination files, subscription books and institution act books are rich sources for schools and schoolmasters, endowed and unendowed, in the seventeenth and eighteenth centuries.[14] However, these requirements were not always observed; they ignored women teachers; and they provide no certain evidence for the continuity of schools. Also important are the various records produced by the bishop's 'primary' and 'ordinary' visitations of his diocese, when schoolmasters were 'called' to appear and 'exhibit' their licences. The preliminary 'visitation articles' addressed to the parish clergy required answers to specific questions, which included the schools in the parish. The published returns for Archbishop Herring's primary visitation in 1743 provide valuable evidence for this period.[15] Archbishop Drummond's primary visitation in 1764 produced equally important returns.[16]

Of the region's endowed grammar schools only Archbishop Holgate's at Old Malton had statutes, and they are printed in N. A. Hudleston, *History of Malton and Norton* (Scarborough, 1962). The archives of the old corporations of Hull and Beverley amply document their respective grammar schools, for which they assumed responsibility after the suppression in 1548 of the religious foundations which had previously maintained them. The Hull Corporation minutes (Bench Books) are not yet in print, but published extracts from the town records of Beverley tell much about its school.[17] Pocklington school is less well documented at this period but it has an admission register with many names added later, ranging from 1626 to 1717.[18] Pupils from these schools traditionally went to Cambridge, seldom to Oxford, and they can be found in college admission books. These may also reveal private schools otherwise unrecorded. Admissions to Gonville and Caius College point to schools (or private tutors) at Beswick and Saltmarshe in 1588, at Hollym in 1591, at South Cave in 1621 and North Cave in 1626.[19] Particularly important for schools in this region are the St John's College admissions. Invaluable biographically for both masters and pupils is J. and J. A. Venn, *Alumni Cantabrigienses,* four volumes to 1751 (Cambridge, 1922-27), six volumes 1752-1900 (Cambridge, 1940-54).

Catholic education, proscribed during penal times, is surveyed with references to its special sources in J. Kitching, 'Catholic education in the North and East Ridings of Yorkshire and the City of York ... 1571-1778', *Durham research review*, 2 no.9 (1958) and no.10 (1959). The same writer's Durham Master of Education thesis (1956) extends the study to 1870. Dom

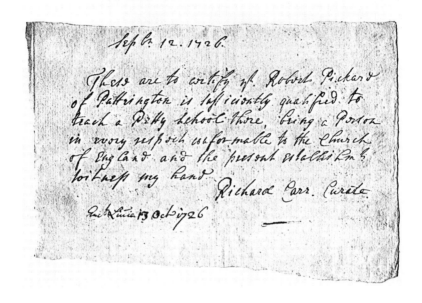

Figure 37: Testimonial for Robert Pickard, petty schoolmaster at Patrington
(BIHR Nom. SM. 1726/13)

Hugh Aveling, *Post-Reformation Catholicism in East Yorkshire 1558-1790* (York, 1960) has references with manuscript sources to clandestine schools and unlicensed teachers.

Source material proliferates during the nineteenth century especially government records with the growing involvement of the state, at first chiefly in elementary education.[20] The old charity schools were now supplemented by day schools promoted by the Church of England National Society, the undenominational British Society and the Associated Catholic Charities (from 1848 the Catholic Poor School Committee). All three bodies published annual reports and have archive collections, notably the National Society, with individual school files and the early annual reports of the York Diocesan Society and the East Riding District Society, both formed in 1812.[21]

Of the nonconformist denominations the Wesleyans were most active in providing day schools; after 1840 these were initiated by circuit ministers through the Wesleyan Education Committee, whose printed and manuscript records are held by the Methodist Education Committee.

Schooling for the poor was surveyed, parish by parish throughout the country, by parliamentary select committees using printed questionnaires in 1816 and 1834;[22] and in 1839 the Manchester Statistical Society investigated elementary education in Hull.[23] From 1840 to 1899 the indispensable source for government-aided voluntary schools is the series of annual *Minutes* (from 1859 *Reports*) of the Committee of Council on Education, providing detailed information about individual schools: their teachers, buildings and equipment, accommodation and attendance, sometimes including Her Majesty's Inspectors' verbatim reports.[24] The 1851 census produced statistics of several categories of individually unnamed schools — public, private, Sunday, workhouse, evening — and a variety of named institutions of adult education, but in registration districts or Poor Law unions, not parishes.[25] Elementary education of all kinds in Hull and the eighteen townships and parishes of the Sculcoates union was examined in the late 1850s by the Newcastle Commission,[26] and references are made to some schools in Holderness and the Wolds in the 1860s in the report of the Royal Commission on the Employment of Children, Young Persons and Women in Agriculture.[27] The returns for Archbishop Thomson's several visitations include information about schools,[28] and another parliamentary survey in 1871 produced returns from civil parishes arranged in census districts giving details in tabulated lists of both grant-aided and private schools, with accommodation and attendance figures.[29]

After 1870 the scene was changed by the rate-aided school boards and also, when compulsory attendance was introduced in 1876, by school attendance committees established by the Poor Law unions to enforce attendance in areas without school boards. Some details of these authorities are given in the annual *Reports* of the Committee of Council on Education. In 1902 on the eve of their dissolution there were forty-two school boards and eleven attendance committees in the East Riding.[30] Voluntary schools of this period are listed with date of foundation, details of trusts and tenure of premises in *Education ... non-provided schools* (1906).[31] During this time individual school records became more plentiful, notably managers' minute books, log books, cash books, and admission registers. HCRO has the managers' minute books of twenty-one schools (the earliest 1840), the records of 117 individual schools (some from 1863) and the records of forty school boards and nine attendance committees.[32] Similar collections in the Kingston upon Hull City Record Office (KHRO) are listed in two schedules of documents: 'Minutes of Kingston upon Hull School Board and its committees 1871-1903' and 'Records of public education in Kingston upon Hull'. The records of the Hull National Union of Teachers, formed in 1871, are in Hull Local Studies Library (HLSL).

Some indications of the relationship between the availability of schooling and basic literacy are to be found in W. P. Baker, *Parish registers*

Figure 38: Holderness Ward British School, Dansom Lane, Hull (1838)

and illiteracy in East Yorkshire (York, 1961). Comparisons and further references are provided by W. B. Stephens, *Regional variations in education during the industrial revolution 1780-1870* (Leeds, 1973).

Secondary education at this time was supplied by the old grammar schools, more recent private 'academies' and from the 1830s by proprietary 'colleges'. Nicholas Carlisle, *The endowed grammar schools* (London, 1818) supplements the Brougham Charity Commission's reports. After 1835 the declining fortunes of Beverley and Hull grammar schools are documented in the committee minutes of their respective new town councils. Endowed schools of all kinds, but chiefly the grammar schools, were investigated by the Taunton or Schools Inquiry Commission; its report in 1868 has detailed information on the eight — mostly decayed — East Riding grammar schools and a tabular list showing the state of thirty-three endowed primary schools.[33] The task of reforming run-down endowed schools passed in 1874 to the Charity Commissioners who until 1900 negotiated new 'schemes' with trustees; their individual school files are in the Public Record Office (PRO) in London (class E27).[34] Private and proprietory schools are to be traced in the directories and in newspaper reports and advertisements. Apart from these, three short-lived proprietary schools in Hull, the precursors of Hymers College, have left little save deeds of settlement, some annual reports to general meetings of proprietors, prospectuses, prize lists and some pupils' reports and magazines.[35]

During this century working-class adult education developed through church and chapel Sunday schools, night schools, adult schools, mechanics institutes, mutual improvement societies, church institutes, public libraries, and finally university extension and its later offspring the Workers Educational Association.[36] Thomas Kelly, *George Birkbeck* (Liverpool, 1957) lists East Riding mechanics institutes in 1850 using the *Annual reports of the Yorkshire Union* ... (Leeds, 1842-1924).[37] J. F. C. Harrison, *Learning and living 1790-1960* (London, 1961) is a comprehensive survey with many Yorkshire references and bibliographical notes. For Church of England night schools there is information in Archbishop Thomson's visitation returns.[38] W. E. Styler, editor, *Adult education in East Yorkshire 1875-1960* (Hull, 1965) is an account by four participants.

Developments in technical education after 1890 are recorded in the minutes of the Technical Instruction Committtes of the new East Riding County Council and Hull County Borough Council. Much ready information about education generally at this time is given in the *Hull and East Riding red book* (Hull, 1899).

For the nineteenth century the directories must be searched, but even more important are the local newspapers.[39] The first of a series of Hull newspapers started in 1787 and all give as much attention to regional as to Hull affairs.[40] For the western parts of the area the York papers are equally informative.[41] Newspapers were later produced in Beverley, Bridlington, Driffield and Filey. The range of educational items in one early newspaper can be seen in K. A. MacMahon, ed., *An index to ... the Hull advertiser...* (Hull, 1955). Representative samples of the abundant educational material available in later periods are to be found in the *Hull advertiser* 1848, the *Eastern counties herald* 1873, and the *Hull news* 1889.

Like the newspapers, autobiographical evidence can animate the official sources. The Sigglesthorne schoolmaster about 1788-1823 is brought to life from his own note books and poems by V. N. Wright, *John Day: a village poet* (Sigglesthorne, 1969). Thomas Jackson, the Wesleyan preacher, in *Recollections of my own life and times* (London, 1878) tells of his schooldays at Sancton in the 1790s. About this time Leavening school is recalled in Robert Addison's manuscript 'Topographical history of Leavening' (1831), copies of which are to be found in the HLSL and Hull University Library (HUL); and schooling in Sculcoates in Christopher Thomson's *Autobiography of an artisan* (London, 1847). How fortuitous rural education could be in the 1830s is shown by the memoirs of J. R. Mortimer, the archaeologist, in J. D. Hicks, ed., *A Victorian boyhood in the Wolds*, EYLHS, 14 (Beverley, 1978). Robert Sharpe of South Cave kept a diary from 1826-38 which shows the varied roles and interests of the village schoolmaster.[42] Mary Simpson, daughter of the vicar of Boynton and Carnaby, in *Ploughing and sowing, or annals of an evening school in a Yorkshire village* (London, 1861), tells of her efforts to instruct and edify the unschooled farm lads of these parishes. In *Yorkshire reminiscences* (Oxford, 1922) M. C. F. Morris remembers Pocklington school in the 1850s, also his church school visits as diocesan inspector of religious instruction from 1874 to 1879; and from an old farm labourer's

Figure 39: St. James' National School, Porter Street, Hull (1844)

recollections he describes, in *The British workman* ... (Oxford, 1928), schools in Nafferton about 1840. Henry Woodcock, *Piety among the peasantry; being sketches of Primitive Methodism in the Yorkshire Wolds* (London, 1889) notes the influence of growing numbers of day and Sunday schools.

From 1903 to 1945 the principal official sources are the records of the new Local Education Authorities (LEAs) — the education committees and their sub-committees of the East Riding County Council, the Hull County Borough Council (both responsible for elementary, secondary and technical education) and the Beverley and Bridlington non-county borough councils (for elementary education only). For Hull an instant source of reference is the Education Committee's *Members' handbook*, annually from 1904-14. Government statistics for each LEA are given in various *Board of Education lists*; for example, *List 21* is of public elementary schools, *List 60* of public secondary schools, *List 70* of independent schools recognised as efficient.[43] Much information is to be found in such annual publications as the *Education committees year book*, the *Education authorities directory and annual*, and the *Schoolmaster's year book*. School records, depending on the type of school may include prospectuses, magazines, governors' minute books, admission registers, staff lists, curriculum and subject syllabuses, inspectors' reports, public examination results, and pupils' exercise books.

173

HOWDEN.

MR. J. G. FITCH'S REPORT.

1. This school continues to be held in an ancient apartment adjoining the church, and apparently part of the original fabric. Its whole resources derived from endowment appear to be 30*l.* per annum, of which the greater portion is derived from a rent-charge of 21*l.* on the property of the Rev. Canon Jefferson of Thicket Priory, who is lord of the manor of Howden, and the representative of Robert Jefferson, Esq., the original testator. The meadow in Saltmarsh bequeathed by Mr. Nelson produces 10*l.* per annum. The vicar of the parish is nominally the head master, but the school is conducted by a substitute who is appointed by him, and who is an undergraduate of Dublin. Twelve of the boys are admitted gratuitously and are selected by the head master; the remaining 14 scholars pay capitation fees varying from 1*l.* 1*s.* to 2*l.* 2*s.* per quarter, according to age.

The teacher has only recently entered on his duties, but is evidently discharging them with skill and care. About half of the boys have made fair progress in compound arithmetic, six have advanced as far as proportion, and three have commenced the study of algebra. Nine are learning the Latin grammar, and of them six have advanced as far as the 22nd exercise in Arnold's first book. The vicar himself attends regularly, and gives lessons in French to ten of the elder boys. The free scholars are divided from the rest, and sit in another part of the room. It does not appear, however, that the instruction they receive is inferior to that of the paying scholars.

The vicar pays out of the entire income of the school a fixed salary of 60*l.* to his assistant, and is willing to permit him the right of taking boarders. This leaves a small surplus, which barely suffices to keep the premises in repair and to provide needful apparatus. The room is in a creditable state, and the almost gratuitous services of the vicar in the instruction have a good effect on the tone of the school. It is to be regretted that there is any obligation to admit free scholars. Such boys would be better provided for at the national school, and the grammar school is impoverished and kept down by their presence.

Figure 40: Howden Grammar School in 1868, *Report* of the Schools Inquiry Commission (London, 1868) vol. 18, p.451.

For completeness local sources may have to be supplemented by unpublished evidence in the national collections, especially the PRO. For example, for some years after 1548 a succession of Hull Grammar School masters are known only by payments of their Crown stipends entered in the records of the Exchequer.[44] After local complaints of neglect or mismanagement, breaches of the trusts of Burton Agnes, Halsham, Pocklington and Sancton schools were investigated at different periods in the seventeenth century by commissioners under the Charitable Uses Act, and their decrees are in the Chancery records.[45] In the British Library (BL) is a draft set of rules for Hull Grammar School made in 1662 and once in the corporation archives.[46] The Bodleian Library, Oxford, has the returns to Christopher Wase's inquiry concerning free schools made in the 1670s, and they include replies from Hull and Pocklington.[47] For unpublished official material relating to individual schools after 1870 the PRO is the chief repository.[48]

HULL GRAMMAR SCHOOL IN 1680: A CASE STUDY[49]

Two documents in the KHRO throw light on the town's grammar school as it was on 23 June 1680. One is a return made to the corporation as school governors by Robert Pell, the headmaster, naming the boys in each class and the books they had read or were still reading on that day.[50] The other is a list of the school library books made on 8 July 1676.[51] How to exploit these two pieces of evidence?

To comprehend the school in its environment then we have the surviving school building and Hollar's pictorial map of Hull about 1640, the older town histories by Gent (1735), Hadley (1788) and Tickell (1798), and more recently the Hull volume in VCH ER and Edward Gillett and Kenneth MacMahon, *A history of Hull* (Oxford, 1980). These show Hull small and compact, walled and moated, a port and garrison town of perhaps 7000 inhabitants, mainly merchants, seamen and craftsmen, governed by a corporation of thirteen aldermen (the Bench), one of them the mayor. They controlled the grammar school, the town's only permanently established school.

Two contemporary works on grammar school curriculum and practice put the school in its educational context — Charles Hoole, *A new discovery of the old art of teaching schoole* (1660) edited by E. T. Campagnac (Liverpool, 1913) and Christopher Wase, *Considerations concerning free-schools* (Oxford, 1678). A modern study is W. A. L. Vincent, *The grammar schools: their continuing tradition, 1660-1714* (London, 1969).

Venn reports Pell's brief university career and the Sheffield parish register shows him baptised there in 1644, son of William Pell, therefore youngest brother of two other Pells at the same Cambridge college, and so perhaps like them previously at Rotherham Grammar School, soon after Charles Hoole was headmaster there.[52]

Bench Book 7 (1664-82) is our most informative primary source. This illustrates clearly the procedures of Pell's appointment in 1677; his

175

application for the post with personal recommendations, interview by a sub-committee of the Bench, drafted terms of employment, confirmation by the whole Bench under the common seal and letter of nomination to the archbishop,[53] followed by subscription and licence at Bishopthorpe.[54] The Bench Book also reveals that Pell was not single-handed in the school: John Simpson, formerly schoolmaster at Campsall, near Doncaster, had been appointed usher in 1676,[55] and Samuel Kent, scrivener, visiting writing master in 1678.[56] It suggests, too, that dissensions between master and usher had led to Pell being asked to answer 'what schollers he hath and what books they read'.[57]

His return lists twenty-nine boys unevenly arranged in five classes, class 1 being the top; one boy is in class 1, two in class 2, five in class 3, eighteen in class 4 and three in class 5. Given only their surnames identification is uncertain, save for five. Venn shows four of these later at Cambridge and provides their ages and fathers' occupations — Samuel Prowde, John Catlyn, Timothy Johnson and Thomas Mason.[58] A chance source reveals that Jonathan Harley in class 4 had come from Newcastle to be schooled under Pell.[59] The parish registers of the two Hull churches show fifteen boys with surnames on the list baptised between 1663 and 1668 and these suggest tentative identifications. If correct and generally typical these would suggest an age range of twelve to seventeen and therefore some preparatory education in one or other of the petty or English schools whose masters appear in the diocesan or parish registers of this time.

Hoole's *A new discovery* and Foster Watson, *The English grammar schools to 1660: their curriculum and practice* (London, 1908) help to identify most of Pell's class books despite their summary titles and show them to be generally representative of grammar-school studies at the time — Latin and Greek grammars, vocabularies and dictionaries, textbook aids to Latin writing and conversation, graduated classical authors, and Latin and Greek testaments.

The catalogue of the school library gives authors and short titles of eighty-seven different works listed in size from folio to duodecimo, which is some help to identification. Except for titles such as 'Virgil', 'Some fragments of Cicero' and 'A peece of Aristotle' most can be traced with the help of A. W. Pollard and G. R. Redgrave, *Short-title catalogue of books* ..., 2nd ed. (London, 1976) and its continuation by Donald Wing, *Short-title catalogue ... 1641-1700*, 3 vols (New York, 1972), together with the BL's *General catalogue of printed books*. Thus the garbled item 'Clarkes Curialis Aulicus' proves to be Bartholomew Clerk's Latin translation of the Italian courtesy book *The Courtier* by Baldassare Castiglione.[60] Apart from the big standard grammars and lexicons for reference there are miscellaneous works on Hebrew and Jewish antiquities, sermons and theology, science and medicine, manners and morality. Only twelve are in English, including 'Lord Bacons Naturall history' and 'Thucydides Englished by Hobs'. The corporation Bench Books and audit books record the purchase of some of these, the earliest in 1575,[61] the most recent in 1678.[62] Of the remnants, some are still in the school, some deposited in the HUL.

The *Dictionary of national biography* notes some of the authors and printers of these books. It also has articles on Matthew Robinson, Pell's principal supporter for the headship in 1677, on Pell's elder brother William, and on Bishop Thomas Watson, who presented the school library with G. T. Vossius, *Aristarchus, sive de arte grammatica* (Amsterdam, 1662) inscribed: 'In usum scholae Kingstoniae super Hullam Thomas Watson ejusdem quondam alumnus dedit 9no Cal. Maii 1666'.

Notes for chapter 11

1. *Calendar of the Committee for Compounding 1643-60*, 3, pp.1924-25
2. C. E. Whiting, ed., *Parish registers of Rillington*, Yorkshire Parish Register Society publications, 117 (Leeds, 1948), pp.59, 89, 106, 118, 127
3. *Select Committee on the Education of the Lower Orders* 1818 HC (426) iv, pp.144-60
4. Pugh, p.44; *Commission to Inquire Concerning Charities*, 32 vols with index volume and digest (London, 1819-43)
5. W. E. Tate, 'SPCK Archives', *Archives*, 3 (1957), pp.105-15. Details extracted from *An account of charity schools* ... (1712) are given in T. Cox, *Magna Britannia* (London, 1720), pp.553, 554, 667
6. M. G. Jones, *The charity school movement* (Cambridge, 1938), pp.352, 362
7. Account book 1785-1880 with abstract of foundation deed in Bridlington public library
8. G. M. Attwood, 'Alderman Cogan's Girls' School Hull 1753-1950', (unpublished M.Ed. thesis, University of Hull, 1961)
9. G. Jackson, 'The foundation of Trinity House School ... an experiment in marine education', *Durham research review*, 21 (1968), pp.313-23
10. J. Lawson, 'The use of ecclesiastical records for the history of education', in *Local studies and the history of education*, edited by T. G. Cook (London, 1972), pp.83-98
11. M. W. Barley, ed., *Parochial documents of the Archdeaconry of the East Riding: an inventory*, YAS record series, 99 (Leeds, 1939)
12. N. K. M. Gurney, *Handlist of parish register transcripts in BIHR* (York, 1976)
13. J. S. Purvis, *An introduction to ecclesiastical records* (London, 1973); D. M. Smith, *A guide to the archive collections in the Borthwick Institute of Historical Research* (York, 1953) and *Supplementary guide* ... (York, 1980). Drawing largely from these records are two studies by J. E. Stephens, 'Yorkshire schools 1660-1700', *Durham research review*, 8 (1977), pp.56-66, and 'Yorkshire schoolmasters 1660-1700', *Durham and Newcastle research review*, 10 (1983), pp.90-94
14. BIHR schools index. York Minster Library has two subscription books (call numbers S3(4)a and S3(4)d) covering the period 1571-1679 and these also have many references to schools
15. S. L. Ollard and P. C. Walker, eds, *Archbishop Herring's visitation returns 1743*, YAS record series, 71, 72, 75, 77, 79 (Leeds, 1928-31)
16. Smith, *Guide*, pp.76, 147
17. A. F. Leach, ed., *Early Yorkshire schools*, YAS record series, 27 (Leeds, 1899); J. Dennett, ed., *Beverley borough records 1575-1821*, YAS record series, 84 (Leeds, 1933); K. A. MacMahon, ed., *Beverley Corporation minute books*, YAS record series, 122 (Leeds, 1958)
18. H. Lawrance, 'Pocklington school admission register ...', *YAJ*, 25 (1920), pp.53-70
19. J. Venn, *Biographical history of Gonville and Caius College 1349-1679* (London, 1887), vol. 1, pp.134, 144, 252, 260, 275
20. W. R. Powell, *Local history from blue books: a select list of the sessional papers of the House of Commons* (London, 1962)
21. Pugh, pp.44-55. For the use of these records elsewhere see M. Sanderson, 'The National and British school societies in Lancashire 1803-1839', in *Local studies and the history of education* ..., edited by T. G. Cook (London, 1972), pp.1-36

22. Pugh, pp.46-47. *Digest of parochial returns . . . to the Select Committee . . . on Education of the Poor 1818*, HC 224 (1819), ix (2), East Riding, pp.1075-1104; *Abstract of educational returns 1833*, HC 62 (1835) xliii, East Riding pp.1078-1099

23. 'Report on the state of elementary education in . . . Hull', *Journal of the Statistical Society of London*, 4 (1841), pp.156-75

24. Pugh, pp.47-49. HUL has near full set. HCRO has 82 school building plans submitted in support of applications for government grant, 1842-73

25. *Great Britain, census 1851, education England and Wales report and tables* (London, 1854). East Riding returns pp.clxi, clxxxiv, 40-41, 185-87, 251

26. *Report, Royal Commission on Popular Education*, HC (1861), xxi (3) pp.215-316; J. Lawson, 'Elementary education in Hull in the 1850s', *Studies in education*, 2 no.1 (1953), pp. 7-26

27. HC (1867-68) xvii, pp.363-73

28. Smith, *Guide*, pp.81-83

29. *Returns relating to elementary education*, HC 201 (1871) lv, pp.466-79

30. Details in *List of school boards and school attendance committees*, HC (1902) lxxix

31. HC 178 (1906) lxxvii, lxxviii

32. Detailed lists in HCRO

33. HC (1867-68) xxviii, (18)

34. P. Gordon, 'Some sources for the history of the Endowed Schools Commission 1869-1900', *British journal of educational studies*, 14 no.3 (1966) pp.59-73

35. J. Lawson, 'Two forgotten Hull schools: the foundation of Hull College and Kingston College, 1836', *Studies in education*, 1 no.6 (1952), pp.7-26; 'Middle-class education in later Victorian Hull: the problem of secondary education 1865-95', *Studies in education*, 3 no.1 (1958), pp.27-49

36. W. B. Stephens, *Sources . . .*, pp.240-47

37. HLSL has Hull Mechanics Institute records from 1825-90

38. Extracts from the 1865 returns are given in W. P. Baker, *Parish registers . . .*, pp.19-23

39. G. E. Laughton and L. R. Stephens, *Yorkshire newspapers: a bibliography with locations* (Harrogate, 1960)

40. *VCH ER* 1 (1969), pp.428-32

41. *VCH York* (1961), pp.537-41

42. HCRO DDX/216/4

43. W. B. Stephens, *Sources . . .*, pp.225-26

44. PRO E319 and LR6

45. PRO C93 *Lists and indexes* X (1899), pp.120-35; J. E. Stephens, 'Yorkshire schools and chancery controls in the seventeenth century', in *Aspects of education 1600-1750*, edited by J. E. Stephens (Hull, 1984), pp.4-19

46. BL Lans. MS. 891, ff.117-18

47. Bodleian. MS. CCC 390, ii, 245, 246, iii, 157, 182

48. Particularly useful are Ed. 7 (Public elementary schools: preliminary statements) and Ed. 49 (Endowment files, elementary education). For other classes see W. B. Stephens, *Sources . . .*, pp.221-23, 235, 247

49. See also J. Lawson, 'Hull Grammar School in 1680: the curriculum and a school register', *Studies in education*, 2 no.3 (1955), pp.228-48

50. KHRO, BRK/1/M361

51. KHRO, BRK/1/M347d

52. Venn, *Alumni*, pt.1, 3, p.337; *The parish registers of Sheffield*, edited by C. Drury and T. W. Hall, Yorkshire Parish Register Society, 60 (1918), p.193

53. KHRO, BB7, pp.494-5

54. BIHR, Sub. Bk. 11 (1673-86), p.22; Ins. AB 8 (1676-83), p.9; KHRO, BB7, pp.496-97

55. KHRO, BB7, p.481; BIHR Sub. Bk. 7 (1663-79), p.134

56. KHRO, BB7, p.561

57. KHRO, BB7, p.670
58. Venn, *Alumni*, pt.1, p.308; 2, p.482; 3, pp.157, 403. For scholarship money paid to these see KHRO BB7, pp.754, 763; BB8, pp.46, 76, 90, 104
59. *Memoirs ... of the life of Mr Ambrose Barnes*, edited by W. H. D. Longstaffe, Surtees Society publications, 50 (Durham, 1867), pp.442-43
60. *B. Castilionis ... de curiali sive aulico libri quatuor, ex Italico sermone in Latinum conversi: B. Clerke ... interprete* (London, 1571); BL *General catalogue*, 35, c.32. Foster Watson, pp.103-4
61. KHRO, BB4, f.128 v
62. KHRO, BB7, p.549

12

THE ARCHITECTURE AND HISTORY OF HOUSES

David Neave

Under the heading of sources for the history of houses a wide range of buildings and methods for their study is encompassed. At one level is the stately home whose architecture can be termed 'polite', and at another is the two-roomed mud-walled cottage which is clearly 'vernacular'. R. W. Brunskill has succinctly defined polite buildings as 'the efforts of professional designers, meeting the more elaborate needs of a formal way of life with the aid of internationally accepted rules and procedures, advanced constructional techniques, and materials chosen for aesthetic effect rather than local availability' in contrast to vernacular buildings which were 'the products of local craftsmen meeting simple functional requirements according to traditional plans and procedures and with the aid of local building material and constructional methods'.[1] It is the polite house rather than the vernacular house in the East Riding that has so far been studied by architectural and social historians and for this reason this chapter will concentrate on the original sources for the history of the smaller rural house.

Whatever the scale of the house being studied it will be necessary to have some general knowledge of architectural history and to be familiar with architectural terms. Many books have been written on these topics but two that I have found perennially useful are John Summerson, *Architecture in Britain 1530-1830*, 7th ed. (London, 1983) and A. L. Osborne, *The Country Life pocket guide to English domestic architecture*, 2nd ed. (London, 1967).

A starting point for any study of houses in the county must be N. Pevsner, *Yorkshire: York and the East Riding* (London, 1972) which, though far from comprehensive, provides a survey of the polite house and background information on topics such as building materials. A major source used by Pevsner is the descriptive lists produced by the Ministry of Housing and Local Government (now Department of the Environment) in the 1960s of buildings listed as of architectural and historic importance. These lists which are at present being updated and extended are held by district and county planning departments with some copies in local reference libraries. Many minor buildings not mentioned by Pevsner are described in these lists.

Information on grander Georgian houses is far more readily available than for domestic buildings of any other type or period thanks to the establishment in 1937 of the Georgian Society for East Yorkshire. Many of the county's country houses, including several that have been demolished, have been the subject of articles in the *Transactions* and *Newsletter* of the Society and in *Country Life*. The principal sources for the history of the country house are the records of the various landed families which are now largely in the Humberside County Record Office (HCRO) and Hull University Library (HUL). What can be learnt from such archives,

180

particularly account books, vouchers, letters and plans, has been illustrated by Ivan Hall in relation to Burton Constable in *William Constable as patron; catalogue of an exhibition* (Hull, 1970) and in articles in *Country Life*.[2] Edward Ingram drew extensively on the archives of the Grimston family to detail the building history of Kilnwick Hall and Grimston Garth in *Leaves from a family tree* (Hull, 1951). The East Riding is not rich in country houses for the generally bleak landscape and the distance from London did not encourage landowners to build and reside in the county. The three houses that are open to the public, Sledmere, Burton Constable and Burton Agnes, are excellent examples of their period but many other fine houses such as Londesborough, Risby, Winestead and Hotham House, Beverley have been destroyed in the past two centuries.

The numerous smaller seventeenth century manor houses such as those at Barmby Moor, Portington, Arram, and Knedlington have received no attention from the architectural historian but there are few documentary sources. Elmswell manor house, historically and architecturally one of the most interesting domestic buildings in the county, is sadly in a near-derelict condition. Something of its history and architecture is recounted in D. Woodward, ed., *The farming and memorandum books of Henry Best of Elmswell 1642* (London, 1984).

Drawings, prints, paintings and photographs are an invaluable source for the history of the larger houses. There are extensive collections of illustrations of Hull and East Riding buildings in Hull Local Studies Library, Beverley Library, York Minster Library and Wakefield Art Gallery. Drawings of many of the county's country houses as they were in c.1720 appear in I. Hall, ed., *Samuèl Buck's Yorkshire sketchbook* (Wakefield, 1979).

Approaches to the study of town houses are excellently illustrated in Ivan and Elisabeth Hall's *Historic Beverley*, 2nd ed. (Beverley, 1981) and *Georgian Hull* (York, 1978). The fine photographs and the accurate dating of the buildings and their internal features, chiefly from local records, provide an invaluable comparative source book. The same authors, with the help of G. P. Brown, have been largely responsible for the useful series of Beverley Friary Open House booklets which have been produced annually since 1975. In their studies of the houses of Victorian Beverley the Halls have drawn heavily on the numerous plans and elevations produced under the Public Health Act of 1848 and a vast collection of these plans also survives in Kingston upon Hull Record Office (KHRO) from 1852. These plans, the memorials of deeds in the former Registry of Deeds in Beverley, maps, rate books and street directories are the main sources on urban housing. There is little in print on the Victorian housing of Hull although displays and pamphlets have been produced on various streets and areas by the Hull Heritage Information Centre. The development of the Avenues area is dealt with in M. Sheppard, S. Rooney and D. Smith, *A short history of the Avenues conservation area* (Hull, 1976) and J. Low has written on Hull Garden Village.[3] There is general coverage of the housing development of Hull in volume one of the *Victoria County History, East Riding* (VCH ER) and one particular aspect of nineteeth century working class housing is examined in C. A. Forster, *Court housing in Hull* (Hull, 1972). For other East Riding towns there are articles dealing with the development of housing in Bridlington, Filey and Withernsea in VCH ER II and V and detailed town trails have been produced by David Neave on the buildings of Howden, Driffield and Pocklington.

For many people the history of the country house or the development of an urban street interests them less than discovering the age of their own house and information about its previous owners and occupiers. However the more modest the house the more difficult it is to discover when it was built and who lived in it. The following sections provide guidelines on dating the smaller house and cottage and the principal sources on ownership and tenancy.

More often than not people assume that their house is older than it really is. The assumption is often based on village tradition or the date of the earliest surviving deed. There are few smaller houses in the East Riding built before the early eighteenth century. This is partly because houses before that date were usually of poor quality building materials and quite modest in size. Documents and other contemporary accounts suggest that the majority of the houses before 1750 were single storey two- or three-bedroomed buildings of mud, timber and thatch. A survey of Leconfield village made in 1797 described twenty of the thirty-five houses as being of mud and thatch.[4] Similarly glebe terriers show that in the eighteenth century many East Riding parsonage houses were surprisingly humble. In 1764 Ulrome parsonage was described as 'a mere cottage built with clay walls and covered with thatch containing 3 rooms'.[5] Only three mud houses, at Beeford and Roos, are now known to exist.

The great lack of timber in the East Riding probably accounts for its limited use as a building material though a few examples of both cruck-framed and box-framed houses survive from the seventeenth century and many more are recorded in documents. A survey made of Settrington in 1599 recorded forty-six houses of cruck construction, the most primitive form of timber-framing whereby pairs of curved timbers form the framework for walls and roof.[6] Good examples of seventeenth century box-framed farmhouses can be seen at South Dalton, Wheldrake and Stillingfleet.

Although local stone was used for churches in the middle ages no pre-seventeenth century farmhouses or cottages built of chalk, cobble or limestone are known to survive. Along the western edge of the chalk Wolds where there are bands of limestone and ironstone there are examples of late seventeenth century stone houses and in eastern Holderness there are cobble houses from the early eighteenth century. The majority of the earliest surviving houses of the county are, however, of brick which had begun to be used for houses on the farmhouse level by 1700. Landowners such as the Burlingtons at Londesborough, the Hothams at Lockington and Scorborough and the Constables at Everingham had their own brickworks and were rebuilding their farmhouses and cottages in brick and pantile by 1750. In the later eighteenth century enclosures, agricultural improvements, urban development and the spread of water

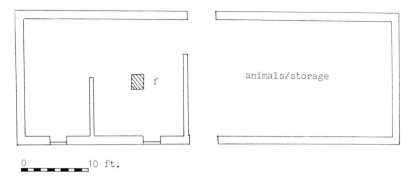

animals/storage

f

0 _____ 10 ft.

Figure 41: Longhouse plan: middle ages to seventeenth century

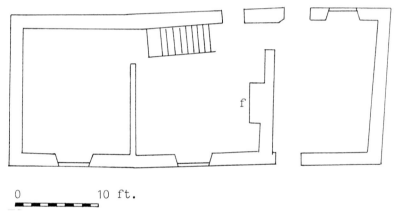

f

0   10 ft.

Figure 42: Hearth-passage plan: mid-late seventeenth century

communications escalated the use of brick and pantile. Slate came into the county by 1800 and often appeared in conjunction with fashionable hipped roofs.

Brick detailing such as tumbled gables, eaves and string courses and brick sizes can be used as dating features but a more important guide to the possible date of a house is the ground plan. One of the first tasks that should be undertaken is the production of an accurate measured drawing. From the plan and a close examination of the building the original layout may be deduced and it may fit into one of the four main plan types common in the East Riding (see figures 41-44).

The dates given are only indications of the approximate periods when this type of plan was common and should not be taken as precluding examples of the plan type occurring at earlier or later periods. B. Harrison and B. Hutton, *Vernacular houses in North Yorkshire and Cleveland*

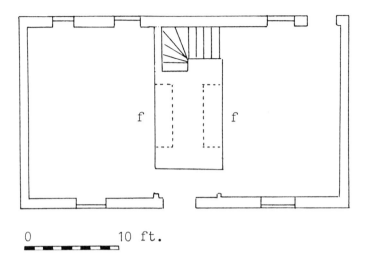

0   10 ft.

Figure 43: Lobby-entry plan: late seventeenth-early eighteenth century

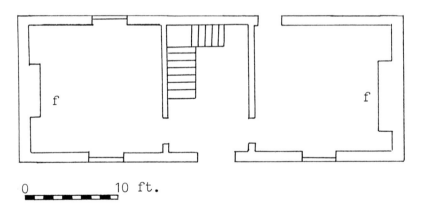

0   10 ft.

Figure 44: End-stack plan: common from 1730s onwards

(Edinburgh, 1984) is an excellent local study and in touching on the East Riding provides a scholarly and detailed coverage of building materials, construction and plan types. See also the general books by Barley, Brunskill, Clifton-Taylor and J. T. Smith listed in the bibliography at the end of this book.

DOCUMENTARY AND PRINTED SOURCES

Any study of an actual building must be accompanied by an examination of printed and documentary sources. A thorough survey of the sources for the history of buildings is given in chapter nine of W. B. Stephens, *Sources for English local history*, revised edition (Cambridge, 1981), and for the smaller house in particular in D. Iredale, *Discovering your old house*, 2nd ed. (Aylesbury, 1980) and chapters two and six in J. R. Ravensdale, *History on your doorstep* (London, 1982). K. J. Allison, *'Hull gent. seeks country residence'*, 1750-1850 (Beverley, 1981) illustrates well the information that can be gleaned on the building, ownership and tenancy of local houses from a wide range of sources.

The following are the most important sources with some comment on their availability in East Yorkshire.

Maps and plans

Maps should be the first source that you consult for they may verify or not the existence of a house on your site at a particular date. There are a wide range of maps available in local record offices or libraries. Begin with the printed plans and then work through the possible range of manuscript plans.

Printed plans

The earliest large-scale printed plans of the East Riding are those produced by T. Jefferys in 1771 and A. Bryant in 1828. These are principally of use in determining the existence or not of farms or other properties at a distance from a settlement.[7]

The first Ordnance Survey (OS) plans of East Yorkshire were published on the scales of one inch and six inches to the mile in the years 1853-56. Second and third editions of the six inch plans were published in 1892-94 and 1910. In 1888-92, 1910 and 1927-28 the county was covered by plans on the scale of twenty-five inches to one mile. In 1853-56 the OS published plans on the scale of five feet to one mile for four East Riding towns, Beverley, Bridlington, Hull and Howden. The first three towns were also covered in 1888-92 by plans on a scale of approximately ten feet to one mile. The three main locations of these plans are Hull Local Studies Library (HLSL), HCRO, and Beverley Public Library.

There are a number of other earlier printed plans of towns. For Hull see T. Sheppard, *The evolution of Kingston upon Hull* (Hull, 1911) and the selection reprinted by Humberside Libraries *The development of Kingston upon Hull shown through maps and views* (Hull, 1974). For Beverley and Bridlington there are plans by John Wood in 1828 but by far the best plans for studying building history are those produced by William Watson covering Market Weighton in 1848 and Pocklington in 1855. These unique plans show the elevation of each property in the towns and give the owners and occupiers and usually the occupation of the latter.

Tithe award plans

A tithe award plan and its accompanying apportionment, usually of the period 1839-50, are the best starting point for researching the history of a house or house site before the mid-nineteenth century. Tithe award plans provide a very accurate large scale map showing and numbering every parcel of land and every building. The plot number of each house can be traced in the accompanying apportionment and the owner and occupier discovered. Armed with this information fuller details on the households can then be obtained from the contemporary census enumerators' returns and changes of ownership searched for in the Registry of Deeds.

Unfortunately it is a minority of East Riding townships that are covered by tithe awards because a large number of places had allotments in lieu of tithes under parliamentary enclosure acts. A full collection of tithe awards is located in the Borthwick Institute of Historical Research (BIHR) (list available in HCRO) and there are some parish copies in HCRO.

Enclosure plans

For many East Riding settlements the earliest surviving plan is one associated with the parliamentary enclosure of the open and common fields in the late eighteenth/early nineteenth century. The majority of these plans show buildings but provide little other information on them. Many farms situated outside villages were built after enclosure and these plans provide an excellent starting point for a farm history. Buildings, however, were of secondary importance to the surveyor and there are cases where not all existing buildings are shown. The seventeenth century Southwold Farm, North Dalton, is not shown on the enclosure plan of the parish made in 1779. For the existence and location of enclosure plans see *Yorkshire enclosure awards*, edited by Barbara English (Hull, 1985).

Estate plans

The earliest plan of any settlement or part of it may be an estate map, dating from the late sixteenth century to early nineteenth century, showing the land and property of an individual owner and these, if also accompanied by a survey identifying the tenants, can be of immense value. Plans and surveys such as those for Settrington in 1599, Burnby in 1725, or South Cave in 1759 provide information on ownership and tenancy for the whole village but often only part of a settlement is covered. Some estate maps have seemingly accurate representations of the houses. The HCRO and HUL have extensive collections of estate plans which are indexed under place.

Title deeds

The deed of title to a property may include conveyances of land, mortgages, probate records, leases and plans and can take the history of a house and its site back to the middle ages. Few collections of deeds however are so extensive or reach back so far and many owners are disappointed to find that their own deeds may be no earlier than the twentieth century. If earlier deeds existed they may now be in the possession of a former owner or his solicitor or they could have been deposited in a record office. There are thousands of title deeds in HCRO and the relevant deeds might be there. However a surer way of tracing the descent of a property in the East Riding is through the register of memorials of deeds, now in HCRO. The Registry of Deeds was established in 1708 and from that date until 1974 all freehold land transactions in the county were supposed to be registered there. There is a place and person index. This excellent source has been effectively used by Keith Allison and by Ivan and Elisabeth Hall to trace the history of properties in Hull and Beverley.

The existence of a title deed is often taken by an owner as confirming the date of a property. The deed however more properly relates to the land on which the house stands and therefore is an indication of the existence or not of a house at a certain time but not usually an exact guide to dating the surviving structure. In some cases deeds can be more helpful and proclaim the building or rebuilding of a property either by recording its first appearance or by stating that it has been recently erected. A lease and release of March 1830 for 1-2 Southgate, Market Weighton describes one of the cottages as 'lately erected by Edward Garwood the elder upon the scite of an ancient cottage',[8] and in the same town 24-28 High Street is described in November 1824 as 'that new erected messuage (now divided into two distinct tenements)'.[9] But be wary of relying on such a statement in one isolated deed for phrases are often copied from earlier ones and the dating of the building will need to be confirmed by architectural evidence.

Manorial records

If there are no known title deeds or memorials in the Registry of Deeds relating to the property you are interested in, or only recent deeds, it may be because it was formerly copyhold, that is, held by copy of manor court roll. This form of land tenure was abolished and became freehold in 1925. The records of manorial courts contain details of 'surrenders' and 'admissions' by which copyhold property was transferred from one party to another. A full collection of court rolls will provide a succession of owners. The ownership of a cobble stone cottage in Southgate, Hornsea was traced back to the late seventeenth century through the court rolls and led to the discovery of a probate inventory relating to the house. The surviving records of many East Riding manors are to be found in HCRO and HUL.

Estate records

Another reason why earlier title deeds do not exist would be because the property was, or was formerly, part of a large estate belonging to a landed family, a charity, the church or a corporation. In this case you might find your researches hampered but if there is an extensive collection of estate papers such as rentals, surveys, maps, leases and building accounts you could possibly discover all you want to know about the date of building, any alterations and a full list of occupiers. The usefulness of estate records is illustrated in the case study below. Many such records, including those for the extensive estates of the Sykes family of Sledmere and the Constables of Burton Constable, are deposited in HCRO and HUL but others are located in more distant archives offices and private collections. The sixteenth to mid-nineteenth century records of the Londesborough estate are at Chatsworth, Derbyshire, those for the Leconfield estate at Petworth, Sussex, and for the Emanuel Hospital estate at Brandesburton in the City of London Record Office. Printed directories (see below) will tell you the names of the main landowners in each settlement in the nineteenth century.

Probate records

Where the names of owners and occupiers are known then it might be possible to find a relevant will in the BIHR. The will may briefly describe the property and also state to whom it is bequeathed. Of greater interest for the history of the house would be the existence, for the late seventeenth or eighteenth century, of a probate inventory in which the goods of the deceased person are listed often room by room, as will be seen in the case study below.

Rates, taxes and electoral lists

The returns of hearth, window and land taxes all provide lists of householders or owners which can add much to the history of an individual property but it would be necessary to know the name of the owner and/or occupier at the relevant dates. Hearth tax returns for the 1670s list all the householders in a town or village and indicate the size of the house by the number of hearths taxed. The original returns are in the Public Record Office but microfilm copies are in HCRO. There are window tax lists, giving the number of windows in individual properties, for places in the county of Hull in the 1770s in KHRO.

Parochial rate assessments listing the ratepayers year by year can assist in determining exactly when a property changed hands and these exist for some parishes from the eighteenth century or earlier and are to be found in the BIHR, HCRO and KHRO. Similar information can be gleaned from the more comprehensive land tax returns in the HCRO for each East Riding settlement for almost every year from 1780 to 1831. These returns initially just give the names of landowners and occupiers and the amount of tax paid but the later returns provide more information on the type of property taxed but do not identify it by name. Iredale shows how land tax returns can be used.[10]

After 1832 printed registers of electors were produced and these later become increasingly more informative in identifying the place of residence of the elector. Copies are kept in the HCRO.

Census enumerators' returns

If you know the Victorian occupiers of the house you are researching then you will be able to populate the house from the information supplied by the detailed census enumerators' returns which are available for 1841, 1851, 1861, 1871 and 1881. The returns themselves do not often identify the house by name or number except for larger or isolated properties and therefore it is necessary to be sure of the occupier in a census year. Microfilms of the returns are to be found in HLSL and Beverley Public Library.

Directories

Directories which list the main inhabitants of towns and villages are usually of limited value for tracing the occupiers and use of properties until the latter part of the nineteenth century and even then it is not usual, except in the case of towns, to give property names or street numbers. The best of the later directories, T. Bulmer's *History, topography and directory of East Yorkshire* (Preston, 1892; reprinted 1985), provides the majority of house numbers only in the case of Driffield and Bridlington but gives a detailed street directory for Hull. Certain properties such as inns and outlying farms are however generally named. The first directories for Hull and Beverley were produced in 1791 and the first for all the settlements in the East Riding in 1823. From 1840 there are two or three county directories each decade until 1937. The towns, particularly Hull, Beverley and Bridlington, are more fully covered in the later nineteenth century by street directories. The local history libraries in Hull and Beverley have the fullest collections of local directories.[11]

CASE STUDY: BURNBY HOUSES

The small village of Burnby, two and a half miles south-east of Pocklington, has been chosen to illustrate how the history of houses can be unravelled because it has an interesting collection of both buildings and documentary sources. Burnby was largely owned by the Anderson family of Kilnwick Percy, near Pocklington, and Lea, near Gainsborough, Lincolnshire. They inherited the estate in 1637 and retained it until 1917 and a search of their family papers, now fortunately deposited in the Lincolnshire Archives Office and HCRO, provided much useful information on the housing and tenants.

The first task was to walk around the village making notes on, and sketching and photographing, each of the older houses. A wide range of housing was evident which externally appeared to date from the early eighteenth to mid-nineteenth century. By the position of their stacks two whitewashed farmhouses and two cottages looked as if they could be early eighteenth century lobby-plan houses while a further pair of altered cottages seemed to have the bases of two timber posts in the front wall and would repay further investigation. The other houses were apparently nineteenth century including the large former rectory and two double-pile brick houses with hipped slate roofs and overhanging eaves.

Documentary and printed sources were turned to and a search made for surviving plans. Burnby is well covered in this respect and estate plans of 1725, 1825 and 1927 were discovered in the family papers. There is no enclosure plan as the parish was enclosed by private agreement in 1731 but a tithe award plan of 1849 is in the BIHR. On consulting these plans and the first edition six inch OS plan of 1852 some changes to the original opinion on the dating of these houses was necessary. Three of the possible lobby entrance plan houses were not on the 1825 and 1849 plans but were there by 1852; the rest of the present house sites were shown as built upon in 1725.

189

Figure 45: Hearth-passage plan: Oak Cottage, South Dalton (seventeenth century)

Figure 46: Lobby-entry plan: Bangram Hill Farm, Riccall (c.1700)

190

Attention was again paid to the houses and they were more closely investigated. Home Farm, which has an interesting centrally placed stack and could have been of around 1720, turned out to be of about 1850 and an old photograph produced by the owner of the house before it was whitewashed clearly showed Victorian brickwork with decorative window surrounds. The house attached to the former smithy, which from map evidence was built around 1850, has a similarly positioned stack and it is likely that both these were estate houses consciously copying an older style. A closer look at the pair of cottages to the north-east of the old rectory was disappointing as there was no indication of its possible timber framing from a limited examination of the interior although information supplied by one of the residents suggests that it might be cruck-framed. It was a chance remark however concerning the existence of 'old beams' that led me to the most interesting house in the village.

Sykes Farm

Externally one could be forgiven for supposing that Sykes Farm was built in the nineteenth century. At a distance the whitewashed walls, window openings and slate roof suggest a date of c.1850 (see figure 48). But once one is inside and sees the extensive timber framing of the east elevation an earlier and more complex building history is revealed (see figure 49). It is impossible to be definite about the dating of the various features and alterations but an accurate measured drawing made things much clearer (see figure 50).[12]

The seventeenth century house was apparently of two builds: a three-bay timber-framed lobby entrance farmhouse, with a later single-bay timber-framed addition at the southern end. At some point, possibly in the early eighteenth century, a single storey stone outshot containing kitchen, pantry and dairy was built on the east elevation and the front of the house was rebuilt in stone. In the mid-nineteenth century the house was extended westwards with a brick addition and a contiguous contemporary farm building; it was also heightened in brick and gives a gabled porch and overhanging slate roof. This century the south end collapsed and was rebuilt in brick. Internally the upstairs floors, which were cracked and distorted with age, were made of plaster, possibly gypsum plaster, which has the appearance of concrete and was a safeguard against a thatch fire spreading too quickly. The timber-framing is characteristic of the Vale of York although the braces on the older section which curve down from the post to the middle rail are more unusual than that on the southernmost bay which curves up to the wall plate.

Documentary sources helped to fill out the house's history. The 1725 plan gives all the owners and tenants of the houses in Burnby and Sykes Farm was then occupied by William Wilkinson. A William Wilkinson, husbandman, was buried on 30 June 1726 and a will and inventory for him were located in the BIRH.[13] Wilkinson, described as yeoman in his will, made three days before his burial, left a wife, Dorothy, and six children, three sons and three daughters. The accompanying inventory which no doubt relates to Sykes Farm names three parlours, a kitchen, a back room

Figure 47: End-stack plan: Bar Farm, Holme-on-Spalding Moor (c.1780)

Figure 48: Sykes Farm, Burnby from south west

192

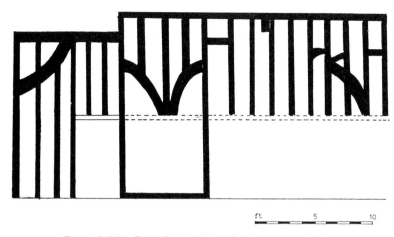

Figure 49: Sykes Farm, Burnby: timber-framing on east elevation

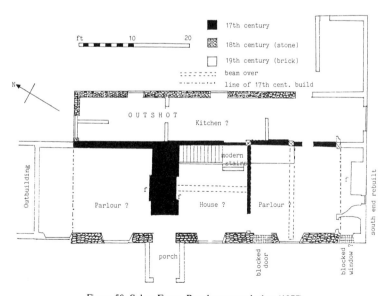

Figure 50: Sykes Farm, Burnby: ground plan (1977)

193

and chambers and suggests the existence of a main living room commonly called 'the house':

> An inventory of all and singular the good chattells and creditts of William Wilkinson of Burnby in the County of York (late deceased) apraised the seventh day of July Anno Domini 1726 apraised by us whose names are underwritten

	£	s	d
Imprimis his purse and aparrell	5	0	0
Item goods in three parlours two beds one table with chests chairs and other utensils	6	0	0
Item goods in the [house] one table one cupboard with pewter and brass and other implements	4	0	0
Item goods in the kitchin and in a back room one cpper one table and other lumber	2	0	0
Item goods in the chambers two beds	2	0	0
Item corn in the chamber and in the barn	16	0	0
Item wool in the chamber	5	10	0
Item beans stakht and helm which they stand upon	6	0	0
Item old hay stackt	5	0	0
Item corn standing upon the ground	98	0	0
Item arders and manures upon the fallows	10	0	0
Item waggons and ploughs and lumber belonging	10	0	0
Item six oxen and four heifers	50	0	0
Item tenn milk kine	20	0	0
Item seven fat kine	21	0	0
Item young beasts on the common	28	0	0
Item draught horses and other horses	53	10	0
Item 85 old sheep 35 lambs	23	0	0
Item swine and poultrey	3	0	0
Item debt owing to the deceased	70	2	0
Total	438	2	0

Appraised by us:
Robert Yare his marke
George Hesletine
William Clarke
Richard Oxtoby

It is likely that it is a far from complete list of the household goods but something of the life-style of the time can be reconstructed.

Wilkinson was a comparatively wealthy man and he probably farmed the same 180 acres of land in the open field of Burnby that his son Richard was farming in 1730. The farm passed through a further three generations of the family with Isaac Wilkinson being shown as the tenant in the tithe apportionment of 1843. By 1851 however the tenant was Charles Weddall who as well as farming the 180 acres of Sykes Farm acted as the local agent for the Andersons. The census enumerators' returns for 1851 show a large household: the farmer, his wife and widowed mother, a son and five

daughters, a house servant and three farm labourers living in — a total of thirteen. Twenty years later the returns record Weddall farming 250 acres with a household of ten.

Research in documentary sources at Lincoln, Beverley and York then helped piece together the history of the other early houses at Burnby. That Sykes Farm was not untypical is shown by a drawing discovered in Lincolnshire Archives Office, probably by Sir Charles Anderson, baronet, 1804-91, a noted antiquary who was non-resident squire of Burnby. The drawing, which is of a timber-framed house pulled down in 1856 (figure 51), is annotated 'Old farm at Burnby where Scott's New House is' and this can be identified from the tithe award plan as Burnby Grange. The 1725 plan shows it then tenanted by William Harper who when he died three years later left goods valued at £311 4s. His probate inventory records a house with six rooms, a house, a great parlour, two little parlours, a kitchen and a chamber.[14]

Two other mid-nineteenth century drawings of Burnby buildings were located in the York Minster Library. They are supposedly exterior and interior views of a massive marquee-like cruck-framed barn although in scale the two drawings do not seem to relate to each other. The exterior view shows a box-framed farmhouse in the distance which might be Grange or Sykes Farm. The drawings show the more substantially built houses for we know from an interesting contemporary comment that mud and thatch was the more typical building material of the village. In about 1813 the son of a Pocklington grocer, William Ullathorne, who was to become Roman Catholic bishop of Birmingham, was sent with his brother to school at Burnby and records that they lodged at the blacksmith's:

195

We slept in a dark attic under the thatch of their cottage, illuminated only by one pane of glass ... we sat, in the winter evenings, by the fire in the brick-floored room which served for kitchen, parlour, and hall ... the school house had mud walls, thatched roof and a clay floor.[15]

Hearth tax returns reveal that 80% of the thirty houses at Burnby in 1672 had only one hearth and these were probably one or two roomed. Only some of the farmhouses and the rectory would have been larger. Today the two largest houses in the village are the Old Rectory and Burnby House. The history of the former was traced through glebe terriers in the BIHR. A house but with no details is recorded in glebe terriers of 1716, 1726 and 1743 but not in 1764. This may mean that the nine roomed brick and tile house with cellar, pantry, dairy and 'other conveniences' mentioned in 1770 was newly built. A barn, thirty feet by fifteen, which stood in the parsonage grounds had been built between 1716-1726 of wood daubed with mortar and covered with thatch, and there were also a dovecote and a thatched brick stable. The terrier of 1781 names the dining room, the hall, the common sitting room, the kitchen, pantry and dairy with chambers over them. The house remained substantially the same until between 1825 and 1849 when the Reverend Charles Carr, rector 1818-61, 'materially enlarged and improved' it giving it a slate roof. As with the other houses in the village we can repopulate the rectory from the census enumerators' returns which show that on the night of 30 March 1851 the rector was absent and the household comprised his wife, two daughters, an aunt, a niece, housekeeper, housemaid, cook and footman.

Unlike the rectory the attractive Burnby House is substantially of one date. Deeds relating to the purchase of this former freehold property by Sir Charles Anderson in 1876 show that the land and a house divided into three tenements were acquired from the Ringrose family in 1830 by Simeon Templeman of Everingham.[16] Templeman is recorded as the owner and occupant of the house in 1843 but on the census night in March 1851 he and his wife were away and the house was occupied by his two young children, two young female house servants and two grooms. These facts suggest that this substantial house was built between 1830 and 1843 and the chance discovery of an article in the *Pocklington weekly news* for 24 August 1895 confirms this and provides an interesting story. Templeman it appears was a jockey who in 1837 rode the winner of the Derby for Lord George Bentinck. He was rewarded with £2000 which the newspaper records he used in 1840 to build 'a handsome mansion known as Burnby House, with grounds and gardens, evidently a gentleman's place' within sight of a thatched cottage where he formerly lived.

Much more could be written about the houses of Burnby and their occupants and with luck and diligent reseach similar material can be compiled on the houses of other villages.

Notes for chapter 12

1. R. W. Brunskill, *Vernacular architecture of the Lake Counties* (London, 1974), p.15
2. *Country Life*, 171, nos.4418-21 (1981)
3. J. Low, 'The founding of Hull Garden Village', *Landscape design*, 141 (1983), pp.27-8
4. West Sussex Record Office, Petworth House Archives 3075
5. J. Lewin and A. G. Parton, 'Building materials and glebe terriers: the case of the East Riding', *The local historian*, 8 (1968), p.48
6. A. Harris, *Survey of the Manor of Settrington*, YAS record series, 126 (Leeds, 1962)
7. See A. Harris, *The rural landscape of the East Riding of Yorkshire 1700-1850: a study in historical geography*, 2nd ed. (Wakefield, 1969), p.71
8. HCRO RD EK 84/94
9. HCRO RD DT 329/385
10. D. Iredale, *Discovering your old house*, 2nd ed. (Aylesbury, 1977)
11. For a list of local directories published before 1900 see the East Yorkshire Local History Society *Bulletin* no.3 (1971), pp.3-4
12. Mr and Mrs Dickinson kindly allowed me to survey Sykes Farm
13. BIHR York Wills August 1726
14. BIHR York Wills August 1728
15. W. Ullathorne, *Autobiography of Archbishop Ullathorne* (London, 1891), pp.8-9
16. HCRO DDAN

PUBLIC HEALTH AND PRIVATE MEDICINE

J. A. R. Bickford

There are no models for the comprehensive study of sources for the medical history of an area. Nor has there ever been a clear division between private medical treatment, with the doctor being paid directly by, or on behalf of his patient, and public provision, where an appropriate administrative body pays for treatment either pro rata, or on a contract basis. For the sake of clarity, as much as because material is scarce, the medical man as an individual will be considered towards the end of this chapter; but it should be remembered that at every stage he was the agent by whom the sick were directly affected.

Understandably medicine, both curative and preventative, has historically been more advanced in the town than in the country. For example, it is probably true to say that, in the nineteenth century at least, Hull was twenty five years ahead of the smaller towns in the East Riding, and that the rural areas lagged another twenty five behind them. Over many years legislation led inexorably towards the raising of standards even in the most backward areas. With the National Health Service (NHS) both private medicine and public health reached their apotheosis.

Some of the earliest medical provision — for maternity, fevers etc. — was made for paupers in workhouses. Information about sickness and treatment yielded by Poor Law records will be examined, together with ways in which parish and other records can be used to supplement them. Until some widespread epidemic struck — such as plague, cholera and, to some extent, smallpox — the health of the public generally was not regarded as a proper subject for concern. And until the causes of disease were understood there could be no rational approach to the problem. Generally speaking public health provision is well documented in East Yorkshire. As the bodies concerned multiplied in the course of the nineteenth century, so the information they collected proliferated. A brief review of what relates to health and sickness in the county will be attempted. Institutions, whether originally charitable or municipal, will be dealt with together. Some of the sources discussed will be used to outline the history of provision for pauper lunatics (as they were then known) in the East Riding from 1807, and the establishment of an asylum, now Broadgate Hospital, Beverley. It must be emphasised that access to hospital records is strictly limited. Unless they have been deposited with the appropriate record office application should be made to the administrator of the relevant Health Authority. Your local archivist will be able to advise on how this should be done.

Records of the Poor Law

Each parish made some provision for its sick, poor and incompetent elderly: by 1601 it was compulsory. The poor rate was assessed and levied by the churchwardens and administered by overseers, all usually local men. At first their accounts may appear only as a brief statement of moneys collected and disbursed. But they become fuller during the course of the seventeenth century; and often a separate book was kept. Before 1700 few of the many records extant for the East Riding parishes contain specific references to the condition for relief. Probably allowance was made for the surgeon's fees when relief was being calculated.[1] Reference to parish registers may help to decide the reason for awarding relief. Sometimes accounts name 'the itch', a fracture or 'being brought to bed', as well as the surgeon called in. His fee, and occasionally the cost of medicine, may be given; and soon after 1700 there are notes of payments to midwives. By the nineteenth century pregnant female paupers were commonly attended by both surgeon and midwife, who also had their travelling expenses paid.[2] In the 1700s many appeals were made to the Justices of the East Riding by the aged poor, the chronically sick, and disabled soldiers and sailors begging that allowances paid to them by the overseers should be increased. Few decisions are recorded.[3]

In Hull the situation was different. The problems inherent in the fluctuating population of a town and port placed unusual burdens on the two city parishes (Holy Trinity and St Mary the Virgin). The corporation was supervising the overseers of the poor by 1600; and in 1698, following the precedent set by London and Bristol, Hull obtained a private Act of Parliament permitting a 'Corporation of the Poor' to administer poor relief for the whole town. It is therefore necessary to search municipal rather than parish records for instances of medical care of Hull paupers. The appointment of a matron to the workhouse (known as Charity Hall) is noted in 1631, and reimbursement on a surgeon's bill in 1692.[4] A physician was appointed in 1700.[5]

Boards of Guardians had taken the place of overseers by 1837, at least so far as medical relief was concerned. They were responsible for much larger areas; but each 'union' of parishes was divided into 'districts', and in each of these a salaried, part-time surgeon was engaged, to attend the pauper sick and provide them with medicines. Generally he was paid extra for midwifery and special attentions. Treatment requiring the assitance of a colleague, e.g. an amputation, also commanded a fee. Prescriptions for extra food had, however, to go through the Board: in earlier days it could have been done directly. And instead of sending for a consultant from Hull, patients might be sent to York County Hospital or to Hull General Infirmary, where those Boards who thought it worth while had an annual subscription. Minutes of Board meetings also indicate the variable success of the campaign for vaccination against smallpox, and the reasons for that. The Guardians were not entirely autonomous: building alterations had to be reported to the Poor Law Board, and progress against smallpox to the Privy Council.[6]

Prison records

East Riding Quarter Sessions' books record provision of a sickroom in Beverley Gaol in 1793;[7] and minutes of Hull Gaol Committee contain details, for a somewhat later date, of an infirmary and the surgeon's concern for the health of his prisoners.[8] The attitude of a Beverley prison surgeon to the prisoners is referred to in a recent article by John Markham.[9]

Public health

Hull

Local Boards of Health were established in Hull and Beverley following the passage of the Public Health Act of 1848. This dealt with the supply of pure water and sanitation, the abatement of nuisances, the prevention of noxious occupations in residential areas and the regulation of lodging houses, slaughter yards, etc. The Local Government Act of 1858 added the responsibility of ensuring that all new buildings were supplied with water and drainage; and that all unsuitable habitations were condemned. Measures had to be taken to prevent the spread of infectious diseases (cholera, smallpox) from ships by quarantine, and by isolation of victims in special hospitals. The whole town council of Hull constituted its local Board of Health. In 1876, Boards of Health were renamed Urban Sanitary Authorities. Hull Sanitary Committee became in turn the Health Committee (1912-29), Health and Public Assistance Committee (1929-38) and Health Committee again (1938-74). Minutes are, in effect, continuous from 1851.[10] Reports were produced on, for example, cholera (1893-94), maternity and child welfare (1918-29), the blind (1920-49) and mental deficiency (1914-50). In urban areas, Boards of Guardians were made responsible for executing the provisions of the Diseases Prevention Act, which sometimes resulted in conflict with the Hull Board of Health, especially with regard to quarantine. The responsibility continued under the Public Health Act of 1872.

The sanitary state of Hull has been well covered in successive general histories. Among specialist studies, George Patrick's summary of measures taken up to 1980, and Bernard Foster's vivid description of the hazards to which the inhabitants were exposed in the nineteenth century, deserve to be read in conjunction.[11]

East Riding

The Public Health Act of 1872 nominated the Guardians as sanitary authorities in rural areas. Reports now kept in the Humberside County Record Office (HCRO) deal with the familiar preoccupations of pure water, substandard dwellings and the disposal of sewage; and are available for Beverley (class RSBE), Driffield (RDSR), Howden (RSHO), Skirlaugh (RSSX), Patrington (RSPA), Cottingham and so on, for varying lengths of time. Later material for parts of Cottingham and Sculcoates which were incorporated in Hull by various boundary extensions may be found in the Kingston upon Hull Record Office (KHRO).[12] There were powers for dealing with nuisances, for which separate reports, again in the HCRO, by the Inspector for Patrington survive (RDPA). The Bridlington authority — successively a Board, an Urban District and a Borough — produced very full proceedings: these reports are also in the HCRO but have yet to be classified. No major progress was made until the Council in Bridlington appointed its own Medical Officer of Health (MOH) in 1906. Against the wishes of many rural authorities a tuberculosis officer was appointed; and dispensaries and eventually a sanatorium were established.[13] The official diary of the MOH for Withernsea covers the period 1898-1924, and that for Driffield 1932-47.[14]

Typical issues

Pure water
The provision of drinking water was a problem for every local authority, and particularly difficult for Hull. Before the cholera epidemic of 1849 the connection between impure water and the spread of diseases was not fully realised. The story of Hull water undertaking (including the dramatic episode of Newington Waterworks) is told in a quincentenary publication by the Corporation Water Department of 1947.[15] It can be amplified by a whole series of Water Bills, etc., to be found in KHRO. The state of hygiene in Beverley can be surmised from petitions against the Water Bill for that town heard by a Select Committee of the House of Lords in 1874 and 1881: these can be consulted in Beverley Public Library (BPL).

Child health
As parochial schools were gradually incorporated in a national educational system so the health of schoolchildren came within the purlieu of the MOH. Many log books are in existence, some now deposited in record offices, some still with the school. From about 1870 they report outbreaks of infectious disease, and sometimes the fatal outcome, which can often be traced further in the registers and annals of the parish. By 1900 some attempt was being made to correct children's defects. Those with poor eyesight and hearing were noted and, where possible, treated, and special provision made for their schooling, as well as for young epileptics and defectives, outside the county. Such concern lay behind the founding of an orthopedic hospital at Kirkby Moorside, North Yorkshire, which was principally for children with tubercular bone and joint lesions. Reports of the Medical Officer to the Education Department were published annually from 1908 and are now in the HCRO. Comparable material for Hull, located in the KHRO, starts a little later.

Hospitals and dispensaries

Local authority hospitals
Until quite recent times a 'hospital' meant an almshouse. The hospitals of the present day have usually evolved either from charitable institutions or from workhouses. The latter were commonly provided with infirmaries. As a result, a rudimentary medical service developed, to take care of the sick paupers of the neighbourhood, and the indigenous population of orphans, deserted wives, elderly and vagrants. Lying-in wards were common. One was specifically licensed in 1809 (perhaps not solely

for paupers) in conjunction with the poorhouse at Bishop Burton, for that parish, Etton and Leconfield.[16] Further specialisation during succeeding decades resulted in separate wards for the elderly, for consumptives and lunatics, and the appointment of a surgeon whose sole duty lay in the workhouse. During the cholera epidemic of 1849 Sculcoates Union employed many extra doctors, some of whom contracted the disease and died.[17]

A much better service was already being provided for the more fortunate poor by voluntary hospitals (see below); but they could not reach everyone who needed in-patient treatment. The Sanitary Committees sought to remedy this by establishing medical and surgical wards in space allotted to them by the Boards of Guardians in workhouses. Specific legislation was necessary for the building of separate fever and maternity hospitals.

Voluntary hospitals

The large medical institutions in Yorkshire — York County Hospital (founded 1740), Leeds Infirmary (1767) and Hull General Infirmary (1782) — were the result of private effort, primarily by members of the local medical 'faculty'. They were built with money raised privately and maintained by voluntary subscription, with the consultants giving their services free. For Hull General (later Royal), there are some annual reports from 1811, and a fairly complete run from 1881, to be found in Hull Local History Library. Less easily available are minutes of the Board of Governors, lists of staff medical and lay, account books and reports (none complete or consecutive), and more ephemeral material like commemorative programmes on the occasion of a royal visit, or an extension opening.[18] This material has been used, variously, in the compilation of histories of the infirmary published in 1873, 1888, 1948 and 1982, which are listed in the bibliography for this chapter. There is also a little documentation for the Victoria Hospital for Sick Poor Children (now merged with Hull Royal Infirmary), and some references to Princess Mary Hospital, Sutton. Lloyd Hospital and Dispensary, Bridlington, is also a voluntary foundation. It has a competent published history, and its records are deposited in the HCRO.[19]

Mental hospitals

Psychiatric hospitals in this area were preceded by a number of private asylums for which lists of patients, returns, correspondence and plans survive.[20] Applications for licences were made to the Justices in Quarter Sessions.[21] A brief account by J. A. R. and M. E. Bickford of the fourteen houses so licensed was published in 1976 entitled *The private lunatic asylums of the East Riding*. The Hull and East Riding Refuge (which originated as Sculcoates Refuge in 1814) catered largely for paupers; and was purchased by the City Council in 1849 to become the Hull Borough Asylum. Records of patients, correspondence and accounts are in the KHRO; its history was summarised in 1981.[22] A new asylum for the city was built at Willerby, East Yorkshire in 1883, and renamed De la Pole Hospital in 1939. Asylum Committee minutes up to 1948, with other records not currently accessible, are also at the KHRO; some plans and photographs are with the East Yorkshire Health Authority. A centenary history was published in 1983.[23]

For Broadgate Hospital, Beverley (formerly East Riding County Asylum) there is material of administrative interest, together with the County Council's Asylum Committee minutes, at HCRO. Sources will be looked at in more detail in connection with the case study later in this chapter. Reports of the Commissioners in Lunacy, and of the Boards of Guardians, for both Broadgate and De la Pole, are at HCRO and KHRO respectively.

National Health Service

In 1948 workhouses as such ceased to exist. Sculcoates Workhouse had been taken over by Hull Corporation some years earlier, and now became Kingston General Hospital. The Western General Hospital — whose site was later used for a new Infirmary — arose from Hull Workhouse.[24] Part of Beverley Workhouse was developed as the Westwood Hospital.[25]

The transfer of both voluntary and local authority hospitals to the NHS is chronicled in Hospital Management Committee (HMC) minutes. General hospitals in Hull were administered by 'A' group HMC, and special hospitals by 'B' group. The minutes cover the 1948-74 period, as do records of the Leeds Regional Hospital Board and of East Riding hospitals (now in the HCRO). Those of Bridlington, formerly included with Scarborough, are also now at Beverley. The *Hospitals' year book* (incorporating Burdett's *Hospitals and charities* in 1899, and later becoming the *Hospitals and health services year book*) gives useful statistical information, and enumerates lay, as well as medical, staff of hospitals and local health authorities. The *Victoria County History, East Riding* inevitably remains the best published general account of the subject.

General and specialist dispensaries

Dispensaries, charitably funded, were an early form of out-patient department. They required little paper work, and for that reason must be traced chiefly in newspapers and directories. Medicine was issued free to the poor, domiciliary visits being made if required. The York General Dispensary began as early as 1740. None is so far known in the East Riding before 1800; but in 1812 a young doctor from Seamer was said to be Dispenser to the Sculcoates Guardians. This may have been the Dispensary which in 1817 amalgamated with one set up three years earlier in Hull. The 'Hull and Sculcoates' had a panel of consultant physicians and surgeons, and a resident medical officer. Assistant dispensers were usually senior students from the Hull and East Riding School of Medicine and Anatomy, until it closed in 1869. The Dispensary later opened two branches, listed in the Hull Community Council's *Social services in Hull*, published in 1930. In 1957 its assets were converted to a Trust for the sick poor, and its main premises (in Baker Street, Hull) were turned over to the NHS for mass radiography.[26] There are a few late annual reports in Hull Central Library. The low maintenance costs of dispensaries made them suitable for smaller centres. There was one in Driffield by 1822. The following year one opened in Beverley, and some public correspondence and reports of about 1831 are to be found in BPL. Another opened in Bridlington a few years later.

No specialist dispensaries are known in the county; but in Hull several sprang up in the course of the nineteenth century. A lying-in charity, for poor but respectable mothers, was inaugurated in 1802. The matron could call on a number of surgeons and midwives from her office located between Dock Street and George Street. It was absorbed into the Corporation Midwifery Service in 1926. Also in 1802, a vaccination centre was set up in Whitefriargate; this transferred to the Infirmary a few years later. The first of several dispensaries for diseases of the eye and ear was in existence by 1822, but probably did not survive the death of its founder in 1850.[27] One such did: the Orthopedic Hospital, founded by surgeon Robert Hagyard (1858-94), which treated mainly out-patients from 1887, was in operation (though under another name) until 1928. Several homeopathic dispensaries made their appearance from about 1850 and one, at least, was still here a century later. During much the same period the friendly societies had a combined dispensary in Hull.

Friendly societies

For working men who hoped never to be classed as 'pauper', yet feared to find themselves unable to afford medical fees, an early form of insurance was provided by friendly societies. Weekly payments were guaranteed to members, once their sickness or incapacity was certified as genuine by the society's registered surgeon or apothecary. The sum was usually reduced after the first year. A lump sum (of about £3) was payable on the death of a wife. In many cases such a subscription obviated the need for accommodation in the workhouse for a sick man and his family.[28]

Medical biography

The identification of medical men before 1845 is far from easy. Talbot and Hammond found no one practising in Hull during the medieval period though they were unable to examine all provincial archives; they did, however, find several at work in Beverley and district.[29] The small number of physicians, including a number of surgeons and apothecaries, who took up the freedom of Hull can be traced from about 1400 in the Bench Books of Hull Corporation. So, too, can their apprentices, who frequently practised elsewhere in the county later. Diocesan archives may also be useful here. Some of the nominations received by the Archbishop of York for licences for surgeons and midwives relate to the East Riding for the period 1660-1790. There are fewer relevant subscription and attestation papers: surgeons had to produce testimonials from colleagues; a midwife required signatures of women, safely delivered, who would vouch for her skill in her 'mystery'. Both were required to swear loyalty to Church and state: examples are to be found in the Borthwick Institute of Historical Research.

Local directories begin to be useful just before 1800. The *Medical directory* commenced annual publication in 1845. Alphabetical entries give professional qualifications, and details of posts and publications. Useful on provincial institutions, it is one of the few sources for the Hull and East Riding School of Medicine and Anatomy (1831-69). Local MOHs are also listed. The compilers relied in large measure on information supplied to them and, particularly during the first decade of publication, this was not necessarily correct. Specialist journals such as *The Lancet* and the *British medical journal* contain obituaries and other useful material, but are not readily available. On the other hand, Munk's *Roll of the College of Physicians*, and Plarr's counterpart for the Royal College of Surgeons, will be found in larger reference libraries.[30] Practitioners in Hull from 1400 to 1900 are included in a recent biographical index by J. A. R. and M. E. Bickford, *The medical profession in Hull* ... (Hull, 1983), in which the sources and methodology of medical biography are also discussed in a manner equally applicable to the county as a whole.

CASE STUDY: THE CARE OF THE MENTALLY ILL IN THE EAST RIDING

The history of provision for the mentally ill paupers of the Riding can be traced largely through the indexes to Justices' minute and order books in the HCRO.[31] Accommodation for pauper lunatics was first discussed by the Justices in 1807, when their conclusion was that, for such small numbers, the county gaol in Beverley could be adapted. This was nearly twenty years after lunatics in Hull had been moved from the House of Correction into the Workhouse.[32] In the event, no action was taken. In 1811 the Justices informed the General Sessions in York that they would provide for their own lunatics, and not in cooperation with neighbouring counties. By 1815 they had decided to do neither, perhaps because private asylums were being established in the Riding, and they proposed to use them instead.

The Refuge was founded in Sculcoates in 1814; and five years later the Justices instructed the building committee to contract with the proprietors to receive their vagrant and pauper lunatics. By 1828 there was dissatisfaction with Sculcoates Refuge and it was resolved in 1834 to remove all East Riding paupers to Mrs Taylor's house in Cottingham.[33] In fact there were so many insane to be provided for that the Refuge (by then the 'Hull and East Riding') still held seventeen paupers in 1847. There were also eleven at Dunnington, another small private house, four at Hessle and one at Moor Cottage, Nunkeeling.

John Beal, proprietor of Moor Cottage, had first been licensed in 1811 to conduct an asylum at Gate Helmsley,[34] North Yorkshire, moving to Nunkeeling in 1820-21. The Dunnington Asylum lasted till 1880. It sometimes placed advertisements in the *Medical directory* (see figure 52). The original proprietor was a Preston Hornby — noted in volume two of Baines' *History, directory and gazetteer of the County of York* (Leeds, 1823) — apothecary of York who had first been licensed for a house at Osbaldwick, North Yorkshire. There he was succeeded by a widow, Mrs Frances Hotham, some of whose land in Dunnington he later purchased.[35]

PRIVATE HOUSE OF RETIREMENT,

(FOR THE RECEPTION OF INSANE PERSONS OF BOTH SEXES,)

DUNNINGTON HOUSE, NEAR YORK.

This Establishment is in a retired and healthy situation, about four miles from York. Its domestic comforts, gardens, and pleasure-grounds attached, render it equal to any other Establishment in the kingdom. The Patients are under the immediate superintendence of Mr. and Mrs. HORNBY, and partake of all the enjoyments of a domestic life. **The amusements** are varied and numerous. The Billiard Table and Bowling Green afford ample exercise for those whose unhappy situation renders walking or riding exercise from home improper. The house is attended by an eminent Surgeon, *but the friends of any Patient may make their own choice of a Medical adviser when occasion requires.* Patients attended from their own residences, travelling expenses only charged. The terms will vary according to the accommodation required.

Figure 52: Advertisement for Dunnington House, near York (from the *Medical directory*, 1869, p.1069)

The East Riding Justices again considered having their own asylum in 1841. Two years later they agreed with their colleagues in the North Riding to erect a joint institution, with the total costs and responsibilities to be divided proportionally. In 1845 land was purchased from Earl de Grey in Clifton, near York; and the North and East Ridings' Asylum opened in 1847, only just in time to comply with the recent legislation on the subject.[36] At this time there were thirty-eight pauper lunatics confined to the county though, according to the regular returns of the overseers of the poor, others were cared for at home, or were confined in workhouses.[37]

Despite enlargement in 1851 the asylum was overcrowded by 1864. A year later the decision was taken to dissolve the union between the two Ridings, and a Committee of Visitors was set up by the East Riding Justices to plan the erection of its own asylum. The building contract was signed in 1867, and four years later the asylum opened.[38] Reports of the Asylum Committee (East Riding County Council from 1889) were published annually to 1947. They record changes to the buildings, the provision of heating, etc., staff changes and major epidemics among the inmates.

Minutes of Number Five Hospital Management Committee (E.R.) note, in 1948, alteration of the name of the asylum to Broadgate Hospital, and the many changes that followed in subsequent years. Some references can also be found in the minutes of the Mental Health Committee of Leeds Regional Hospital Board, now in the HCRO. Remarks about the hospital water supply were made in the petition against the Beverley Water Bill, referred to earlier. Much earlier, the second report of the County Council Asylum Committee (1890) recorded eight cases of typhoid, with one death. A consultant engineer gave evidence that asylum sewage contaminated the Beverley Water Works well, from which the asylum drew its water.

Information about doctors at the asylum is given in successive medical directories. The most distinguished of these doctors was evidently E. B. Whitcombe, described as 'surgeon' in 1880. He had qualified in 1868 from

206

Sydenham College, Birmingham, and published papers in the *Journal of mental science* in 1870 and 1876. From Walkington he went to the City Asylum at Winson Green, Birmingham, later becoming Professor of Lunacy and Mental Diseases at Mason College (afterwards Birmingham University). He was president of the Medico-Psychological Association in 1891.[39]

M. D. Macleod succeeded him as medical superintendent. He was a graduate of Edinburgh University, and had been employed at the Cumberland and Westmorland Asylum in Carlisle. He died in 1908, at the early age of fifty-six. There is a memorial in Beverley Minster and a stone in the graveyard at Walkington Parish Church.

M. A. Archdale, although medical superintendent, moved to a similar post at Fulbourn in Cambridge (where he obtained the Diploma of Psychological Medicine in 1922) and then to the Borough Mental Hospital, Sunderland. He had been a Major in the Royal Army Medical Corps, attached to the 3rd Northumberland Field Ambulance, in the First World War. Other doctors, employed for short periods, often settled afterwards in private practice, and may easily be traced in the directories.

The returns of the census of 1871, to be found in BPL, might have been expected to name some of the staff for the asylum due to be opened that October. In March, however, the buildings were not yet complete, and only a bricklayer, his wife and child, his mother-in-law and two male 'boarders' were resident on the site. Amongst privileges enjoyed by senior resident staff was the purchase of provisions at cost price. Dr Macleod's bill for one quarter of 1896 was £29 (Clerk & Steward's petty cash book). James Owen, the Chief Attendant, had emoluments worth £40, and earned £90 per annum in 1918 (Officers' and Staff wages book). Retiring after thirty-six years his pension was £103 (Superannuation book). Previous asylum experience (if any) was noted in the Service Register of staff employed, with details of their current responsibilities.

From time to time a substantial number of paying patients was accepted (Private Patients' book) to help with the Asylum's finances. Injuries were recorded in the Casualties' book; and if a post-mortem was necessary the signature of the doctor who carried it out was often counter-signed by the Medical Superintendent (Post Mortem book). Pauper patients came from all parts of the county (Boards of Guardians' report books). In addition, for the best part of twenty years considerable numbers of pauper lunatics were accommodated (under contract) from asylums managed by the London Boroughs. Complaints were made by one such patient to Alice Holtby, J.P. (mother of the novelist Winifred Holtby) that 'the food was not what they were accustomed to; and they were given *cocoa* ...' (Reports of the East Riding Committee of Visitors). If straightjackets or isolation were employed a note had to be made (Mechanical Restraint and Seclusion book). The Pharmacy book makes clear how little medicine was used in the early days.

The wealth of sources for Broadgate Hospital (and to a lesser extent for De la Pole) serves to emphasise the paucity of pre-1948 material for the voluntary institutions. The reasons for this may lie in accountability.

Figure 53: Rear view of Broadgate Hospital c.1920, showing exercise 'gardens' for female patients and perimeter wall

Asylum officers derived their authority from the general public, whereas those of voluntary hospitals were responsible only to their subscribers. Furthermore, prior to the passage of the Voluntary Treatment Act of 1930, people were admitted to asylums only in consequence of a judicial order; and legal records are never destroyed lightly. To an extent this is true for parish records, for example those of the overseers of the poor. As the years passed doubts as to their relevance, and the inability to store them properly, led to the destruction or decay of much early material.

That medical practitioners kept records too is self-evident. Yet, except for a chance find in collections of family papers, they might never have existed. An account paid, a debt collected, a doctor's decease, almost always led to the clearing away of such unconsidered trifles. When a workhouse was enlarged or merged with another, or reorganisation took place at a higher level, wholesale destruction of papers referring to earlier phases normally took place. The past can then only be reconstructed from references in the press, or the transactions of other bodies. Early medical care has to be traced mainly in records that are non-medical in origin; and the student of more recent times will find that his access to many sources is restricted to protect individual privacy.

Notes for chapter 13

1. See G. Oxley, *Poor relief in England and Wales, 1601-1834* (Newton Abbot, 1974), pp.65-67
2. Parish account books may be found in the BIHR and HCRO
3. HCRO/QSP
4. KHRO Bench Book 5, 275 and 8, 319
5. KHRO Workhouse minute book, 1698-1737
6. HCRO and KHRO/PU
7. HCRO/QAG
8. KHRO/TCM
9. J. Markham, 'The East Riding House of Correction, Beverley and Robert Peddie, its most famous prisoner', *Journal of local studies*, 1 (1980), pp.21-46
10. KHRO/BHH
11. G. Patrick, *A plague on you, sir!: a community's road to health* (Hull, 1981); B. Foster, *Living and dying: a picture of Hull in the nineteenth century* (Hull, [1983])
12. KHRO/BHB-BHN
13. County Council Reports, HCRO
14. Both in the HCRO
15. Hull Corporation Water Department, *History of the water supply of Kingston upon Hull* (Hull, 1947)
16. HCRO/QSV/2/2 H303
17. Minutes of Sculcoates Board of Guardians 1848-50, KHRO/PUS
18. Hull Health Authority, refer to the Administration
19. T. R. Wilson, *Lloyd Hospital, Bridlington 1868-1968* (Beverley, 1968)
20. HCRO/QAL
21. HCRO/QSV
22. J. A. R. Bickford, *The old Hull Borough Asylum 1849-83* (Hull, 1981)
23. J. A. R. Bickford, *De la Pole Hospital 1883-1983* (Hull, 1983)
24. Some minutes KHRO/PUH
25. Beverley Union Minute Book HCRO/PUA
26. VCH ER I p.384
27. A certificate of competence given to a trainee is in KHRO at DMM 48
28. HCRO QDC 2/1 1789 and QSV 1-9 1782-1805; KHRO CQB 102
29. C. H. Talbot, and E. A. Hammond, *The medical practitioners in medieval England: a biographical register* (London, 1965)
30. W. Munk, *The roll of the Royal College of Physicians of London*, 5 vols (London, 1878-1968); V. G. Plarr, *Plarr's lives of the Fellows of the Royal College of Surgeons*, 2 vols (London, 1930)
31. HCRO/QSV
32. VCH ER I p.439
33. J. A. R. and M. E. Bickford, *The private lunatic asylums of the East Riding*, EYLHS, 32 (Beverley, 1976), p.17
34. This is recorded in the Quarter Sessions Records, York Minster Library
35. Manor Court Rolls, BIHR
36. See W. L. Parry-Jones, *The trade in lunacy: a study of private madhouses in England in the nineteenth century* (London, 1972)
37. HCRO/QAL; KHRO/CQB
38. B. Vickerman, *Centenary of Broadgate Hospital, Beverley* (Hull, 1971)
39. Further information obtainable from the Royal College of Psychiatrists, 17, Belgrave Square, London

14

LOCAL HISTORY IN THE CLASSROOM

Jane Lancaster

In the late sixties when I was training to be a teacher local history was occasionally mentioned as being 'a good thing'; but living as I then did in Birmingham where everything old seemed to be in process of demolition, I assumed that local history must apply to somewhere else and that I could concentrate on Elizabeth I or the industrial revolution and not worry about these new fangled ideas. Now had I lived in the East Riding not even I, in my extreme ignorance, could pretend that there was no local history. It seems unavoidable. Look at an Ordnance Survey (OS) map of the area and in gothic script it says "Tumuli", or in small capitals ROMAN ROAD. Walk around Beverley and you can see ancient churches and an old gate with a notice proclaiming it cost less than a hundred pounds to build. Go into Hull and you can see abandoned docks and warehouses, and even a golden statue of a man on a horse astride a public lavatory.

This visibility makes it easy to interest children in the past which is literally all around them. Younger pupils are naturally observant; the task of the teacher is to show them how to interpret what they see. As they get older their level of understanding will increase, but one of the beauties of local history is that it can be studied with most age groups and any level of ability, and all children will learn something about their environment and why it looks the way it does.

The 'new' history

Since the mid-seventies the new approach to history has infiltrated many secondary schools. Based on the Schools Council Project it aims to teach historical skills by using primary evidence and to avoid history as 'just one damn thing after another'. A key part of the syllabus is entitled 'History around us', and here the students study a local topic, coursework on which represents up to 20% of the final mark in both 'O' level and CSE.[1] The topic is chosen by the teachers and the scheme of work must satisfy three criteria: the students must:

(i) describe and interpret something in the local environment and explain how and why it developed;
(ii) use and evaluate the available evidence, both primary and secondary, in order to find out information for themselves;
(iii) acquire an empathetic understanding of people in the past.

In the section which follows I shall describe in some detail how the study of local history is approached in secondary schools with reference to these three objectives which seem to me necessary if local studies are to rise above the anecdotal or antiquarian level. There are, however, more open-ended or impressionistic approaches possible which are more suited to non-examination classes of all ages in both primary and secondary schools, and some projects which are less teacher-directed are also discussed.

SOME LOCAL HISTORY PROJECTS

The study of a street

The detailed study of a street has immense educational potential; providing the street is carefully chosen, much of the history of a town can be discovered. What I have to say applies to Whitefriargate, Hull, but the same approach could be used on any street more than about 150 years old. Students of mine have successfully studied some of Hull's less prominent streets like Dagger Lane or Finkle Street, or shorter streets like Land of Green Ginger, with great success. One boy managed to write eighty A4-sized pages on Nelson Street, and won a local history prize in the process. Although this study is aimed at fifteen to sixteen year olds of a wide ability range, there is no reason why much younger children could not attempt it.

Old maps provide an ideal introduction. Humberside County Leisure Services has produced a set of twelve maps and views of the city which are easily obtainable, relatively inexpensive, and so fascinating to children that it is hard to tear them away from them.[2]

A simple preliminary exercise is to locate the street in question, note variations in its name which might be complete changes or simply altered spelling, and then by use of a dictionary of place names get an idea of the meaning of the word. Written work at this stage would consist of comprehension questions on the maps plus sketches of the location of the street.

The next stage would be to show the class photographs or slides of different architectural styles and teach them to tell the difference between, say, Georgian, Victorian and Edwardian buildings. They can easily learn to recognise Georgian windows and it does not take them long to realise that if these small panes are on a dormer bungalow on a new housing estate they are unlikely to date from the eighteenth century. Most pupils like drawing, perhaps because it seems less like hard work than writing, and sketches of different types of windows and doors together with notes on the different sizes of bricks would reinforce this lesson.

Only at this stage would I take the class to look at the site. One of the important aspects of the visit is to get them to look above eye level to see what is above the shop fronts or offices. Practice for this could be during a journey on the top deck of a bus — for once in their lives the students could legitimately do their homework on the way to school! Blocked up windows, faded notices, carvings, dates, even statues; many of these can be seen in any shopping street. Even an area as historically unpromising as a 1950s housing estate is not without possibilities. One unexpectedly sunny autumn day I took a small group around such an estate, and they became very adept at spotting changes that had been made and asking questions such as why is this pub called the *National* (I think we solved that one) and why is that pub called the *Marrowbone and Cleaver*? However, unless the site visit is very

Whitefriargate Survey		Name	
		Date of Survey	

Number of Building	ground floor	first floor	second floor
	(a) name of shop or business	(a) what is it used for?	(a) what is it used for?
	(b) what type of shop or business?	(b) sketch and label a window	(b) sketch/ describe any carvings you can see
	(c) what materials are used in the shop-front?		

Figure 54: Street survey form: Whitefriargate, Hull

212

Whitefriargate through the ages - how do we know about its past?

Here is some information about developments in the street over the last 800 years. By looking carefully you can find evidence in the street about each piece of information.

The evidence takes many forms; it could be a carving, a sign, a style of architecture, or a name.

1. There was a Carmelite friary on the south side of the street

   clue (1)

   clue (2)

2. After the Reformation, when the friary was closed down, its land was bought by a man called Thomas Ferres.

   clue (1)

   clue (2)

3. Thomas Ferres later gave this land to the Brethren of Trinity House

   clue (1)

   clue (2)

4. King Charles I was refused entry to the town in 1642. This marked the beginning of the English Civil War, 1642-45

   clue:

5. There was a large inn built by George Pycock, called the Neptune

   clue:

6. The Neptune Inn was built between 1794-97, which means it is a Georgian building.

   clue:

7. Hull's foreign trade grew in the eighteenth century, and they collected more customs duties.

   clue:

8. The prosperity of Trinity House grew with the prosperity of Hull.

   clue:

9. The buildings on the North side of the street have a lot of different owners, while the buildings on the south side are all owned by Trinity House.

   clue:

10. Until 1851, there was a workhouse on the site now occupied by Littlewoods, where over 350 poor people lived.

    clue:

Figure 55: Street survey form: Whitefriargate through the ages

213

informal, the class must be provided with a worksheet to direct their search in the right direction. In the case of Whitefriargate this could be very simple, as in figure 54. Having completed this systematic survey, they would be asked to complete a further questionnaire, as in figure 55 to see if they can interpret the visual evidence, to use it as clues to the past.

Back in the classroom, after discussing what has been observed, I would introduce them to the Department of the Environment's list and description of buildings of special architectural or historical interest (accompanied by a glossary, since the vocabulary is very specialised), which they could incorporate into their report on what they saw. The report might go something like this:

'On March 1st 1983 we visited Whitefriargate, Hull. It is a pedestrianised street and was busy with shoppers. We started at the east end of the street.

Numbers 1-2 are occupied by *Thrifty Clothes*. The building has plate glass windows and an orange coloured plastic sign. It was built in the early nineteenth century and is made of red brick and painted stone. The window overlooking the corner of Trinity House Lane has curved glass in it'.

This is a combination of observation and use of the DOE list to supply extra information; after that exercise is finished work on the historical explanation can begin.

First they could look at old photographs and drawings, of which the Local Studies Library in Hull has an excellent collection. These will have to be photocopied after copyright has been checked, but the new machines reproduce photographs very clearly. Pictorial evidence can be used in two ways: firstly, to show what a site looked like in the past; and, secondly, to stimulate discussion on the validity of primary evidence — in other words, does the camera lie? For example, one of the photographs available shows Whitefriargate in 1867 with Beverley Gate at the west end of the street. It had apparently been put up in honour of a royal visit and was soon taken down again but without that piece of information the student could easily be misled.

After the photographs, the trade directories. The Hull directories were printed in streets rather than alphabetically by name from the 1840s. If a sequence of directory entries is taken at, say, twenty-year intervals, they can be analysed to see what differences in trade and residence have taken place. This could be a rather sophisticated idea for younger or less able children, but the broad pattern of change from dwelling houses through workshop to retail shops and to multiple stores can probably be seen.

The next stage is to look at the census returns. The 1841 census is probably not worth the effort required since the amount of information contained in it is limited. The 1851 census is much better. More able or older students can usually read the enumerators' returns in the original handwriting, although having them use the microfilm readers in the local history library is a recipe for frustration. It is possible to obtain a copy of one page of the returns to enable the students to get the flavour of the documents, but a typed transcript is much easier for the students to handle.

Some simple statistical work can be done, for example plotting family size, numbers of servants, or migration patterns. This can either be done manually or by using one of the computer programs designed to handle census material. If the data is only from one street it may not, of course, be very typical of the whole town but statistical validity is probably of less importance with thirteen to sixteen year olds than learning something of the past by handling the actual data.[3]

The final stage is to use secondary sources to look for an explanation of what has been discovered by observation on site and by using the documentary evidence and to explain the clues found in figure 55. To continue with the Whitefriargate example, the students would need to know about the White Friars, Trinity House, Thomas Ferres, Charles I and the Civil War, the Poor Law and the Workhouse, the growth of trade in Hull, the expansion of the city, and the reasons for the decline and subsequent revitalisation of the Old Town. The problem here is that much of the printed material available is far too difficult for the average school child and as there is no short, simple history of Hull, materials such as information from the *Victoria County History*,[4] Storey's *History of Trinity House*,[5] or Sheahan's *History of Hull*,[6] it will have to be summarised or predigested by the teacher.

To conclude, I have gone into some detail to show an approach to local history teaching based firmly on two of the criteria outlined earlier. The third aim, empathetic reconstruction, could be based on material relating to Charles I being refused entry to the town, or on newspaper reports of conditions in the Workhouse shortly before it was closed in 1851. By studying a street in this way the student will have learnt some historical skills as well as something of the history of the town.

The development of Hull's docks

This is a local history project which has been carried out successfully for a number of years.[7] It fulfils two educational criteria. First, the personal investigation and description of a site; in this case, the eighteenth and nineteenth century docks ringing Hull's Old Town. Second, putting what is observed on site into historical context: in other words explaining the impact the industrial revolution had on Hull, how the merchants and others reacted to the growth of trade, and why alternative uses have had to be found for many of the docks and warehouses.

To carry out this project, students are given a resources pack which contains maps, statistics, and summaries of much secondary material on the development of Hull's docks. They are taken on a full day field visit, with a question sheet which encourages them to observe and to express their own opinions. Examples of these questions are:

A. *Posterngate: The Waterfront*
   1. What was the Waterfront used for before it became a hotel? (Clue: look upward)
   2. What evidence of restoration work can you see?

215

B. *Princes Street*
1. What is new in this street?
2. What is old in this street?
3. Do you like the restoration work? Yes/No. Why?
4. Would you like to live in one of these houses? Yes/No. Why?

C. *Humber docks and Humber dock basin, 1809*
1. What was the basin used for?
2. Can you find evidence of where the old dock gates used to be? Sketch the evidence.
3. Why were the lock gates needed?
4. Who was the moveable bridge built by and when was it built?
5. Why was the moveable bridge added on do you think?
6. What is the old lock keeper's house used for today?
7. What is the Humber dock used for today? Do you think this is a good use for the dock?

These questions are basically very simple; this is necessary when dealing with a wide ability range, but responses could be at different levels, and careful observation is necessary.

The second aim is to put the site into historical context. An 'O' level student guided by questions such as:

1. Why was a third dock necessary by 1818?
2. Why wasn't it built then?
3. What primary evidence do you have that Humber dock was overcrowded?

can write:

At the end of the French wars there was a massive trade boom creating a need for a third dock. By 1818 the volume of shipping at Hull went over the limit laid down in the 1802 Dock Act for the building of a third dock. Merchants, shipowners, the Hull Corporation and Trinity House met with the directors of the Dock Company to discuss a third dock, but the Dock Company wanted to change duties on river boats in return for financing the new dock. The merchants wouldn't agree, so nothing was done. By 1824 congestion was so bad that the Company was forced to agree to build a third dock. A parliamentary committee reported about the congestion in 1825. 'Many instances have lately occurred of ships having performed their voyages from St. Petersburg and other parts of the Baltic to the port of Hull in less time than ships have of late been able to pass from the River Humber to the Old Dock.'

The boy who wrote this achieved a C grade in his 'O' level examination. A better candidate would have shown more depth of understanding of the historical background. In this type of project, the teacher guides the student through pre-selected material, but the Old Town visit acts as an important stimulus, and sometimes leads to small moments of comedy. Last year one report from a member of my group contained an extremely blurred photograph, a study in blue and grey which was captioned: 'The River Humber on a dark afternoon'.

Joseph Pease's diary

This is another very successful component of the local history section of the 'O' and C.S.E. courses at Kelvin Hall School, Hull, and is designed to 'promote empathetic understanding of an earlier period'.

Joseph Pease (1688-1778) was a very successful Hull merchant, banker and industrialist. The students' task is to discover a few entries from his 'lost' diary. They are given a folder containing evidence almost entirely from primary sources.[8] This includes:

Joseph Pease's account of expenses and income for 1751
A letter from his sister Abigail, 1752
His grandson, J. R. Pease's jeweller's bill, 1778
Will of Abigail Pease
Memorandum 1776, engaging a new coachman
Eighteenth century pictures of Hull
Joseph Pease's share certificate in the Calder and Hebble Navigation 1776
Pages from Battle's *Hull Directory* for 1791.

Here is a typical entry:

A letter dated 26th October from Robert in Holland reached me today, after travelling on my new ship the *Beverley Gate.*

He is now enjoying learning the business with Clifford in Harlem. Robert is a most industrious young man, whilst learning the business he is also studying geography with the money I sent for his instruction.

The Dock Co. are fast gaining shareholders. I notice both Joseph and Henry Maister have shares in the Company.

The new dock is to be built with an entrance to the River Hull next to the Blayde's warehouse. Today I took a walk to see how things were going on. Nowadays I must walk with the aid of a stick, and today I stumbled as one of the drunken navvies kicked it away from me.

Hull is more and more like this nowadays, with the influx of navvies places like the Black Boy and Ye Olde White Hart are reaping extremely high profits as nearly all the ten shillings a week paid to them is spent on beer, women and cockfighting. It is a most terrible state of affairs.

This was written by a fifteen year old in the 1980s and despite some errors in context and vocabulary he has assimilated the evidence well, and understood something of life in eighteenth century Hull. Most of the students like the Pease diary section of the course, which proves to be an enjoyable way to learn history.

Graveyard surveys

So far I have looked at systematic, teacher-directed learning of local history. The next project is more discovery-based, and allows the students to collect their own data and follow up those topics which attract their interest. Obviously a few well-timed suggestions may be necessary but with favourable conditions, that is plenty of time, warm weather, and a teacher-pupil ratio of about 1:10 much can be achieved.

I have always been fascinated by graveyards. Our school, in common with an increasing number of secondary schools, has a so-called 'activities week' in July when the timetable is abandoned and pupils choose from a variety of options ranging from water skiing to vegetarian cookery, from camping to making a video film. I decided to call my week in the Western General Cemetery, Spring Bank, Hull, 'Down among the dead men', which proved surprisingly attractive, although one or two pupils who remembered that I had done some archaeology the previous year had to be disabused of the notion that we might be digging amongst the graves. So, armed with pens, but no spades, tape measures and the British Council for Archaeology recording forms, we set forth.[9]

The form is not easy for thirteen year olds to use, but we soldiered on and after five days had recorded most of the cemetery, which although it is very large had been so vigorously tidied up in the early seventies that only a fraction of the headstones remained. This meant that our record was of little historical use, since:

— using unskilled child labour leads to inaccuracies
— the form is not meant to provide demographic data
— the surviving stones were a non-random sample (largest, best preserved, most interesting) of a non-random sample (the wealthiest) of those buried in the cemetery.

Despite this the students learnt a little geology, in distinguishing the materials, a little history about shipwrecks, local notables, cholera, and the high infant mortality rate, and had a lot of fun.

The following summer, under the title 'The dead centre of Hull', we tried again, this time looking at church memorials and town centre burial grounds. By this time I had devised a new form (figure 56) more geared to producing demographic data, so the students used this in Sculcoates Cemetery where we were beset by wasps and the scent of mint humbugs (the Cemetery is next door to Needler's factory), in Holy Trinity Church and St Mary's Lowgate, in Spring Bank, and the Holy Trinity burial ground at the corner of Mytongate and Anlaby Road. The students made a lot of grave rubbings and with the help of members of Hull Architecture Workshop they took photographs.[10] When they started to write up their findings, the approach was far more impressionistic than I had intended. The students chose interesting or puzzling memorials and headstones and tried to explain them. The sort of questions they tried to answer were:

```
┌─────────────────────────────────────────────────────────────────────┐
│                                                                     │
│  GRAVEYARD _____   SURNAME ON GRAVE _____  │
│                                                                     │
│  DATE OF SURVEY _____                                     │
│                                                                     │
│  NAME OF SURVEYOR _____   REFERENCE NUMBER OF GRAVE _____   │
│                                                                     │
│                     DETAILS  OF  INSCRIPTION                        │
│                                                                     │
│  ┌──────────────┬───────┬───────────────┬─────┬──────────────────┐  │
│  │              │       │               │     │                  │  │
│  │ FULL NAMES   │  M/F  │ DATE OF DEATH │ AGE │ ANY OTHER DETAILS │  │
│  │              │       │               │     │                  │  │
│  ├──────────────┼───────┼───────────────┼─────┼──────────────────┤  │
│  │              │       │               │     │                  │  │
│  │              │       │               │     │                  │  │
│  │              │       │               │     │                  │  │
│  │              │       │               │     │                  │  │
│  └──────────────┴───────┴───────────────┴─────┴──────────────────┘  │
│                                                                     │
│                     DETAILS  OF  MEMORIAL                          │
│                                                                     │
│  MATERIAL(S) USED _____        │
│                                                                     │
│  TYPE(S) OF LETTERING _____        │
│                                                                     │
│  ANY CARVING?  DESCRIBE _____        │
│                                                                     │
│  ANY RHYME?  COPY IT OUT _____        │
│                                                                     │
└─────────────────────────────────────────────────────────────────────┘
```

Now sketch the memorial stone below:

Figure 56: Graveyard survey form

Why were new burial grounds necessary about 1800?
Why is there a Victorian monument to John Ferres, who died in 1650?
What styles of monument were popular at different periods?
Why is Dr John Alderson important for the health of Hull people?
Why is there a big momument to the Captain of the whaling ship *Diana*?
When were the cholera epidemics?
Why was the infant death rate so high?

With a lot of practical assistance from the Hull Architecture Workshop we researched and mounted photographs and text to try to answer all these questions. The end-product looked very professional and the students were proud of what they had helped to produce — and they had learnt a lot of local history in the process.

School history
This worked well with a group of thirteen year olds with reading or writing difficulties, and is an introduction to oral history. Their families were all local; many of the schools their parents or grandparents had attended were still operating. The students devised a questionnaire, including questions such as:

What is your first memory of school life?
What punishments were there?
How did you travel to school? How far?

One girl used a tape recorder when she interviewed her father, then played the tape to the class. Another girl, whose mother and grandmother had attended the same school as she had drew plans of the classrooms, 'then and now'. A third girl who had been at a special school interviewed her grandfather who had been at the school two generations ago when it was an open air school for 'delicate' children. All he remembered was a 'tortus' (tortoise) and being given the cane. His granddaughter remarked that now they only got lines.

If a teacher wanted to pursue the idea of school history, punishment books and school logs are an excellent primary source. I have always been wary of this, however, since the Hull pupils' strike of 1911 might give present day students some undesirable ideas.

A study of a house and its inhabitants
The obvious place to start for owner-occupiers is with the deeds, but these are more often than not kept deep in a solicitor's safe and not readily available. One solution is for the teacher to choose a house. I have had sixth formers studying the history of my house which has the advantage of being old; there is therefore a wide range of evidence available. Briefly, this evidence includes:

memorials of deeds (in the County Record Office, Beverley)
census enumerators' schedules (in the local history library)

poll books and electoral registers (in the local history library)
local newspapers (in the local history library)
old maps, particularly large scale OS maps (local history library)
former residents of the house

As well as tracing changes of ownership they also note physical changes in the house, by working out which alterations were made, when and why. This works well, mainly because having worked through the material I know where the dead ends are. If students are asked to study their own house they usually get stuck, either because the deeds are not available or because of the relative newness of their house there is no census material available. David Iredale has written a useful guide to the study of a house.[11]

Some other projects in brief
Brass rubbings, grave rubbings, masons' marks

All students seem to like doing rubbings. It is quick and easy, the results display well, and it can stimulate historical research.

Model making

Junior schools are often particularly good at this. I have some excellent models of the Ferriby boat and of a variety of buildings.

Archaeological dig in the school grounds

A class at a Brough primary school did this. They dug a neat trench, labelled the strata; they found a lot of Victorian pottery but also some earlier remains. This could stimulate further research, or make a museum visit more interesting.

The history of a local sports team

This could legitimise a student's consuming interest, as long as he or she could be persuaded to look at what was going on outside the football, rugby or other club.

Study of place names

If pupils are given information about Saxon, Viking etc. place name derivations, they could colour code onto a map the pattern of settlement in the East Riding, and study migration and invasion routes.

Family history

The student could be encouraged to interview elderly relatives and write down or tape what they have to say either about the family or about the place they lived in and what they can remember about, say, the Second Word War, or the General Strike.

A recent problem

The decline of the fishing industry can be studied by reference to local newspapers and official reports, all to be found in the local history library.

Local teachers could add many more suggestions; this is far from an exhaustive list of what can be, and is being done, in schools in the East Yorkshire area.

The teacher, the librarian and the archivist

Local history librarians and archivists are unfailingly helpful to teachers in search of materials for their students, but they become understandably harrassed when thirty children turn up at different times during half term saying 'We've got to do a project on the whaling industry'. Good relations will continue only if teachers prepare their pupils adequately before setting them loose amongst the documents.

The first stage in any local history project should be a visit by the teacher to the library to see what material is available, and to discuss the project with the librarian or archivist. The second stage is to decide whether to use the actual materials, photocopies, or transcripts. If the actual material is to be used the students should be taken on a preliminary visit when the location of each type of evidence — the photographs, the maps, the directories — can be indicated and the various card index systems can be explained. In my experience the librarians would far rather spend half an hour doing this than show the documents to thirty individuals, one at a time. If photocopies of the material are to be used, great care has to be taken over copyright, but if transcripts are used this is expensive in terms of labour. The third stage is to provide the students with clear guidance on what they have to do, in terms of gathering and interpreting the material.

These three stages are a counsel of perfection. In practice teachers can be very short of time to prepare materials; and this may prevent some teachers from embarking on local history because of the amount of preparation it entails. At the moment there is a lot of first rate work going on in isolation; in each school there are teachers preparing material and in some cases unknowingly duplicating what has been done elsewhere. A beginning has been made in the Humberside College of Higher Education to produce materials for use in all Humberside schools but it would seem to me a most useful task if someone were to act as a local studies co-ordinator, to work with the schools passing on information about what materials are already available, and to work with local librarians and archivists to produce the materials which the teachers want but do not have enough time to produce for themselves.

Conclusion

Local history is fun, for teacher and pupil alike. It can fulfil the most abstract pedagogic criteria while being stimulating to any age of students. Like anything else in teaching, success stems from thorough preparation but this is difficult because of the lack of comprehensive and simple textbooks. Relations with librarians and archivists are likely to become strained if teachers send under-prepared pupils to 'find out all about ...' but if the problem of access to materials can be overcome satisfactorily, it can provide pupils with a lasting interest as well as an understanding of their environment, and with that some hope for the sensitive future development of our villages, towns and cities.

Notes for chapter 14

1. Courses in local history leading to GCE 'O' level and CSE certificates are taught in a number of local schools. Details may be obtained from the secretary of the Southern Universities Joint Board. There is also an alternative Ordinary GCE examination in local history offered by the Joint Matriculation Board

2. Humberside Libraries, *The development of Kingston upon Hull shown through maps and views* (Hull, 1974)

3. I. Kilberry, *Census analysis* (Longman Micro Software, 1983)

4. VCH ER I

5. A. Storey, *Trinity House of Kingston upon Hull*, 2 vols (Hull, 1967-1969)

6. J. Sheahan, *History of the town and port of Kingston upon Hull* (Hull, 1864)

7. This scheme was developed by my colleagues at Kelvin Hall School, Ken Bore and Sue Price, as was the Pease diary material

8. The original documents are in the archives at Wilberforce House

9. These may be obtained from the Council for British Archaeology, 112, Kennington Road, London, SE11 6RE

10. Hull Architecture Workshop: a voluntary body situated at 44, High Street, Hull

11. D. Iredale, *Discovering this old house*, 2nd ed. (Aylesbury, 1977)

GLOSSARY

almshouse: a charitable institution providing care for the poor or sick

Augmentations, Court of see *Court of Augmentations*

Augustinians: order of friars observing the precepts of the writings of St Augustine, who died in A.D.430

banns: notice in church of intended marriage

Baptists: nonconformist body believing in spiritual regeneration through adult baptism

Benedictines: order of friars or nuns founded in A.D. 529 by St Benedict

Black Death: outbreak of bubonic plague in Europe in the fourteenth century

boss: carved or sculptured projection at the intersection of ceiling ribs

buttress: projecting support to a wall

Carmelites: members of a mendicant order of friars founded in the twelfth century at Mount Carmel in Palestine

carr: common land, usually marshy

Carthusians: order of monks founded by St Bruno in 1086 and named after Chartreuse in France

cartulary: compilation of charters, which are documents recording grants

carucate: the amount of land which could be ploughed in a year using one plough

chalice: eucharistic wine cup

chancel: part of a church near the altar used by the clergy or choir

chantry: usually a chapel within a church, but sometimes just an altar therein, endowed by an individual to ensure the singing of masses for his or her soul

chantry certificates: give an estimate of the number of communicants in a parish in 1545

charter: document recording a contract largely concerned with grants of land

chartulary see *cartulary*

Cistercians: offshoot of the Benedictines, named after Citeaux in France where they were founded in 1098

Compton Census: census in 1676 of worshippers and non-worshippers, named after Henry Compton, Bishop of London

Congregationalism: branch of nonconformism in which local churches are autonomous and which believes in the priesthood of all believers

copyhold: a form of land tenure originally carrying obligations to perform certain services for the lord, later commuted to money payments

cordwainer: shoemaker

Council of the North: established by Richard III to adminster the North of England and eventually abolished in 1641

Court of Augmentations: created in 1536 to administer lands, possessions and revenues of the dissolved religious houses; abolished in 1554 when its functions were transferred to the Exchequer

crossing: intersection of church nave and transepts

crucks: pairs of curved timbers holding up the ridge beam of the roof of a timber frame house

Curia Regis: royal court of the Norman and Angevin kings

Dissolution of the Monasteries: suppression of monastic houses and the transfer of property to the Crown between 1536 and 1540; most of the property was sold by the Court of Augmentations

Domesday Book: detailed record of taxable property ordered by William I, carried out during 1086

Dominicans: order of friars and nuns named after St Dominic, founded in 1215

factor: merchant buying and selling on commission

Franciscan: friar or nun of the order founded in 1209 by St Francis of Assisi

friendly society: group of individuals associated to provide mutual insurance against illness or old age

garth: yard or enclosure

Gilbertines: monastic order for women founded by St Gilbert in 1131 at Sempringham, Lincolnshire; it later also included men

glebe land: land included in the property of a parish church

glebe terriers: surveys of lands and benefices belonging to a rectory or vicarage

green lane: grassed right of way, originally probably a road to market

Guardians of the Poor: Boards established by the 1834 Poor Law Amendment Act; agents of the Poor Law administration

Hearth Tax: tax on fire hearths collected twice a year from 1662 to 1689

indult: in the Roman Catholic Church, the Pope's licence for something not sanctioned by the common law of the church

jamb: side post of doorway or window

lancet: a narrow window moving up to a sharply pointed arch, usually associated with thirteenth century architecture

letters patent: open letters, usually embodying a grant of a holding or privilege

manor court rolls: record of the decisions of the manor court, some dating from the thirteenth century

mark: a unit of currency, originally valued at 10s 8d., later revalued at 13s 4d.

Methodism: Protestant body originating in the eighteenth century evangelistic movement of Charles and John Wesley and George Whitefield; emphasised individual salvation and the love of God

Monasteries, Dissolution of the see *Dissolution of the Monasteries*

mortmain: untransferable lands held by an ecclesiastical or other body

Mortmain, Statute of see *Statute of Mortmain*

mullion: vertical bar separating the lights of a window

muster book: book for registering military forces and giving the number of able-bodied men in a parish

nave: main part of a church from the west door to the chancel

Overseer of the poor: parish officer established to levy a poor rate and supervise its distribution; duties passed to the Guardians of the Poor in 1834

oxgang: measure of land which varied with soil quantity but originally the amount which could be cultivated using one ox; normally one eighth of a carucate

pantile: S-shaped roof tile with one curve larger than the other

parcel gilt: partly gilt

parish chest: a strong chest in which the records of a church and parish could be locked away

parish register: book recording baptisms, marriages and burials at a parish church

patent rolls: record of royal grants of privileges, offices or lands

piscina: basin, with drain, used for washing vessels used in Mass; usually set on the south wall of a church near the altar

plinth: square projecting base of a column

poll books: lists of voters at parliamentary elections

poll tax: form of personal tax introduced in 1222

Poor Rate: rate or assessment for the relief of the poor

Presbyterian: Protestant sect in which the church was governed by elders, all (including ministers) of equal rank

Privy Council: sovereign's private counsellors; functions taken over by the Cabinet in the eighteenth century

probate: verified copy of will with certificate

Protestation: protest against the possible imposition of an arbitrary and tyrannical government arranged by Parliament in 1641; the Protestation Returns of 1642 give the names of all males aged eighteen and above who subscribed to the Oath of Protestation

Puritans: English Protestant sect who wished to rid the church of all Roman Catholic elements

Quakers: popular name for the (Religious) Society of Friends, established by George Fox in the mid-seventeenth century; no written creed or ordained ministers; members devoted to peaceful principles, and formerly noted for plainness of dress and simplicity of living

Quarter Sessions: meetings of the county justices held four times a year

recusants: term applied to people who refused to attend Church of England services and after 1570 usually meaning Roman Catholics

register: official list of, for example, births, marriages and deaths, or persons entitled to vote

reticulated: arranged in small squares or with intersecting lines

roll: document consisting of a number of single sheets attached end to end

rood: quarter of an acre

Schools Council History 13-16 Project: established at Leeds in 1972, it aimed to devise suitable objectives for history teachers, and resulted in a new type of syllabus designed to teach history in a way suited to the needs and interests of adolescents

scrivener: drafter of documents, copyist, writer

sedilia: seats, usually on the south side of the chancel and three in number intended for the priests who celebrated mass

Statute of Mortmain: passed in 1279, this limited grants of land to the church

string course: raised horizontal band running round the face of a building

thegn: in feudal society, member of a class higher than an ordinary freeman but lower than the hereditary nobles; held land in return for services performed for his lord

tithe: tax, for the upkeep of the church, of one tenth of the earnings or produce of an inhabitant of a parish

title deeds: legal document concerning ownership or occupation of real estate

Toleration Act: passed in 1689, it allowed English nonconformists their own places of worship, teachers and preachers

tracery: pattern formed by interlacing stone work at the top of a window; there are several forms which can be used as a guide for dating windows

transept: the cross-wise part of a cross-shaped church

tumulus: burial mound of earth or chalk

turbary: right of digging turf on common or other ground

vault: arched roof or ceiling

villein: in feudal society, not a freeman, but obliged to pay sums of money to his lord on various occasions; farmed in return for services performed

Visitation Books: records of cathedral and church administration, giving details of parishes visited

wapentake: an administrative subdivision of the shire or county, in areas of England where there was a large Danish population

workhouse: building constructed or rented by the parish to house paupers

USEFUL ADDRESSES

This section lists some of the most important local and national resources for the local historian. Readers are advised to check details such as opening times (which are inevitably subject to variation) before making a personal visit. Access to archive, university, college or record office collections can be restricted; it is usually essential to write to or telephone such institutions in advance. All information is the most up-to-date available at the time of writing.

ARCHIVES
Borthwick Institute of Historical Research
Address: St Anthony's Hall, Peasholme Green, York, YO1 2YW
Telephone: (0904) 642315

Doncaster Archives Department
Address: King Edward Road, Balby, Doncaster, DN4 6NA
Telephone: (0302) 859811

Durham County Record Office
Address: County Hall, Durham, DH1 5UL
Telephone: (0385) 64411 ext. 2474/2253

East Riding Registry of Deeds
Now incorporated in the Humberside County Record Office (see below)

General Register Office
Address: St Catherine's House, 10, Kingsway, London
Telephone: (01) 242 0262

Humberside County Record Office
Address: County Hall, Beverley, HU17 9BA
Telephone: (0482) 867131 ext. 3393/94

Kingston upon Hull Record Office
Address: 79, Lowgate, Hull, HU1 2AA
Telephone: (0482) 222015/6

Lincolnshire Archives Office
Address: The Castle, Lincoln, LN1 3AB
Telephone: (0522) 25158

Methodist Archives and Research Centre
Address: John Rylands University Library of Manchester, Deansgate, Manchester, M3 3EH
Telephone: (061) 8345343

National Register of Archives
Incorporated in the Royal Commission on Historical Manuscripts (see below)

North Yorkshire County Record Office
Address: County Hall, Northallerton, DL7 8SG
Telephone: (0609) 3123 ext. 455

Principal Registry of the Family Division
Address: Somerset House, The Strand, London, WC2 1LP
Telephone: (01) 405 7641 ext. 3097

Public Record Office
Medieval and early modern records
Address: Chancery Lane, London, WC2 1AH
Telephone: (01) 4050741
Modern records
Address: Ruskin Avenue, Kew, Richmond, Surrey, TW9 4DU
Telephone: (01) 8763444

Royal Commission on Historical Manuscripts (incorporating the National Register of Archives)
Address: Quality House, Quality Court, Chancery Lane, London, WC2A 1HP
Telephone: (01) 2421198

University of Hull
Address: Brynmor Jones Library, University of Hull, Cottingham Road, Hull, HU6 7RX
Telephone: (0482) 46311

York City Archives
Address: Exhibition Square, York, YO1 2EW
Telephone: (0904) 51533

York Minster Archives
Address: York Minster Library, Dean's Park, York, YO1 2JD
Telephone: (0904) 25308

Yorkshire Archaeological Society
Address: Claremont, Clarendon Road, Leeds, LS2 9NZ
Telephone: (0532) 456362

LIBRARIES
Bodleian Library
Address: University of Oxford, Oxford, OX1 3BG
Telephone: (0865) 44675

British Library
Address: Great Russell Street, London, WC1B 3DG
Telephone: (01) 6361544

Humberside College of Higher Education
Address: Inglemire Site Library, HCHE, Inglemire Avenue, HU6 7LU
Telephone: (0482) 42157

Humberside County Libraries
Beverley Public Library
Address: Champney Road, Beverley, HU17 9BQ
Telephone: (0482) 867108
Bridlington Public Library
Address: King Street, Bridlington
Telephone: (0262) 72917
Hull Central Library
Address: Local Studies Library, Central Library, Albion Street, Hull, HU1 3TF
Telephone: (0482) 224040

University of Hull
Address: Brynmor Jones Library, University of Hull, Cottingham Road, Hull, HU6 7RX
Telephone: (0482) 46311

MUSEUMS, etc.
Bridlington Art Gallery and Museum
Address: Sewerby Hall, Bridlington
Telephone: (0262) 73769

Ferens Art Gallery
Address: Queen Victoria Square, Hull, HU1 3DX
Telephone: (0482) 222750

Goole Museum and Art Gallery
Address: Market Square, Goole, DN14 5DR
Telephone: (0405) 2187

Heritage Information Centre
Address: Waterguard Offices, Minerva Pier, Hull, HU1 1XP
Telephone: (0482) 228608

Hull Architecture Workshop
Address: 44-46 High Street, Hull, HU1 1PS
Telephone: (0482) 224726

Museum of Army Transport
Address: Flemingate, Beverley, HU17 0NG
Telephone: (0482) 860445

National Maritime Museum
Address: Romney Road, Greenwich, London, SE10 9NP
Telephone: (01) 8584422

North Holderness Museum of Village Life
Address: 11, Newbegin, Hornsea, HU18 1AB
Telephone: (04012) 3443 or 3430

Town Docks Museum
Address: Queen Victoria Square, Hull, HU1 3DX
Telephone: (0482) 222737

Transport and Archaeology Museum
Address: High Street, Hull
Telephone: (0482) 222737

Trinity House, Hull
Address: Trinity House Lane, Hull, HU1 2JG
Telephone: Hull (0482) 24956

Wilberforce House and Georgian Houses
Address: High Street, Hull
Telephone: (0482) 222737

SOCIETIES

Beverley and District Civic Society

Address: 16, Limetree Avenue, Beverley, HU17 9PQ
Telephone: (0482) 860462
Contact: The Secretary
Aims: '... to conserve the character of a town listed as one of the 40 most historically important in the country, and also to encourage developments leading to improved conditions for living and working in the area'
Activities: Lectures and films; excursions and social events; studies of the local area and advice to the local authorities
Publications: *Newsletter* (quarterly)

Bridlington Augustinian Society

Address: Flat 3, 26, St John's Avenue, Bridlington, YO16 4NG
Telephone: (0262) 601310
Contact: The Scribe
Aims: '... the collecting of all matters and objects relating to the history of Bridlington and district, the encouragement of an interest in local history and the study of objects of general antiquarian interest...'
Activities: Lectures; visits to places of historical interest; collection of objects for the Bayle Museum, and involvement in its running; maintenance of a library of historical and antiquarian books
Publications: Occasional booklets of photographs

British Association for Local History

Address: The Mill Manager's House, Cromford Mill, Mill Road, Cromford, Matlock, Derbyshire, DE4 3RQ
Telephone: (062982) 3768
Contact: The Secretary
Aims: '... to advance understanding and knowledge of local history'
Publications: *The local historian* (quarterly)

Cottingham Local History Society

Address: 7, George Place, George Street, Cottingham, HU16 5QR
Telephone: (0482) 848323
Contact: The Secretary
Aims: The study of local history in Cottingham, Hull and the East Riding
Activities: Meetings and lectures; excursions
Publications: Journal (irregular, supplemented by newssheets); occasional pamphlets

Council for British Archaeology

Address: 112, Kennington Road, London, SE11 6RE
Telephone: (01) 582 0494
Contact: The Director
Aims: '... to co-ordinate archaeological activities in the British Isles; to promote research in archaeology and the preservation of ancient monuments and historic buildings'
Publications: *Annual report*; *Archaeological bibliography for Britain and Ireland* (annual); *Calendar of excavations* (nine times a year)

East Riding Archaeological Society
Address: 14, Kenilworth Avenue, Hull, HU5 4BH
Telephone: (0482) 443873
Contact: The Secretary
Aims: 'Preservation, investigation and restoration of the antiquities in the East Riding of Yorkshire'
Activities: Meetings; research; study groups; visits and excursions
Publications: *East Riding archaeologist* (irregular); *Archaeology and redevelopment* (irregular; publication of the Sub-committee)

East Riding Dialect Society
Address: 3, Clarence Avenue, Bridlington, YO15 3DW
Telephone: (0262) 73995
Contact: The Secretary
Aims: No details
Activities: No details
Publications: No details

East Yorkshire Family History Society
Address: Iona House, 9, Stepney Grove, Scarborough, YO12 5DF
Telephone: (0723) 63760
Contact: The Secretary
Aims: '... to bring together those interested in the study of family history either living in the East Riding or with East Riding ancestry'
Activities: Meetings; genealogical searching; preservation of archival material by transcription, indexing and publishing; recording of monumental inscriptions (gravestones); special projects
Publication: *The Banyan tree* (quarterly); miscellaneous publications including directory of members' interests

East Yorkshire Local History Society
Address: Beverley Library, Champney Road, Beverley, HU17 9BQ
Telephone: (0482) 887108
Contact: The Secretary
Aims: 'To encourage the study and appreciation of local history and to assist those interested in the subject'
Activities: Meetings, talks and discussions; occasional research groups
Publications: *Bulletin* (twice yearly); booklets on aspects of East Yorkshire local history

Georgian Society for East Yorkshire
Address: The White Hall, Winestead, Hull, HU12 0NJ
Telephone: (0964) 30242
Contact: The Secretary
Aims: '... to preserve from destruction or disfigurement buildings, especially those of the Georgian period, of architectural and historic interest in Hull and the East Riding ... to stimulate public appreciation of the architectural and historic heritage of Hull and the East Riding'
Activities: Lectures; visits to buildings of interest; advice to owners and public authorities on the preservation and repair of buildings, and on the uses to which they might be adapted
Publication: Annual notes

Hedon and District Local History Society
Address: 24, Wylies Road, Beverley, HU17 7AP
Contact: The Secretary
Aims: The study of the history of Hedon and Holderness, and other historical interests
Activities: Meetings and lectures; excursions; current project involving transcribing and indexing Hedon parish registers
Publications: *Newsletter* (annually); *Hedon local history series*; *Hedon town trail*

History of Education Society
Address: Institute of Education, University of London, 20, Bedford Way, London, WC1H 0AL
Telephone: (01) 636 1500
Contact: The Secretary
Aims: '... to further the study of the history of education'
Publications: *History of education* (quarterly); *Bulletin* (twice yearly)

Howden Civic Society
Address: Community Council of Humberside, 14, Market Place, Howden, DN14 7BJ
Telephone: (0430) 30904
Contact: The Secretary
Aims: '... to encourage the conservation and enhancement of buildings and the general environment in the town of Howden'
Activities: Buildings and gardens awards; drawing, painting and photographic competitions in local schools
Publications: Frequent newsletters; 'Looking around Howden' (folder)

Hull Civic Society
Address: 163, Westbourne Avenue, Hull, HU5 3JA
Telephone: (0482) 43588
Contact: The Secretary
Aims: '... to look after the existing features which make Hull unique, by retaining and improving the waterspaces, preserving and restoring the best buildings and conserving groups of buildings which form interesting townscapes ...'
Activities: Talks and discussions; excursions; fund-raising; acts as a pressure group and advises on planning applications
Publications: *Newsletter* (three times a year); miscellaneous publications

Hull Maritime Society
Address: Town Docks Museum, Queen Victoria Square, Hull, HU1 3DX
Telephone: (0482) 222737
Contact: The Secretary
Aims: '... to encourage and promote an interest in maritime affairs and give support to the Town Docks Museum'
Activities: talks and visits; purchase of items for the Town Docks Museum; support of maritime causes such as the Humber Keel and Sloop Preservation Society
Publications: No details

Royal Commission on Historic Monuments
Address: Fortress House, 23, Savile Row, London, W1X 2BT
Telephone: (01) 734 6010
Contact: The Secretary
Aims: '... to make an inventory of the ancient and historical monuments and constructions connected with or illustrative of the contemporary culture, civilisation and conditions of life of the people in England ...'
Publications: Reports and Inventories

COURSES

Non-vocational courses

Most local education authorities organise non-vocational day-time courses. Examples of courses running in the 1984/85 session include 'Tudor and Stuart Yorkshire' (South Hunsley Institute of Further Education) and 'Society and change in 17th century East Yorkshire' (Hessle Institute of Further Education). You should contact your nearest public library for details of all courses currently being offered in your area.

The following institutions also provide non-vocational courses at various centres in the East Riding:

University of Hull
Address: Department of Adult Education, University of Hull, 49, Salmon Grove, Hull, HU6 7SZ
Telephone: (0482) 46311

Workers Educational Association
Address: Albermarle Youth Centre, Ferensway, Hull, HU2 8LZ
Telephone: (0482) 28562 (Mon.-Fri. 10 a.m.-12 noon)

Vocational courses

The following institutions provide full- and part-time examination courses:

Humberside College of Higher Education
Address: Inglemire Avenue, Hull, HU6 7LU
Telephone: (0482) 45157
Courses: Include the B.A. Humanities (part-time), which includes two units in local/regional history; Diploma in Professional Studies, which includes an environmental studies option which contains some local history — this course is for practising school teachers; the B.Ed. degree course is currently being revised to include a unit on local/regional history

University of Hull
Address: Department of Adult Education, University of Hull, 49, Salmon Grove, Hull, HU6 7SZ
Telephone: (0482) 46311
Courses: Part-time certificate and degree in regional and local history. The certificate is obtained after two years of part-time study. Students can go on to take the degree in local and regional history, which is taken over a further four years. Although there is to be no intake to the course in 1985, it is hoped to run the course in future years

SELECT BIBLIOGRAPHY

GENERAL
Allison, K. J., ed., *A history of the County of York, East Riding*, volumes 1-5, Victoria history of the counties of England (London, 1969-1984)

Beresford, M. W., *History on the ground: six studies in maps and landscapes*, new ed. (Gloucester, 1984)

Dymond, D., *Writing local history: a practical guide* (London, 1981)

Harley, J. B., *Maps for the local historian: a guide to the British sources* (London, 1972)

Harley, J. B., *Ordnance Survey maps: a descriptive manual* (Southampton, 1975)

Hepworth, P., *How to find out in history: a guide to sources of information for all* (Oxford, 1966)

Hoskins, W. G., *Fieldwork in local history*, 2nd ed. (London, 1982)

Hoskins, W. G., *Local history in England*, 3rd ed. (London, 1984)

Iredale, D., *Discovering local history*, 2nd ed. (Aylesbury, 1977)

Madden, L., *How to find out about the Victorian period: a guide to sources of information* (Oxford, 1970)

Mulholland, H., *Guide to self-publishing: an A-Z of getting yourself into print* (Little Neston, 1984)

Munby, L. M., 'Publishing your own local history', *Local historian*, 16 (1984), pp.90-92

Norton, J. E., ed., *A guide to national and provincial directories of England and Wales, excluding London, published before 1856* (London, 1950)

Pugh, R. B., *How to write a parish history*, 6th ed. (London, 1954)

Ravensdale, J. R., *History on your doorstep* (London, 1982)

Richardson, J., *The local historian's encyclopedia* (New Barnet, 1974)

Riden, P., *Local history: a handbook for beginners* (London, 1983)

Rogers, A., *Approaches to local history*, 2nd ed. (London, 1977)

Stephens, W. B., *Sources for English local history*, The sources of history: studies in the use of historical evidence, rev. ed. (Cambridge, 1981)

BY CHAPTER TOPIC
1 Local libraries and guides
Dickens, A. G. and K. A. MacMahon, *A guide to regional studies on the East Riding of Yorkshire and the City of Hull* (Hull, 1956)

Drewery, R. F., *A select list of books on Hull and district: a guide to collections in the Local History Library* (Hull, 1968)

Hobbs, J. L., *Local history and the library*, 2nd ed. (London, 1973)

Hull Public Libraries, *William Wilberforce, 1759-1833: a catalogue of the books and pamphlets on William Wilberforce and slavery in the Reference Library of Kingston upon Hull Public Libraries* (Hull, 1959)

Humberside Libraries, *The development of Kingston upon Hull shown through maps and views* (Hull, 1974)

Humberside Libraries, *A select bibliography of the County of Humberside* (Hull, 1980)

Laughton, G. E. and L. R. Stephen, *Yorkshire newspapers: a bibliography with locations* (Harrogate, 1960)

MacMahon, K. A., ed., *An index to the more important local historical information contained in the files of the 'Hull Advertiser and Exchange Gazette'* ... (Hull, 1955)

Ollé, J. G., *A guide to sources of information in libraries* (Aldershot, 1984)

2 Archives
Armstrong, J., compiler, *Directory of corporate archives* (London, 1985)

Emmison, F. G., *Archives and local history*, 2nd ed. (Chichester, 1974)

Emmison, F. G. and I. Gray, *County records* (London, 1973)

Emmison, F. G., *How to read local archives, 1550-1700* (London, 1973)

234

Emmison, F. G., *Introduction to archives* (London, 1977)

Foster, J. and J. Sheppard, *British archives: a guide to archive resources in the United Kingdom* (London, 1981)

Hector, L. C., *The handwriting of English documents*, 2nd ed. (London, 1966)

Iredale, D., *Enjoying archives*, 2nd ed. (Newton Abbot, 1985)

Kingston upon Hull Record Office, *Guide to the Kingston upon Hull Record Office: Part 1* (Hull, 1978)

Martin, C. T., *The record interpreter: a collection of abbreviations, Latin words and words used in English historical manuscripts and records* (London, 1892; reprinted Dorking, 1976)

Morton, A. G. and G. Donaldson, *British national archives and the local historian* (London, 1981)

Oxley, G. W., *An introduction to the history of local government in Kingston upon Hull* (Hull, 1975)

Public Record Office, *Guide to the contents of the Public Record Office*, 3 vols (London, 1963-68)

Royal Commission on Historical Manuscripts, *Record repositories in Great Britain: a geographical directory*, 7th ed. (London, 1982)

Smith, D. M., *A guide to the archive collections in the Borthwick Institute of Historical Research*, Borthwick texts and calendars: records of the Northern Province, 1 (York, 1973)

Smith, D. M., *A supplementary guide to the archive collections in the Borthwick Institute of Historical Research*, Borthwick texts and calendars: records of the Northern Province, 7 (York, 1980)

Tate, W. E., *The parish chest: a study of the records of parochial administration in England*, 3rd ed. (Chichester, 1983)

Thorp, J., 'Books on palaeography: sixteenth to eighteenth century handwriting', *Local historian*, 16 (1985), pp.327-334

3 Medieval history

Beresford, M. W. and J. G. Hurst, *Deserted medieval villages* (London, 1971)

Beresford, M. W. and J. K. St Joseph, *Medieval England: an aerial survey*, 2nd ed. (Cambridge, 1979)

Darby, H. C., *The Domesday geography of eastern England*, 3rd ed. (Cambridge, 1971)

Davis, G. R. C., *Medieval cartularies of Great Britain: a short catalogue* (London, 1958)

Elton, G. R., *England, 1200-1640*, The sources of history: studies in the uses of historical evidence (London, 1969)

Gooder, E. A., *Latin for local history: an introduction*, 2nd ed. (London, 1978)

Grieve, H. E. P., *Examples of English handwriting, 1150-1750 ...* (Chelmsford, 1954)

Lamplough, E., *Medieval Yorkshire* (London, 1884)

Latham, R. E., *Revised medieval Latin word-list from British and Irish sources* (London, 1965)

Newton, K. C., *Medieval local records: a reading aid*, Helps for students of history, 83 (London, 1971)

Taylor, C. C., *Fieldwork in medieval archaeology* (London, 1974)

4 Medieval church history

Barlow, F., *The English church, 1000-1066: a history of the later Anglo-Saxon church*, 2nd ed. (London, 1979)

Bond, E. A., ed., *Meaux Chronica*, Rolls series, 3 vols (London, 1866-68)

Bond, F., *Gothic architecture in England ...* (London, 1906)

Burton, J. E., *The Yorkshire nunneries in the twelfth and thirteenth centuries*, Borthwick papers, 56 (York, 1979)

Child, M., *Discovering church architecture* (Aylesbury, 1976)

Clapham, Sir A. W., *English Romanesque architecture after the Conquest* (Oxford, 1934)

Cocke, T., and others, *Recording a church*, 2nd ed. (London, 1984)

Dymond, D., *Writing a church guide* (London, 1977)

Earle, A., *Essays upon the history of Meaux Abbey* ... (London, 1906)

Farrer, W. [then] C. T. Clay, eds, *Early Yorkshire charters* ..., YAS record series: extra series, 12 vols (Leeds, 1914-65)

Foster, R., *Discovering English churches* (London, 1981)

Harvey, J. H., *The medieval architect* (London, 1972)

Kitching, C. J., 'The chantries of the East Riding of Yorkshire at the Dissolution in 1548', YAJ 44 (1972), pp.178-94

Knowles, M. D., *The religious orders in England*, 3 vols (Cambridge, 1948-59)

Lancaster, W. T., compiler, *Abstracts of the charters and other documents in the Chartulary of the Priory of Bridlington* (Leeds, 1912)

Owen, D. M., *The records of the established church in England, excluding parochial records* (London, 1970)

Owen, D. M., 'What to read on English religious history', *Local historian*, 16 (1984), pp.151-60

Platt, C., *The abbeys and priories of medieval England* (London, 1984)

Platt, C., *The parish churches of medieval England* (London, 1981)

Power, E. E., *Medieval English nunneries c.1275 to 1535* (Cambridge, 1922)

Purvis, J. S., *The archives of York Diocesan Registry: their provenance and history* (London, 1952)

Rodwell, W., *The archaeology of the English church: a study of historic churches and churchyards* (London, 1981)

Turner, J. H., *The coats of arms of the nobility and gentry of Yorkshire* ... (Idle, 1911)

5 Post-Reformation religion

Ambler, R. W., 'The 1851 census of religious worship', *Local historian*, 11 (1975), pp.375-81

Aveling, H., *Post-Reformation Catholicism in East Yorkshire, 1558-1790*, EYLHS, 11 (York, 1960)

Baker, F., *The story of Methodism in Newland* (Hull, 1958)

Darwent, C. E., *The story of Fish Street Church, Hull* (London, 1899)

Davison, J., *The life of the venerable William Clowes, one of the founders of the Primitive Methodist connexion* (London, 1854)

Jackson, T., *Recollections of my own life and times*, edited by B. Frankland (London, 1878)

Kendall, H. B., *The origin and history of the Primitive Methodist Church*, 2 vols (London, c.1906)

Miall, J. G., *Congregationalism in Yorkshire: a chapter of modern church history* (London, 1878)

Ollard, S. L. and P. C. Walker, eds, *Archbishop Herring's visitation returns 1743*, YAS record series, 71-2, 75, 77, 79 (Leeds, 1928-1931)

Purvis, J. S., *Dictionary of ecclesiastical terms* (London, 1962)

Sheils, W. J., 'Sources for the history of dissent and Catholicism at the Borthwick Institute', *Borthwick Institute bulletin*, 3 (1983), pp.11-28

Thistlethwaite, W. P., *Yorkshire quarterly meeting (of the Society of Friends) 1665-1966* (Harrogate, 1979)

Thompson, W. H., *Early chapters in Hull Methodism, 1746-1800* (Hull, 1895)

Trout, A. E., 'Nonconformity in Hull', *Transactions of the Congregational Historical Society*, 9 (1924-26)

Watts, M. R., *The dissenters: from the Reformation to the French Revolution* (Oxford, 1978)

Woodcock, H., *Piety amongst the peasantry; being sketches of Primitive Methodism on the Yorkshire Wolds* (London, 1889)

6 Family history

Barrow, G. B., *The genealogist's guide: an index to printed British pedigrees and family histories, 1950-1975* (London, 1977)

Camp, A. J., *Wills and their whereabouts ...*, 4th ed. (London, 1983)

Cox, J. and T. Padfield, *Tracing your ancestors in the Public Record Office*, 3rd ed. (London, 1984)

Currer-Briggs, N., *A handbook of British family history: a guide to methods and sources* (Flitwick, 1979)

Hamilton-Edwards, G., *In search of ancestry* (Chichester, 1974)

Hawgood, D., *Computers for family history: an introduction* (London, 1985)

Humphery-Smith, C. R., *A genealogist's bibliography*, 2nd ed. (Chichester, 1981)

Humphery-Smith, C. R., ed., *The Phillimore atlas and index of parish registers* (Chichester, 1984)

Leary, W., *My ancester was a Methodist: how can I find out more about him?* (London, 1982)

Mander, M., *How to trace your ancestors* (London, 1977)

Needham, S., *A glossary for East Yorkshire and North Lincolnshire probate inventories*, University of Hull Department of Adult Education studies in regional and local history, 3 (Hull, 1984)

Rayment, J. L., *Notes on the recording of monumental inscriptions*, 2nd ed. (Plymouth, 1978)

Rogers, C. D., *The family tree detective ...* (Manchester, 1983)

Steel, D. J., *Discovering your family history* (London, 1980)

Steel, D. J. and L. Taylor, eds, *Family history in focus* (Lutterworth Press, 1984)

Steel, D. J., ed., *Sources for nonconformist genealogy and family history* (London, 1973)

Wagner, A., *English genealogy*, 2nd rev. ed. (Chichester, 1983)

Webb, C. C., *A guide to genealogical sources in the Borthwick Institute of Historical Research* (York, 1981)

7 Urban settlement and town histories

Baines, E., *History, directory and gazetteer of the County of York*, 2 vols (Leeds, 1823; reprinted as *Baines Yorkshire*, Newton Abbot, 1969)

Barfoot, P. and J. Wilkes, *The Universal British Directory of trade and commerce*, 6 vols (London, 1791-98)

Barley, M. W., *The history of Great and Little Driffield* (Hull, 1938)

Bedell, E. W., *An account of Hornsea in Holderness* (Hull, 1848)

Boyle, J. R., *The early history of the town and port of Hedon* (Hull, 1895)

Bulmer, T., *History, topography and directory of East Yorkshire* (Preston, 1892; reprinted 1985)

Calvert, H., *A history of Hull* (London, 1978)

Clark, P., *The early modern town* (London, 1976)

Clarke, T., *History of Howden* (Howden, 1851)

Duckham, B. F., *The inland waterways of East Yorkshire*, EYLHS, 29 (York, 1973)

Gent, T., *Annales Regioduni Hullini; or, The history of the Royal and beautiful town of Kingston-upon-Hull ...* (York, 1735)

Gillet, E. and K. A. MacMahon, *A history of Hull* (Oxford, 1980)

Hadfield, C., *The canals of Yorkshire and North-East England*, 2 vols (London, 1972)

Howorth, P., *Driffield: a county town in its setting 1700-1860* (Hull, 1980)

Jackson, G., *Hull in the eighteenth century: a study in economic and social history* (Oxford, 1972)

MacMahon, K. A., *Beverley: a brief historical survey* (Beverley, 1965)

Neave, D., *Great Driffield: a town trail* (Beverley, 1981)

Neave, D., *Howden explored* (Hull, 1979)

Neave, D., *Market Weighton portrayed* (Beverley, 1981)

Neave, D., *Pocklington: a small East Riding market town, 1600-1914* (Beveley, 1970)

Neave, D., *South Cave: a market village community in the eighteenth and nineteenth centuries*, 2nd ed. (South Cave, 1983)

Neave, D., 'Transport and the early development of East Riding resorts', in *Ports and resorts in the regions*, edited by E. M. Sigsworth (Hull, 1981), pp.101-119

Nicholson, J., *Capital of the Yorkshire Wolds* (Hull, 1901)

Noble, M., *Change in the small towns of the East Riding of Yorkshire 1700-1850*, Hedon local history series, 5 (Hull, 1979)

Noble, M., 'Inland navigations and country towns', in *Ports and resorts in the regions*, edited by E. M. Sigsworth (Hull, 1981), pp.79-100

Noble, M., 'The land tax assessments and physical development in country towns', in *Land and property: the English land tax 1692-1832*, edited by M. Turner and D. R. Mills (London, 1985), chapter 6

Noble, M., 'Land tax returns and urban development', *The local historian*, 15 (1982), pp.86-91

Patten, J., *English towns 1500-1700* (London, 1978)

Poulson, G., *Beverlac; or, The antiquities and history of the town of Beverley*, 2 vols (London, 1829)

Purvis, J. S., *Bridlington charters, court rolls and papers* (Hull, 1926)

Ross, F., *Contributions towards a history of Driffield and the surrounding Wolds district* (Driffield, 1898)

Sheahan, J., *History of the town and port of Kingston upon Hull* (Hull, 1864)

Slater, W., *Yorkshire directory* (Leeds, 1849)

Sutcliffe, A., 'What to read on urban history', *The local historian*, 16 (1984), pp.67-72

Tickell, J., *History of the town and county of Kingston upon Hull ...* (Hull, 1798)

Unwin, R. W., 'Tradition and transition: market towns of the Vale of York', *Northern history*, 17 (1981), pp.72-116

West, J., *Town records* (Chichester, 1983)

West, J., *Village records*, 2nd ed. (Chichester, 1982)

White, W., *General directory and topography of Kingston upon Hull and York* (Sheffield, 1851)

8 Population

Armstrong, A., *Stability and change in an English county town: a social study of York, 1801-51* (London, 1974)

Beresford, M. W., *The unprinted census returns of 1841, 1851, 1861 for England and Wales* (Canterbury, 1966)

Bradley, L., *A glossary for local population studies*, 2nd ed. (Matlock, 1978)

Drake, M., ed., *Population studies from parish registers: a selection of readings from 'Local population studies'* (Matlock, 1982)

Flinn, M. W., *British population growth, 1700-1850* (London, 1970)

Hoskins, W. G., *Provincial England: essays in social and economic history* (London, 1963)

Lawton, R., 'Rural depopulation in nineteenth century England', in *English rural communities: the impact of a specialised economy*, edited by D. R. Mills (London, 1973), pp.195-219

Palliser, D. M., 'What to read on population history', *The local historian*, 16 (1984), pp.207-212

Redford, A., *Labour migration in England 1800-1850*, 3rd ed. (Manchester, 1976)

Schofield, R., 'Crisis mortality', *Local population studies*, 9 (1972), pp.10-21

Smith, M. H., *Parish histories and population history in southern Holderness*, Hedon local history series, 3 (Hull, 1976)

Stapleton, B., 'Sources for the demographic study of a local community from the sixteenth to the mid-nineteenth century', *Journal of regional and local studies*, 4 (1984), pp.1-26

Thirsk, J., 'Sources of information on population', *Amateur historian*, 4 (1959), pp.129-33 and 182-4 (reprinted in her *The rural economy of England*, London, 1984, pp.17-26)

Tranter, N., *Population since the Industrial Revolution: the case of England and Wales* (London, 1973)

Wrigley, E. A., ed., *An introduction to English historical demography from the sixteenth to the nineteenth century* (London, 1966)

Wrigley, E. A. and R. S. Schofield, *The population history of England, 1541-1971* (London, 1981)

9 Agriculture

Allison, K. J., *The East Riding of Yorkshire landscape* (London, 1976)

Beresford, M. W., 'Glebe terriers and open-field Yorkshire', YAJ, 37 (1951), pp.325-68

Best, S. E. J., *East Yorkshire: a study in agricultural geography* (London, 1930)

Boer, G. de, 'Rural Yorkshire', in *Great Britain: agricultural essays*, edited by J. B. Mitchell (Cambridge, 1962), pp.373-95

Crowther, J., 'Parliamentary enclosure in eastern Yorkshire, 1725-1860' (unpublished Ph.D. thesis, University of Hull, 1984)

English, B., ed., *Yorkshire enclosure awards*, University of Hull Department of Adult Education studies in regional and local history, 5 (Hull, 1985)

Fussell, G. E., *Farming systems from Elizabethan to Victorian days in the North and East Ridings of Yorkshire* (York, 1946)

Harris, A., 'The agriculture of the East Riding before the parliamentary enclosures', YAJ, 40 (1959), pp.119-28

Harris, A., 'The lost villages and the landscape of the Yorkshire Wolds', *Agricultural history review*, 6 (1958), pp.97-100

Harris, A., *The milk supply of East Yorkshire, 1850-1950*, EYLHS, 33 (Beverley, 1977)

Harris, A., *The open fields of East Yorkshire*, EYLHS, 9 (York, 1959)

Harris, A., *The rural landscape of the East Riding of Yorkshire, 1700-1850: a study in historical geography*, 2nd ed. (Wakefield, 1969)

Sheppard, J. A., *The draining of the Hull valley*, EYLHS, 8 (York, 1958)

Sheppard, J. A., *The draining of the marshlands of South Holderness and the Vale of York*, EYLHS, 20 (York, 1966)

Sheppard, J. A., 'Field systems of Yorkshire', in *Studies of field systems in the British Isles*, edited by A. R. H. Baker and R. A. Butlin (Cambridge, 1973), pp.145-87

Ward, J. T., *East Yorkshire landed estates in the nineteenth century*, EYLHS, 23 (York, 1967)

Wilkinson, O., *The agricultural revolution in the East Riding of Yorkshire*, EYLHS, 5 (York, 1956)

Woodward, D. M., ed., *The farming and memorandum books of Henry Best of Elmswell, 1642*, British Academy records of social and economic history: new series, 8 (London, 1984)

10 Maritime history

Barron, W., *Old whaling days* (Hull, 1895; reprinted London, 1970)

Bolton, R. V. and F. J. Bryan, eds, *Marine transport: a guide to libraries and sources of information in Great Britain*, 2nd ed. (London, 1983)

Boswell, D., ed., *The fishing log of Edwin Green Smith, 1884-8* (Grimsby, 1967)

Cox, N., 'Sources of maritime history: the records of the Registrar General of Shipping and Seamen', *Maritime history*, 2 (1972), pp.168-188

Credland, A. G., *The Diana of Hull*, Kingston upon Hull Museums bulletin, 13 (Hull, 1981)

Credland, A. G., *Iron and steel shipbuilding on the Humber: Earles of Hull*, Kingston upon Hull Museums bulletin, 15 (Hull, 1982)

Credland, A. G., *Whales and whaling: the Arctic fishery* (Aylesbury, 1982)

Davis, R., *The trade and shipping of Hull 1500-1700*, EYLHS, 17 (York, 1962)

Dyson, J., *Business in great waters: the story of British fishermen* (London, 1977)

Hepton, P., *Sailings of the Hull whaling fleet from the port of Hull 1843 to 1869*, Malet Lambert local history originals, 24 (Hull, 1985)

Jackson, G., *The British whaling trade* (London, 1978)

Jackson, G., *The trade and shipping of eighteenth century Hull*, EYLHS, 31 (Beverley, 1975)

Lubbock, B., *The Arctic whalers* (Glasgow, 1937)

Magnolia, L. R., *Whales, whaling and whale research: a selected bibliography* (Redondon Beach, Calif., 1977)

March, E. J., *Sailing trawlers ...* (London, 1953; reprinted Newton Abbot, 1970, 1978)

Matthews, K., 'Crew lists, agreements and official logs of the British empire, 1863-1913, now in the possession of the Maritime History Group, Memorial University, St John's, Newfoundland', *Business history*, 16 (1974), pp.78-80

Matthews, L. H., ed., *The whale* (London, 1968)

Oxley, G., *Transport by sea, rail and inland navigation*, KHRO subject guides, 2 (Hull, 1983)

Pearson, F. H., *The early history of Hull steam shipping* (Hull, 1896; reprinted 1984)

Ritchie, L. A., *Modern British shipbuilding: a guide to historical records* (London, 1980)

Rodger, N. A. M., *Naval records for genealogists* (London, 1984)

Scoresby, W., *An account of the Arctic regions . . .*, 2 vols (Edinburgh, 1820; reprinted London, 1969)

Spence, B., *Harpooned: the story of whaling* (London, 1980)

Storey, A., *Trinity House of Kingston upon Hull*, 2 vols (Hull, 1967-69)

Taylor, J. A., *Ellermans: a wealth of shipping* (London, 1976)

Tunstall, J., *The fishermen* (London, 1962)

Warner, W., *Distant water: fate of the North Atlantic fishermen*, new ed. (Harmondsworth, 1984)

Watts, C. T. and M. Watts, 'Unravelling merchant seamen's records', *Genealogists magazine*, 19 (1979), pp.313-21

11 Education history

Armytage, W. H. G., *Four hundred years of English education* (Cambridge, 1941)

Bamford, T. W., *The evolution of rural education: three studies of the East Riding of Yorkshire*, University of Hull Institute of Education research monographs, 1 (Hull, 1965)

Bateman, R., *Yorkshire school history: a bibliography: publications held by Yorkshire libraries, with locations* (Leeds, 1969)

Cook, T. G., ed., *Local studies and the history of education* (London, 1972)

Elton, E. A., *Secondary education in the East Riding of Yorkshire 1944-72*, Educational administration and history monographs, 2 (Leeds, 1974)

Jordan, W. K., *The charities of rural England 1480-1660* (London, 1961)

Lawson, J., *The endowed grammar schools of East Yorkshire*, EYLHS, 14 (York, 1962)

Lawson, J., *Primary education in East Yorkshire, 1560-1902*, EYLHS, 10 (York, 1959)

Lawson, J. and H. Silver, *A social history of education in England* (London, 1973)

Lawson, J., *A town grammar school through six centuries: a history of Hull Grammar School against its local background* (Oxford, 1963)

Purvis, J. S., *Educational records* (York, 1959)

Sands, P. C. and C. M. Haworth, A history of Pocklington school, East Yorkshire, 1574-1950 (London, 1951)

Seaborne, M., *The English school: its architecture and organization, 1370-1870*, 2 vols (London, 1971-77)

Silver, H., *Education as history: interpreting nineteenth and twentieth century education* (London, 1983)

Stephens, J. E., ed., *Aspects of education, 1600-1750* (Hull, 1984)

Tate, W. E., *A. F. Leach as a historian of Yorkshire education, with an index of the Yorkshire schools (c.730 to c.1770) referred to in his works, etc., and some corrigenda* (York, 1963)

Unwin, R. W., 'Alternative educational arrangements in an English market town 1830-70', *Journal of educational administration and history*, 17 (1985), pp.11-21

Unwin, R. W. and W. B. Stephens, eds, *Yorkshire schools and schooldays: a guide to historical sources and their uses* (Leeds, 1976)

12 Architecture and history of houses

Allison, K. J., '*Hull gent. seeks country residence' 1750-1850*, EYLHS, 36 (Beverley, 1981)

Atkinson, T. D., *Local style in English architecture: an enquiry into its origin and development* (London, 1947)

Barley, M. W., *The English farmhouse and cottage* (London, 1961)

Brunskill, R. W., *Illustrated handbook of vernacular architecture* (London, 1970)

Clifton-Taylor, A., *The patterns of English building*, new ed. (London, 1972)

Hall, I. and E. Hall, *Historical Beverley*, 2nd ed. (Beverley, 1981)

Hall, I. and E. Hall, *Georgian Hull* (York, 1978)

Harrison, B. and B. Hutton, *Vernacular houses in North Yorkshire and Cleveland* (Edinburgh, 1984)

Harvey, J. H., *Sources for the history of houses* (London, 1974)

Iredale, D., *Discovering your old house*, 2nd ed. (Aylesbury, 1977)

Osborne, A. L., *The Country Life pocket guide to English domestic architecture*, 2nd ed. (London, 1967)

Pevsner, N., *Yorkshire: York and the East Riding*, The buildings of England (Harmondsworth, 1972)

Smith, J. T. and E. M. Yates, 'On the dating of English houses from external evidence', *Field studies*, 2 no. 5 (1968)

Summerson, J., *Architecture in Britain, 1530-1830*, The Pelican history of art, 7th ed. (London, 1983)

Woodforde, J., *Georgian houses for all* (London, 1978)

13 Public health and private medicine

Bickford, J. A. R., *De la Pole Hospital 1883-1983* (Hull, 1983)

Bickford, J. A. R. and M. E. Bickford, *The medical profession in Hull, 1400-1900: a biographical dictionary* (Hull, 1983)

Bickford, J. A. R., *The Old Hull Borough Asylum 1849-83* (Hull, 1981)

Bickford, J. A. R. and M. E. Bickford, *The private lunatic asylums of the East Riding*, EYLHS, 32 (Beverley, 1976)

Crowther, M. A., *The workhouse system 1834-1929: the history of an English social institution* (London, 1981)

Digby, A., *The Poor Law in nineteenth century England and Wales* (London, 1982)

Dyer, A., 'What to read on medical history', *Local historian*, 16 (1984), pp.32-5

Foster, B., ed., *Living and dying: a picture of Hull in the nineteenth century* (Hull, 1983)

Hovell, B. C., *The Hull Royal Infirmary, 1782-1982*, edited by S. Bates (Hull, 1982)

Hull Corporation Water Committee, *Kingston upon Hull water undertaking* (Hull, 1947)

Jacobs, M., *Reflections of a general practitioner* (London, 1965)

Lowson, K. J., *Story of Hull Royal Infirmary, 1782-1948* (Hull, 1948)

Neave, D., 'The local records of affiliated friendly societies', *Local historian*, 16 (1984), pp.161-7

Oxley, G., *Poor relief in England and Wales, 1601-1834* (Newton Abbot, 1974)

Patrick, G., *A plague on you, sir!: a community's road to health* (Hull, 1981)

Rockcliffe, W. C., *History of the Hull Blind Institution* (Hull, 1914)

Sandwith, H. and T. Sandwith, *History of the epidemic fever in Bridlington ...* (Hull, 1821)

Shepherdson, W., *Reminiscences of the Hull General Infirmary* (London, 1873)

Simpson, H., *The history of Hull Royal Infirmary ...* (Hull, 1888)

Smith J., *Report on a preliminary enquiry into the sewerage, drainage and supply of water and the sanitary condition of Kingston-upon-Hull* (Hull, 1850)

Vickerman, B., *Centenary of Broadgate Hospital, Beverley* (Hull, 1971)

Wilson, T. R., *Lloyd Hospital, Bridlington, 1868-1968* (Beverley, 1968)

14 Local history in the classroom

Child, M., *Discovering churchyards* (Aylesbury, 1982)

Douch, R., *Local history and the teacher* (London, 1967)

Dundee College of Education, *History in schools: unit 5: using local sources*, Videocassette [56 minutes] (Dundee, 1984)

Dyer, J., *Teaching archaeology in schools* (Princes Risborough, 1983)

Fairley, J. A., *History teaching through museums* (London, 1977)

Gee, A., *Looking at local houses,* History in focus for 13-16 year olds (Batsford, 1983)

Gwynne, T., *Local population studies in schools* (London, 1984)

Haddon, J., *Discovering towns* (Tring, 1970)

Ireland, R. F. J., *Producing guides to local resources* (London, 1979)

Jones, J., *How to record graveyards*, 3rd ed. (London, 1984)

Lovett, P., *Local studies in towns: a teacher's handbook* (London, 1980)

Mackinolty, J., ed., *Past continuous: learning through the historical environment* (Sydney?, 1983)

Mainstone, M. and M. Bryant, 'The use of museums and historical sites', in *Handbook for history teachers*, edited by W. H. Burston and C. W. Green, 2nd ed. (London, 1972)

Manning, F. E., *Beginning English local history* (London, 1982)

Petty, M., 'Local studies and the schools', *Local studies librarian*, 3 (1984), pp.12-13

Pluckrose, H., *Let's use the locality: a handbook for teachers* (London, 1971)

Schools Council History 13-16 Project, *History around us: some guidelines for teachers* (Edinburgh, 1976)

West, J., *Archives for schools* (London, 1971)

242

246

249